Culture and the Literary

Culture and the Literary

Matter, Metaphor, Memory

Avishek Parui

ROWMAN & LITTLEFIELD
Lanham • Boulder • New York • London

Published by Rowman & Littlefield
An imprint of The Rowman & Littlefield Publishing Group, Inc.
4501 Forbes Boulevard, Suite 200, Lanham, Maryland 20706
www.rowman.com

86-90 Paul Street, London EC2A 4NE

Copyright © 2022 by Avishek Parui

All rights reserved. No part of this book may be reproduced in any form or by any electronic or mechanical means, including information storage and retrieval systems, without written permission from the publisher, except by a reviewer who may quote passages in a review.

British Library Cataloguing in Publication Information Available

Library of Congress Cataloging-in-Publication Data

Names: Parui, Avishek, 1983– author.
Title: Culture and the literary : matter, metaphor, memory / Avishek Parui.
Description: Lanham : Rowman & Littlefield, [2021] | Includes bibliographical references and index.
Identifiers: LCCN 2021035475 (print) | LCCN 2021035476 (ebook) | ISBN 9781786615992 (cloth) | ISBN 9781786616005 (paperback) | ISBN 9781786616012 (epub)
Subjects: LCSH: Culture in literature. | Collective memory and literature. | Cognition in literature. | Literature—History and criticism.
Classification: LCC PN56.C85 P37 2021 (print) | LCC PN56.C85 (ebook) | DDC 809/.93355—dc23
LC record available at https://lccn.loc.gov/2021035475
LC ebook record available at https://lccn.loc.gov/2021035476

Contents

Acknowledgements   vii

Introduction   1

1 Culture, Commodity, and Colonial Identity   41

2 Culture, History, Memory, and Forgetting   93

3 Culture, Consumption, and Technology   143

4 Race, Medicine, Matter, and Metaphor   177

Conclusion   207

Index   215

Acknowledgements

This book was born in an airport. The contract arrived in an email as I was heading back from Tokyo, in transit at a terminal in New Delhi. In my mind, that is the perfect chronotope which could have conceived a book on memory, cultural vectors, and storytelling, a fluid space-time which is also a liminal non-place, as Marc Augé theorized it.

This book was finished in a vacant office building, in a city shut down due to a pandemic which changed and is changing our commonly consumed experiences of space, security, trust, and tactility. COVID-19. That's another chronotope, another non-place. Nobody could have theorized it.

This book took one and a half years to write, during which my family and I contracted COVID, suffered together, survived. I was particularly keen on finishing this book during the infection phase, just in case I ran out of time. The best and biggest chunks in this book may have been written during that high viral window. My first and most fundamental gratitude, as always, is to the accident that is life. We who are writing and reading this, we are very lucky. We survived.

This book was commissioned by Rowman & Littlefield after their editors happened to see my NPTEL course Introduction to Cultural Studies. Special thanks to the commissioning editor Gurdeep Mattu from the Rowman & Littlefield London office for approaching me with the idea to write this book and for the long and lovely Skype chat about memory, cultural artefacts, and abandoned objects. That alignment of academic and intellectual wavelengths was very vital for the genesis of this book. Thanks also to Scarlet Furness, Frankie Mace, and Jehanne Schweitzer at

Rowman & Littlefield for their very kind and generous support during the writing process, for being so kindly and creatively flexible and accommodative, especially during the difficult times. It was an absolute joy to work with you all.

This book has drawn organically on my PhD thesis and is squarely situated within my current research interest in memory studies. Special thanks to my PhD supervisor from Durham, Patricia Waugh, who has been and always will be a wonderful mentor and an inspiring benchmark for brilliance, kindness, and human depth. Pat's role throughout the writing process was immediate and profound, from the many emails and messages to the final phase where she kindly shared her latest publication which significantly shaped the conclusion of this book.

I am thankful to my colleagues in the Memory Studies Association who have profoundly and positively influenced my research and understanding of the domain and have directly contributed towards the formation of the Indian Network for Memory Studies (INMS). Special thanks to Astrid Erll, Hanna Teichler, and Jenny Wüstenberg for their kind collegiality and research rapport. The many interactions I have had with these wonderful scholars contributed directly and substantially to this book.

Special thanks to Pramod Nayar for being an excellent friend and mentor, and also for constantly checking on how this book was growing, with his characteristically cryptic dark humour which tries, not very successfully, to conceal his concern and kindness. That always helps, especially during the trying times.

I am very grateful to my colleague at IIT Madras and fellow founder and co-chairperson of the INMS, Merin Simi Raj, for her kind collegial and professional support, and also for her excellent help with the index and references for this book. Thanks also to Merin's wonderful family, Joe and little Paul and Rachel, for their warm and very sincere friendship.

Thanks to my parents, Samir Parui and Nandita Parui, and my sister, Aishwarya, who have always taught and inspired me to honour, produce, and promote positivity, sometimes stubbornly, to value the little acts, gifts, and moments that make life lovely. All three of them have taught me precious lessons in kindness, openness, and revivability, which have stood me in good stead during my many failures. They have always celebrated the smallest things I have managed to do and continue to stay very close emotionally, despite the distance across the different cities. Thanks also to my wonderful in-laws, Paran Krishna Saha, Swapna Saha, and Samudra Saha, for their encouragement and kind appreciation that contribute very positively to my work and life.

My final and fullest note of thanks is for the two people who form what's home for me, my best friend Priyanka and our son Ayanish. Priyanka's work ethic and enterprise, as she runs a company and manages many demanding professional fronts, while also designing our home with an artist's eye, inspire me experientially, not least during the difficult phases of work. It's a unique privilege to be so close to someone you can so look up to, emotionally as well as professionally. I am always grateful for her grace, intuitive intelligence, and her wisdom to know what to choose and what to reject, decisions that shape a book as well as a life. Our beautiful son, Ayanish, teaches me to be curious about the smallest things, pushes me to become a better and more consistent storyteller, and reminds me to never take for granted the one attribute which makes us unique: imagination. Together they create the most precious matter, metaphors, and memories for me, the ones which grow from love, care, happiness, empathy.

This book, like my first one, is dedicated to Priyanka and Ayanish.

May we make many merry memories and travel across many magical stories together in the times to come.

Introduction

If you can fill the unforgiving minute
With sixty seconds' worth of distance run
Yours is the Earth and everything that's in it
And – which is more – you'll be a Man, my son!

Rudyard Kipling's 'If' (Kipling 1994, 605), from where the above lines are taken, was used in a promotional video before the men's singles final at Wimbledon in 2007. The video featured the tennis superstars Roger Federer and Rafael Nadal reciting the poem together with a backdrop of dramatically shot scenes from their sporting triumph. Appearing also at the players' entrance to the Centre Court in Wimbledon, 'If' has consistently been classified as a British favourite by major public polls (Jones 1996). Kipling's 1910 poem was historically motivated by the failed British raid in 1896 against the Boers at Transvaal and the subsequent betrayal suffered by its leader, Leander Jameson, in the hands of the Salisbury-led British government that had supported the raid formerly (Havholm 2008, 140–42). 'If', thus, is a poetic tribute to the British imperialist politician Leander Starr Jameson and a piece of personal advice to the poet's son John Kipling who was subsequently killed in the Battle of Loos during the First World War. The poem ends on an absolute enunciation of ideal manliness after extolling the virtues of undeterred decisive action, unemotional stoicism, strong nerves, and indefatigable energy, in ceaseless service to the nation and its imperial 'missions'. George Orwell's description of Kipling as 'a jingo imperialist' who is 'morally insensitive and aesthetically disgusting', while also acknowledging Kipling's lasting legacy (Orwell 1961,

179), captures the complexity that went into the production and reception of this literary piece. Variously interpreted as inspirational as well as jingoistic, Kipling's 'If' – with its imperious advocacy of being emotionally indifferent to triumph and disaster alike – delineates the *manly attributes* which historically may be seen to have corresponded to an ideal of plucky imperialist masculinity. As the video featuring Federer and Nadal demonstrates, such set of attributes continues to connect to the concept of the ideal white masculine sporting character today.

A dramatic monologue with carefully constructed qualities of manly courage and productively channelized feelings, Kipling's poem has attained the status of a classic in spite of its critics and detractors. Its political legacy as an imperialist poem and its continuing popularity as a piece of profound advice concerning the normative manly character in the Western world serve as the starting point of this book, which is an examination of the complex correspondences, collusions, and critical tensions between culture and the literary. The Kiplingesque construct of masculinity – historically tied to the tenets of its contemporary Boy Scout movements – emerges as an unequivocally well-knit body of zeal and nerves. The enterprising and sporting aspect of masculinity that Kipling promoted in his poetry and fiction make his lines relevant to modern models of *desirable masculinity* (Mangan 1986). Edward Said affirms how Robert Baden-Powell, the founder of the Boy Scouts in Britain, was personally influenced in his ideas about 'boyology' by the Kiplingesque character of imperial authority and resourcefulness. As Said argues, Kipling and Baden-Powell appeared to have concurred on two major points: boys in service to the empire ought to conceive life as governed by unbreakable laws, and secondly, service to the empire was more effective when thought of less as a story and more like a game (Said 1994, 137). The legacy of the poem connects late nineteenth-century imperialist heroes to the sporting superstars of the present day by making a virtue out of manly toughness, indomitable spirit, and self-effacing honour in the ludic landscape. As a literary text born out of the same political and cultural context that promoted the white man's burden in the colonies for the edification of the 'sullen peoples', 'Half-devil and half-child' (Kipling 1994, 334), Kipling's 'If' enacts an indoctrination of *noble manly values* that continue to be circulated and consumed in the liberal Western world today.

'If' is an excellent example of how a literary text becomes a voice and a vehicle of its contemporary culture, while also speaking selectively and stylistically to its subsequent ages which consume it for its literary merit as well as moral message. In its advocacy for 'plucky' masculinity, Kipling's poem inhabits the dual function of representing abstract philosophy and historical materiality, aestheticizing the same with its lyrical quality. It is a suitable text that sets the tone for the scope of this book, which intends to examine and underline the necessity to read literary texts for a fuller and more complex understanding of culture and cultural valences. 'If' also exemplifies how cultural value-based narratives are created, consolidated, and consumed through literary texts that may be variously reinterpreted and recontextualized through a combination of matter, metaphor, and memory. This combination is key to this book, which is largely an enquiry into how literature may be revisited and reread as a special form of representation that refracts how power, privilege, and production may be critiqued as well as formalized in fiction. Culture and literature are both examined as narratives that are constantly coded, constructed, and consumed, narrative being a 'dialectic between what was expected and what came to pass' (Bruner 2002, 15). Thus literature, through a production of possibilities, may be seen as a form of representation whereby matter becomes metaphor, which enters memory with its materiality as well as affectivity, a process alluded to by the very title of this book.

In this reading, the figurative quality in literature and literary texts is not seen as a departure from reality but rather a stylized representation of the same. Rather, reality in the way it is commonly consumed emerges as already always inscribed with symbolic codes that are further foregrounded by literary language and forms of representation. Such stylization may be defamiliarizing, descriptive, distancing, or a combination of all. Added to this is the question of focalization and perspectival position, which entails a situatedness of the subjective frame inside or around objects and objective events that inform history and materiality. In the process, this book aims to invoke the necessity of close reading of literary texts for a fuller understanding of culture through matter, metaphors, and narratives of remembering. If culture may best be examined as an entanglement between a superorganic omniscient order and local epistemic experience, informed by the politics and experience of presence and absence, such combinations manifest themselves most immediately in narratives. If culture and literature may both be considered as narrative categories, which operate with the politics of permutations and privilege, such privilege may also be seen as a function of narrativity and narrative agency.

Literature is studied in this book as a production of possibilities which may be uniquely positioned to critique as well as consolidate cultural constructions and consumptions. By enacting what Paul Ricoeur describes as a 'dialectical treatment' between real history and unreal fiction, literature offers the 'world of the text' (Ricoeur 2004, 262) as the site of alternate possibilities that contain as well as calibrate complex markers of cultural identity and existential agency. This connects closely to Edward Said's argument in *Culture and Imperialism* that the 'power to narrate, or to block other narratives from forming and emerging', had historically been 'very important to culture and imperialism, and constitutes one of the main connections between them' (Said 1994, xiii). This equation of narrative agency and political power bears significant resonances in the context of cultural production and consumption in terms of how a discourse is disseminated and rendered dominant by being narrativized. This reveals a relationship between narration, identity, and agency, while also underlining an understanding of culture as a narrative category, one which operates through complex politics of representation and reification. Drawing on Said's argument, this book attempts to offer a unique understanding of literature as a complex negotiation with culture in terms of being a play between consolidation, complicity, and critique, sometimes simultaneously. Secondly, and in keeping with the perspective that binds fiction (storytelling) with discourse and lived reality, the book offers a complex study of the entanglement of matter, metaphor, and memory in their discursive and experiential components. It thus explores how matter (things and events) becomes metaphors (semantic and semiotic codes) which enter the space of memory collectively through a combination of remembering and forgetting.

Drawing on the cognitive philosopher Jerome Bruner's definition of narratives as 'accounts of the intrusion of the unexpected on the expected', containing as well as violating 'presupposed notions of shared ordinariness' (Bruner 2008, 36), this book will study how such intrusions, violations, and resolutions in fiction are reflective of the ontological and epistemic qualities constituting cultural productions and predilections. By situating literature and literary texts as a field of play of culture and cultural identities, this book will underline what Wolfgang Iser describes as the 'ineluctable doubleness' of representation and reflexivity underlining the 'interrelation between absence and presence' in a literary text. Such doubleness in literature and literary language often foregrounds how the politics of presence is continually subverted 'till it turns into a carrier for absence of which we would otherwise not know anything' (Iser 1996b, 336). In the process, literature becomes an articulation of absence as well as a self-reflexive representation of the unsayable in culture and cultural narratives. Elsewhere, in *The Fictive and the Imaginary*, Iser examines how the fictionalizing act dramatized by literature 'converts the reality reproduced into a sign, simultaneously casting the imaginary as a form that allows us to conceive what it is towards which the sign points' (Iser 1996a, 2). Literature thus emerges as a process of encoding, transforming the real into signs while also mapping inward experiential first-person narratives onto external third-person ones. As Iser's study shows, culture as a narrative is constituted by codes as well as their absences, and literature as a representative medium becomes an instrument whereby such cultural codes are dramatized, consolidated, and subverted. By drawing on memory studies, this book examines key questions about the relationship between things, events, and their affective associations in lived experience as well as in fictional frames. Therefore, this book offers a unique understanding of how history, remembering, and forgetting inform culture, its constructions, and consumptions. Equally, by offering a unique combination of material engagement theory and affect studies frames, the book examines the entanglement of commodity, consumption, and identity as represented in literary and cultural narratives. Lastly, through a detailed study of fictional as well as nonfictional texts, the book offers a unique perspective into the relationship between body, technology, race, and waste in the world we inhabit today.

Before moving on to the primary content frame of this work, it is worthwhile to unpack the theoretical frames appropriated for this study. Drawing on a complex combination of thing theory, material engagement theory, memory studies, race studies, and affect studies, this book examines fiction as a production as well as a play between reality and possibility, whereby historical and collective memories are mediated through phenomenal frames and affective objects. Affect will be examined in this book as a form of contagion, drawing on Sara Ahmed, as something which sticks, moves, and 'sustains or preserves the connection between ideas, values, and objects' (Ahmed 2010, 29). This stickiness between affect and object produces, as Arjun Appadurai argues, a two-way signifying system inasmuch as things are semantically situated by a phenomenal frame whose consciousness itself is informed by its engagement with 'things in motion' (Appadurai 1986, 5). Literature may be viewed as the narrative/phenomenal frame which captures things in motion and the manner in which the human mind perceives the same. As a moving medium embedded as well as extended in language between cognition and culture, literature inhabits and exhibits a unique privilege of representation. As the movement of materiality which underlines the ontology of materiality itself, literature may be seen as the self-reflexive vehicle in language which dramatizes the discursivity, affectivity, and textuality of culture. In the process, it highlights what Judith Butler describes as the 'temporality of matter' (Butler 1993, 250) whereby the *meaningfully material* body is informed by temporal markers which make it sentient as well as socially signifying, establishing the dynamic between interiority and performativity foregrounded in Butler's philosophy. This complex of affect and materiality is significant for this study, especially amid an academic awareness of how affect as a critical category is increasingly acknowledged in cultural studies which examines the 'contagiousness of affect' operating 'through the medium of the text' (Gregg 2006, 9). In this theoretical frame, literature emerges as a unique medium of representation embedded in language and cognition, one which cuts the cultural/phenomenal axes, articulating memory and materiality through 'the messiness of the experiential, the unfolding of bodies into worlds, and the drama of contingency, how we are touched by what we are near' (Ahmed 2010).

Presenting as its fundamental philosophical frame that self-consciousness is materially and intersubjectively mediated (Malafouris and Ihde 2019), material engagement theory (MET) accentuates the affective markers of materials and how those may be mapped onto storytelling selves situated in culture, its construction, and consumption. The affective material engagement and *relative ontology* informing such processes of materiality and intersubjectivity may be seen as major players in cultural narratives and their representations, incorporating in their wake issues of identity and agency. Intersubjectivity is a key category in this study as an affective and material condition that connects selves and their extended embodiments through markers of memory and narrativity, remembering and retelling. As an affective, experiential, and discursively determined condition, intersubjectivity is a cultural as well as an existential phenomenon and may be uniquely examined in literary representations which generate empathy and possibilities in fiction. Intersubjectivity entails affective association between subjects as well as affective engagement with materials, making it a major representational category in fiction with its play between interiority, interconnectivity, and the production of shared identities. This idea of intersubjectivity corresponds to the distributive model of cognition corroborated by philosophers such as Andy Clark who describes the human mind as a 'leaky organ, forever escaping its "natural" confines and mingling shamelessly with body and with world' (Clark 1997, 53). This has significant bearings on an understanding of culture as a form of contagion that is distributive, interactive, and intersubjective, whereby the social and phenomenal frames fuse asymmetrically to form affective and material markers through which processes of identity and memory materialize. In its study of literature's location in culture by mapping materials, metaphors, and memories, this book examines the equation between intersubjectivity, interactivity, and intertextuality, the last category being the self-reflexive system through which texts reflect, retell, and remember other texts in a nodal network of association, emergence, and difference. The primary emphasis of this argument is that subjectivity as a moving mutable process is materially, textually, and interactively determined. The affective subject situated in culture and cultural vectors is thus studied as a narrative and textual category inasmuch as it connects to other subjects through texts and their contexts. This compares closely to Catherine Belsey's argument that 'subjectivity is an effect of culture', culture being the 'range of signifying practices' that the subject is born out of. The very function of the subject, in Belsey's argument, emerges from an effort to 'reproduce or to challenge the meanings inscribed in the signifying practices' (Belsey 2005, 9). Literature emerges, in this enquiry, as the representational mode through which the textuality of the subject and the subjectivity of the text are affectively articulated.

The fundamental premise of material engagement theory – that humans and things are endlessly entangled and co-constituted (Malafouris 2013) – offers a complex view of subjectivity as at once internal/embedded and material/extended. It generates the notion that all forms of subjectivity are intersubjective in nature, mediated through as well as shaped by experiential engagement with materials. This is particularly pertinent to the premise of this book, which argues that literature as an affective order of representation is uniquely situated as an insider as well as an outsider to forms of cultural determination, its *relative autonomy* (a term used by Louis Althusser which will be unpacked later) in close correspondence to the *relative ontology* foregrounded by material engagement theory. Drawing on affect theory and material engagement theory, this book argues that literature offers an excellent understanding of the complex processes through which materials becomes metaphors, facts become figurative through forms of representation in cultural systems, reflective of the 'ontological coalition' between mind and matter, the 'co-extension of the mental with the physical' (Malafouris 2013, 6). If culture may be seen as a form of contagion that produces affective markers that need to be consumed through memory and materiality, literature emerges as the best device in language about the play between matter and the mind, about the human subject's situatedness in social settings with all its unreliability, precarity, and possibility.

Memory studies as a theoretical and philosophical framework forms the primary interpretative system in this book. Examining the relationship between remembering and forgetting, at the collective/discursive and private/experiential levels, memory studies also explores cognition and its various forms of cultural representation. Culture emerges, in this reading, as a play between remembering and representation, through contagious and affective experiences as well as through material markers. As a theoretical frame, memory studies is particularly relevant in exploring the location of literature and fiction apropos of cultural identities, their production, reception, and dissemination. As Richard Terdiman argues in *Present Past: Modernity and Its Memory Crisis*, 'how a culture performs and sustains' its modes of memory may be 'distinctive and diagnostic' (Terdiman 1993, 15). In other words, memory, at a collective level, may be seen as a significant mode as well as a mutable marker of cultural production and preservation whereby the matter and manner of remembering (through events, monuments, and texts) determine the discursive and diachronic quality of a given culture. Equally, forms of forgetting factor into the politics of erasure constituting cultural production as well as preservation of absence. What connects both functions is the narrativity that informs remembering and forgetting. Forms of forgetting corroborate the narrative quality of institutional memory which constitute, as Charlotte Linde examines, 'ephemeral narratives' and the 'retold tales' (Linde 2009, 72–73). While the former happen to be episodic in quality and do not eventually materialize into privileged modes of memory that receive institutional backing, the 'retold tales' are the ones ontologically compatible with hegemonic versions of history and institutional identity. Examining the complex relation between memory and iterability, Linde studies how remembering and reiterating form functions of cultural consolidation through reproduction. If fiction is a production of possibilities which are mutable and unpredictable, operating through cognitive bias, affect, and intersubjectivity, the role of remembering as an affective vector in culture and the self's situatedness in the same connects literature and memory as narrative categories.

This view of memory as a representational and narrative medium finds rich resonance in the works of major neuroscientists and philosophers such as Eric Kandel, Paul Ricoeur, and Marc Augé, who examine remembering and forgetting not as ontological opposites but as cognitive components of each other at psychological as well as cultural levels. If memory is a form of representation, like literature, it also offers a perspective on absence as an order of production open to interpretation, famously exemplified in philosophy in Jacques Derrida's reading of Hamlet's father as a spectral presence which is hauntological in quality. Fiction thus emerges, to quote Jorge Luis Borges, as a combination of 'memory and oblivion' (Borges 1982, 20) whereby remembering and dismembering become cognitive as well as representational processes. Seen in this light, forgetting too emerges as an act of production in fiction, whereby spectrality is produced as an articulation of absence. This connects to literature's position as a complex category of representation, one which is a production of possibilities and self-reflexivity apropos of cultural realities and identities. This dialectic between possibility and reflexivity is achieved in the fictional frame of *as-if*, which Paul Armstrong examines as the structure that allows the play of difference whereby negation becomes an act of production. The mimetic reproduction of reality through possibility connects to the broader experience of simulation, as 'simulating what we are not allows us to explore and perhaps become what we might want to be' (Armstrong 2013, 169).

As Astrid Erll examines, literature and memory share several key characteristics such as condensation, narration, and genre, through which events and experiences are compressed, conveyed, and encoded in the mind as well as in the text (Erll 2011, 146–49). If culture operates through narrative orders, literature with its fictional privilege can appear interdiscursive through representations of connected as well as contesting memories. This dual potential to be intersubjective and interdiscursive lends literature a unique location in cultural memory and its politics of identities. As postmodern historiographic metafiction makes amply evident, literature can be memory productive as well as memory reflexive, sometimes simultaneously. This play of productivity and reflexivity in literature is achieved through what Wolfgang Iser defines as *fictionalizing acts*, whereby 'extratextual reality merges into the imaginary, and the imaginary merges into reality' (Iser 1996a, 3). The role of literature in memory narration is thus accentuated by its fictionality which flags how fact and fantasy, presence and absence, may be simultaneously negotiated and articulated. In the process, literature becomes an act of construction through which memory and meaning making in culture are not simply represented but, as Paul Ricoeur puts it, 'iconically augmented' (Ricoeur 2008, 81). The intersection of literature and memory studies thus opens up and underlines the play between extratextual reality and fictionality, remembering and forgetting, offering a deconstructionist view on event, identity, and materiality. As subsequent sections on deconstruction corroborate, this securely situates literature as a major player in cultural studies, whereby affect, history, memory, and materiality may be represented by a play of production and possibilities.

In its theoretical premise, this book engages with some fundamental questions, such as What is culture? What are the abstract and material markers of culture as a category? How do culture and the textuality of culture emerge as entanglements of experiential and discursively determined processes? How is culture invested with and shaped by political, social, medical, and technological events? An examination of these fundamentals will then connect to questions about the role and responsibilities of cultural studies as a discipline, its history within academia, and its key figures, subjects covered subsequently in this introduction. Chapter 1 examines the cultural production and consumption of identities, especially in politically complex conditions such as colonialism. Titled 'Culture, Commodity, and Colonial Identity', this chapter studies the processes of commodification and the cultural production of identity in discursively determined settings, focalized through the unreliable and nervous narrators in the selected works of fiction. Particularly relevant in this chapter is an examination of imperial identity as a politically constructed as well as an ambivalently experiential process. Drawing on philosophers and theorists such as Michel Foucault, Homi Bhabha, and Judith Butler among others, the chapter offers close readings of Joseph Conrad's *Heart of Darkness* and George Orwell's 'Shooting an Elephant' and *Burmese Days*. In examining Conrad's and Orwell's *misadventure fiction* and their depictions of melancholic white imperial masculinities, the chapter highlights the processes through which colonial commodities (ivory and teak in Conrad's and Orwell's novels, respectively) and human identities become enmeshed as constructed and consumable categories. Chapter 2, 'Culture, History, Memory, and Forgetting', examines the role of memory as a form of representation apropos of cultural location. It studies stereotypes as an economy of expectations and exaggerations and showcases how memory and the act of remembering often deconstruct shared narratives of history. Drawing on cultural theorists as well as cognitive theorists, this chapter is interdisciplinary in quality and offers close readings of selected short stories of Saadat Hasan Manto and Milan Kundera's *The Book of Laughter and Forgetting*. In its study, the chapter examines memory as a political and existential category that also foregrounds forgetting as an agentic activity against the cultural backdrop of the 1947 India-Pakistan Partition and the 1968 Prague Spring.

Chapter 3, 'Culture, Consumption, and Technology', examines the entanglement of organic and inorganic orders of cultural production and consumption. Particularly relevant in this chapter is the network of affect and affective identities mediated through machines and objects of consumption invested in subject formation and re-formation. Drawing on material engagement theory, actor network theory, and philosophies on embodiment and technology, the chapter offers close readings of Oscar Wilde's *The Picture of Dorian Gray* and Will Self's *Dorian* in an examination of corporeality and virtuality in the fin de siècle and postmodern cultural imaginary. It also highlights how the fictional frame of the two selected novels offers the liminal site which sees subjects and objects blend, exemplified by the ageless body and ageing portrait in Wilde's novel and the free-floating human images disseminated and consumed across television screens in Self's sequel. Chapter 4, 'Race, Medicine, Matter, and Metaphor', examines how cultural identities and normative narratives are formed and re-formed through prisms of biomedical and racialized discourses. It also studies the complex collusions of cultural and political identities in relation to the production and consumption of waste. Drawing on biomedical studies, race studies, waste studies, phenomenology, and affect theory primarily, this chapter offers close readings of Frantz Fanon's *Black Skin, White Masks* and *The Wretched of the Earth* and Ian McEwan's *Saturday*. While Fanon's works are examined as accounts of experiential violence and unsettled embodiment under the biomedical and racially reifying colonial gaze which are narrative in quality despite their nonfictional nature, McEwan's post-9/11 neuro-novel is read as a fictional work that dramatizes an affective unlearning of the privileged order of medical science, followed by a more modest acceptance of the mutability and messiness of the human mind. The conclusion re-examines the broader strands studied in the rest of the book and re-addresses the questions with which the introduction opened, especially in relation to the collectively experienced pandemic COVID-19. By routing the responses through the literary works already studied and examined in the chapters, the book ends on the increasing and renewed relevance of an interdisciplinary dialogue between literary and cultural studies in the globalized *crisis chronotope* we share and internalize today (Parui and Raj, forthcoming).

The *Oxford English Dictionary* defines the word *culture* thus: 'way of life . . . the customs and beliefs, art, way of life and social organization of a particular country or group'. Thus the most commonly consumed meaning of culture corresponds to collective activities that include rituals and art forms, ones that organize and orient a group towards a uniform and standardized identification. What is also evident in the definition is the coded quality of such organizational behaviour, codes that are shared, circulated, and consumed by a group of people living under shared material conditions. At the very outset, it is thus important to recognize culture as a process of iteration, inscription, and internalization, through which certain signifiers which are material as well as abstract are produced and perpetuated through repetition and consumption. This entanglement of materiality and abstraction is key to this book, especially as it aims to examine *literature as a special situation of culture*, one which is reflective and also sometimes subversive. In the economy of affect and materiality which constitutes culture, literature emerges as an activity as well as a network of ideas, one which is inconstantly collusive and critical in relation to dominant discourses. As a system of signification which is always already embedded with cultural codes and linguistic referents, literature is an insider of culture, while at the same time being uniquely situated to expose cultural narratives' fault lines and ontological interruptions. Literature emerges as the finest form of culture's economy of signs, a sophisticated consolidation within a culture's sign-map. Equally, it can also become a subversion of such signs at the precise point at which it perfects semantic mappings. Like Joseph Conrad's Kurtz in *Heart of Darkness*, literature may be the highest point in culture and also its most immediate threat due to its *over-appropriation of signs*. This book is an attempt to examine this complex relationship, this discursive *double entendre* that underlines literature's location in culture and its politics of production and consumption. Examining culture as a narrative category that is determined by production, dissemination, and consumption, this book draws on Jerome Bruner's theory of culture as a complex and self-reflexive form of storytelling, whereby it becomes a 'maker and enforcer of what is expected but it also, paradoxically, compiles, even slyly treasures, transgressions' (Bruner 2002, 15).

In locating literature as a significant function and reflection of culture, this book draws on Mircea Marghescou's notion of *regime of texts* whereby a semiotic and stylized textual system autonomously and creatively informs interpretations of values in a given culture amid its economy of information (Marghescou as cited in Frow 2002, 47). This idea of the textual or literary regime may be extended as a function of affective engagement with culture, one which is 'ontologically impure' and is composed of 'codes, practices, organized bodies of texts, physical spaces (libraries, bookshops, bedrooms), modes of authority, and people and things interacting (all at once) physically, semiotically, and socially' (Frow 2005, 51). This understanding of literature as a marker of interaction with and interpretation of cultural contexts and valences entails a consideration of culture as a code field, one where the production and consumption of affect and materiality inform changing landscapes of values and meanings. Seen in this light, textuality and the conditions which produce it become connected categories that foreground the constructed quality of meaning making and value production, simultaneously debunking and deconstructing grand narratives of identity and history. This symbiosis of literature and culture as categories of narrativity is corroborated and voiced by Antonio Gramsci who stated in his *Prison Notebooks* that 'literary history is a part and an aspect of a much larger history of culture' (Gramsci as cited in Frow 2005, 158). If cultural studies as an academic discipline may be defined 'as a concern with the social relations of textuality' (Frow 2005, 54), the idea of the textual regime informing and informed by cultural coordinates as theorized by Marghescou offers a unique understanding of the entanglement of culture and the literary, through matter, metaphor, and memory. It underlines the urgency of examining cultural studies and literature as mutually symbiotic representational and reading practices.

Raymond Williams is a fine figure to start a study on the interface between the literary and cultural markers in terms of their discursive and experiential components. This complex of discursivity and experientiality is dramatized in an anecdote in the introduction to Williams's *Keywords* (1985) where the author describes his experience on returning to a British university after the Second World War. Coming to a Cambridge college following the Second World War from an artillery regiment in Kiel Canal, Williams experiences his alienation due to a significant shift in language markers, to the extent of having to confess to a comrade that 'they don't speak the same language' (Williams 1985, 11). The change in language and popular linguistic discourses post–Second World War thus emerges as an example of the ever-mutable quality of culture, one that is occasionally accelerated by major political events such as the world wars. Williams's introduction to *Keywords* offers an excellent understanding of culture as a process marked by material and affective signifiers, and this idea is central to the content and scope of this book, not least as it aims to examine literature, literary production, and consumption apropos of culture and cultural conditions. Describing his experience of reading T. S. Eliot's *Notes towards the Definition of Culture* – a work which will be examined shortly in this section itself – as a treatise which he 'grasped but could not accept' (ibid., 13), Williams underlines how the word *culture* came to be indistinguishably associated in his mind with art, class, industry, and democracy. Each of those categories may be seen as an entanglement of emotional and material signifiers and thus correspond to the complex combination of matter, metaphor, and memory which underlines the production and consumption of culture.

Williams's definition of the word *culture* in his *Keywords* offers a flavour of the complexity of the term, through its various etymological and discursive roots and routes. Marking how the word *culture* emerged from the Latin *colere*, which had a range of meanings from *inhabiting* to *honouring with worship*, Williams shows how the same root eventually informed the current meanings of the words *colony* and *cult* respectively. Williams's study shows clearly how the word *culture*, from its very etymological inception, has always had associations with spatial systems of control and conformation which may take political and religious routes at different points of time. It is easy to see how such associations operate along the complex of matter, metaphor, and memory inasmuch as how selected and privileged matter metaphorizes into cultural artefacts and value systems through collective memory which may be controlled politically as well as through other epistemic instruments. Among other things, Williams's study may be used to examine the deep entanglement between colonialism and religion in terms of how both historically drew on similar systems of coercion.

Alluding to the usage of the term in bacteriology and crop production, Williams elucidates three major strands in the contemporary usage of *culture*: production and cultivation in terms of arts and aesthetics; a way of life pertaining to a group or collective identity; and, lastly, a series of artistic and aesthetic activities which is often institutionalized in forms such as a ministry of culture. It is easy to read Williams's definition of culture as a set of codes and coded activities, which are materially determined as well as mutable. The codes are created, consumed, and consolidated by acts of inscription, iteration, and institutionalization. Literature emerges in this reading as a stylized navigation with such cultural codes and, in the process, as a production of possibilities that may be reflective as well as subversive. In its embeddedness in as well as special usage of language, literary production and consumption correspond to all the three categories of culture classified by Williams.

Williams's definition of culture as a combination of material as well as affective markers finds remarkable resonance in the works of the Marxist philosopher Louis Althusser whose significance in a study of the interface between literary and cultural studies can hardly be overestimated. More famous for his theorizations of ideological and repressive state apparatus in an era of capitalist reproductions, Althusser is a key figure in the context of this book due to his formulation of the *relative autonomy* of art and aesthetic production, which was to be seen as non-reducible to economic and ideological overdeterminism. Dividing cultural and social totality into four components – economic, political, ideological, and theoretical – Althusser argued how each enjoys relative autonomy apropos of the others, despite being connected categories. Among other things, Althusser's theorization of *subjectivity-effect* produced by a discourse is particularly pertinent here (Althusser 2003, 33–84). Such subjectivity-effect is a complex of material conditions and affective experience. This brings into play the entanglement of discursivity and experientiality that constitutes cultural codes and their consumption. In the same work, Althusser examines the ontology of aesthetic discourse and defines it as a system where the subject-effect emerges only in relation to an *ambiguous structure of cross-references* (ibid., 50). In such a structure, each centre is only a presence by virtue of its negation of another centre, in an economy of indecision. Althusser's vocabulary here is interestingly similar to the Derridean description of the production of difference in deconstruction, which will be studied subsequently in this book. Defining the aesthetic discourse thus, Althusser reiterates its polycentric quality, stating unequivocally that the lapse into a single centre converts the aesthetic discourse into an ideological one.

Althusser's work is of special significance in this book as his is one of the finest and earliest studies on the convergence of ideology, affect, and the unconscious, bringing the theories of Marx and Lacan into a dialectic that includes materiality and experientiality. This combination of Marxist materialism and Lacanian affectivity offers interesting parallels to the works of Slavoj Žižek, which will be examined at the end of this introduction. Like Žižek, Althusser's position apropos of current cultural studies is complex and contingent, but what gives him special significance (like Žižek) in the context of this book is his engagement with the order of the aesthetic apropos of cultural production and consumption. Althusser's thesis on the polycentricity and ambiguity of the aesthetic discourse perhaps contains the key to his much-debated statement of the relative autonomy of art apropos of ideological identification and material production. His most direct examination of literature perhaps comes with his study of drama and the relation between the dialectical and the non-dialectical orders of time on a theatre stage. In his 'Notes on a Materialist Theatre', Althusser offers a brilliant examination of Bertolazzi's play *El Nost Milan* along with Brecht's *Mother Courage* and *Galileo*, drawing on Marx's study of melodrama in *The Holy Family*. In what appears as an extraordinary reading of performative temporality dramatized in a play, Althusser studies *El Nost Milan* as a theatre piece where non-dialectical time (in which nothing happens, where there is no progression through conflicts) is mapped and exists alongside dialectical time (where action happens and progresses through conflicts). More innovatively, Althusser examines how the dialectical time of conflict, progress, and action is situated in the margins of Bertolazzi's play which continues to foreground the non-events where nothing happens (Althusser 2010, 138–40). In an interesting interpretation which may be mapped onto a reading of Samuel Beckett's *Waiting for Godot* as well, Althusser examines how Bertolazzi's play dramatizes a deferral of the dialectic, inasmuch as how the dialectical time and action constituting conflicts and progress is almost always 'acted in the wings, in one corner of the stage' (ibid., 138). Such deferral, Althusser argues, is also an act of interruption and interrogation which, in the case of *El Nost Milan*, is a critique of bourgeois consciousness.

Moving on to a study of Brecht's plays, especially *Mother Courage* and *Galileo*, Althusser argues that the alienation effect and epic theatre theory have been inadequately examined in Brecht scholarship and underlines again the frame of dialectical and non-dialectical time. As in Bertolazzi's *El Nost Milan*, in Beckett's plays too, Althusser finds 'forms of temporality that do not achieve any mutual integration, which have no relation to one another, which coexist and interconnect, but never meet each other', producing instead 'an internal dissociation, an unresolved alterity' (ibid., 143). In a description that is again strikingly similar to Derrida's discourse on deconstruction, Althusser argues how, in Brecht's plays, 'the centre is always deferred, always in the beyond, in the movement going beyond illusion towards the real' (ibid., 145). This is achieved through a theatrical process which fractures a seamless consumption of ideology and ideological worldview through realism and development-centric temporality and instead produces an *ontological opacity* that interrupts actions and associations. Brecht's theatre, in Althusser's reading, emerges as profoundly political precisely in its refusal to reflect reality through the tools of totality and morality. Such opacity also offers political possibilities for Althusser, generating 'a perception which is not given, but has to be discerned, conquered and drawn from the shadow which initially envelops it, and yet produced it' (ibid., 146).

The politics of literature lies for Althusser in its production of possibilities which interrupt the process of *interpellation*, a term Althusser made famous, one which he defined as 'the precise operation' or *hailing* through which individuals are recruited as subjects (Althusser 2014, 190) and which is an indistinguishable component of ideology and ideological state apparatus. Althusser's final note on the possibilities of political theatre emerges as an affirmation of the potential of the literary word and its performance. In it he underlines how Brecht's theatre contains the possibilities of the 'production of a new consciousness' (ibid., 151) which is incomplete as it situates itself against any commonly consumed tangible totality. Althusser ends by stating how such consciousness is paradoxically promoted by its own incompletion, towards the possibilities of alternate production and subversion. Althusser remains a somewhat understudied figure outside of Marxist scholarship, and his work on the intersection of ideology, interpellation, and affect offers original and fertile fields of enquiry in any study that intends to investigate the complex of metaphor and materiality that constitutes culture and cultural codes. His concept of *relative autonomy*, a notoriously contested and controversial category which breaks away from any notion of economic overdeterminism, has had significant impact on subsequent studies in cultural materialism. It has helped form a more dialogic relation between matter and affect, something embedded in Althusser's idea of interpellation as a material as well as a consciousness-centric activity. This relative autonomy of art and culture apropos of material and economic production has interesting parallels with Saussurean semiotics which argues that there exists a relationship of relative autonomy between language (the system of signs) and reality, making all acts of representation ambivalent, contested, and contingent. Literature emerges in this context, particularly with its figurative coding, as especially suited to interrupt interpellation. If ideology and its interpellation are totalizing and totalitarian categories that constitute culture and its consumption, literature, which is always already embedded in culture's symbolic systems, can further consolidate such ideological interpellation, as in Kipling's 'If' with which this book opened. Alternately, it can also offer an incomplete or confused consciousness which undercuts any myth of completion or closure, as in the misadventure fiction of Joseph Conrad and George Orwell, examined in the first chapter.

Since it reads carefully selected literary texts as complex case studies of refractions and representations of culture, an appropriate point of beginning for this book would perhaps be to highlight some of the definitions of culture offered by literary writers across the ages. Matthew Arnold's *Culture and Anarchy* (1882) may be considered as perhaps the first systematic attempt in English at a description of culture and cultural valences from the point of view of humanities education, liberal politics, and literature. In it, Arnold is quick to depart from a definition of culture as a strand of scientific curiosity and instead sees it as *'a study of perfection'* which 'moves by force, not merely or primarily of the scientific passion for pure knowledge but also of the moral and social passion for doing good' (Arnold 1882, 34). In the same work,

Arnold states that culture has two primary passions – sweetness and light – but its greater passion is to make such sweetness and light *prevail* (ibid., 52). Thus one can see how even Arnold's great humanistic project and projection of culture incorporate elements of execution and performance, while at the same time constantly cautioning against any unauthoritative activities such as riots and mob unrest, even if those are staged for supposedly good causes. Arnold's *Culture and Anarchy* may be read as a conservative treatise which sublimates the desirable codes that constitute high culture into a moral message of beauty and conformation to authority, while also highlighting the happy contagion that precludes any anarchy.

The historical location of *Culture and Anarchy* as a text of humanist idealism in response to the cultural panic of Darwinism is significant. As Joseph Carroll argues in his compelling thesis, one fundamental difference between the Darwinian narrative of evolution and the Arnoldian narrative of cultural perfection is that the former presupposes 'no specific goal, and the values of any given culture are relative to a specific adaptive situation' (Carroll 2004, 3). Instead, Arnold's idea of culture was essentially a goal-driven progress narrative, a constant activity towards existential perfection. In a subsequent study, Carroll delineates Arnold's humanistic design as a 'teleological scheme of cultural history, quasi-Hegelian, in which a transcendent force works through history toward a culminating realization of a perfected human condition' (ibid., 264). In the same work, Carroll argues how the postmodernist and deconstructionist turn in post-1960s Anglo-French literary criticism, despite their fractured fault lines and language games, retain two fundamental tenets of the Arnoldian strand of culture study: first, an abiding interest in verbal discourses and, secondly, a preference and celebration of ethical and subjective narratives over objective or fact-driven scientific truths. Arnold's engagements with the possibilities of poetry as the producer of culture, set against the non-teleological nature of Darwin's naturalism and against 'Darwin's bulldog' Thomas Huxley's idea of science as the overarching materialist vision informing the natural order where the human is all but a tiny speck, remains relevant, even when contested, in humanities-centric cultural studies today.

Eliot's work *Notes towards the Definition of Culture* has already been mentioned in the context of Raymond Williams's alienation post–Second World War. In a project structurally and spiritually similar to that of Arnold, Eliot sets out to define *culture* and classifies it as a 'development', one that is aimed towards not individual upliftment but for the entire society. If the Arnoldian tone of holistic collective improvement re-presents itself in Eliot's engagement, what makes the latter work almost strangely striking is Eliot's choice of populist material markers as objects of culture and cultural interests. Thus the description goes:

> Derby Day, Henley Regatta, Cowes, the twelfth of August, a cup final, the dog races, the pin table, the dart board, Wensleydale cheese, boiled cabbage cut into sections, beetroot in vinegar, 19th-century Gothic churches and the music of Elgar. The reader can make his own list. (Eliot 1949, 45)

Eliot's metonymic markers of culture correspond to his fluid description of the category as 'not merely the sum of several activities, but a *way of life*' (ibid., 45). Examining several stages of cultural assimilation in languages, religions, customs, and political interfaces, Eliot goes on to state something that sounds remarkably resonant with subsequent champions of multiculturalism: 'a national culture, if it is to flourish, should be a constellation of cultures, the constituents of which, benefiting each other, benefit the whole' (ibid., 99). Despite the drive for upliftment, what marks Eliot's thesis on culture as distinctly different from Arnold's is his advocacy for the necessary divisions in class and region which would, in Eliot's opinion, create healthy harmony as well as 'conflicts and jealousies which should be profitable to society' (ibid., 34). Thus Eliot's view of the ideal cultural state, unlike Arnold's, does not disregard the productive potential of conflicts and the 'vital importance for a society of *friction* between its parts' (ibid., 100), which are seen as sites of difference as well as dialogues.

Both Arnold and Eliot examine what is essentially a white, Christian culture and the latter's idea of cultural identities is indistinguishable from his Catholic Christian identity. Eliot's project of resurrecting the reception of the Metaphysical Poets may also be seen in connection with his advocacy of Catholic literature and culture, and Arnold's idea of humanism, although not explicitly stated, also embraces a deep-seated Christian sense of faith that seeks to situate itself against the naked naturalism of Darwin and Huxley. The worldview espoused by Eliot is essentially European, and the geopolitical zeitgeist and significance he locates in literary figures such as Goethe and Wordsworth also draw on their impact in a pan-European cultural context. Most strikingly, despite their lengthy and assiduous attempts at enunciating the values of liberty and freethinking, neither Arnold nor Eliot spend a sentence on the impact of English imperialism, although *Notes towards the Definition of Culture* engages with the perceived ills of the Indian caste system and how that has in turn influenced the English imagination. India thus enters Eliot's examination either as an exotic epistemic resource – his pronouncements on the *spiritual richness* of the Vedas and Upanishads are well known – or as a regressive cultural situation which ought to be avoided as a negative example, in classic corroboration of Edward Said's study of Orientalist discourses in European imagination. Said's reading of Arnold's *Culture and Anarchy* is interesting here for in it he examines how Arnold's perspective on culture – an aspiration towards perfection through the best that is known and thought – can quickly become an instrument in identity politics whereby a canonization of the supposedly finest forms of achievements in a national culture can alternately produce pride and xenophobia. As Said would go on to argue, this tendency to consume culture purely as a value-based aesthetic activity has historically informed the humanist inability to connect 'slavery, colonialist, and racial oppression, and imperial subjection on the one hand, and the poetry, fiction, philosophy of the society that engages with these practices, on the other' (Said 1994, xiv). Historically speaking, it is interesting to notice the conspicuous absence of any substantial discussion on imperialism in Arnold's and Eliot's humanistic treatises, as both *Culture and Anarchy* (1882) and *Notes towards the Definition of Culture* (1949) are historically situated at the high point and the immediate end point of imperialism. Among other things, this is comparable to the non-innocence of metaphors that Derrida expounds in his thesis on deconstruction whereby the literary focal point is often a covert consolidation of political proclivities and ideological activities, as instantiated by the canon of Kipling's poetry which this book offered as example earlier.

Derrida's location at the interface of literary and cultural studies is complex and contested and will be studied at length later here as well as elsewhere in this book. But it is important to note and historicize, especially in relation to the discussions on Arnold and Eliot above, their elitism in examining culture and literary artefacts, especially when the latter are regarded as timeless capsules of qualitative knowledge and moral values. A quick look at the endorsement of such a view followed by its critique may be had on examining the different stands of F. R. Leavis and Terry Eagleton. In his 1930 work *Mass Civilization and Minority Culture*, Leavis clearly classifies culture and literature as categories created and controlled by the *fit few* as opposed to the common majority. Delineating Dante, Shakespeare, Baudelaire, and Hardy as markers of high literature and culture, Leavis is quick to pronounce how their worth is determined and protected by the minority who have the 'power of profiting by the finest human experience of the past', who uphold 'the implicit standards that order the finer living of an age' (Leavis 1948, 144–45). Culture emerges in Leavis's study as a value-added activity, understood and executed only by the select few with higher gifts of reason and understanding. Most importantly, and from a literary point of view, culture to Leavis is the use of heightened language which informs fine living and which helps determine the difference in quality of spirits.

Leavis's examination and articulation of culture is a complex combination of the desirable and the perishable. Culture is thus that which must be desired as well as protected, and he is careful to situate the same in binary opposition to mass production and consumption. The difference, according to Leavis, lies in the depth of human experience and genuine human response which is markedly different from the formulaic, stereotypical quality of markers of mass production. Particularly critical of Hollywood and its designed address to what he considers the lowest common denominator of human intelligence, Leavis's study encompasses what he considers as the decadence in reading and broadcasting and the monstrous growth of the popular cinema industry, among other issues. What emerges in Leavis's reading is an examination of how the 'inherited codes of habit and valuation' experience a 'breach in continuity that threatens', through a process of passive consumption, that 'what has been inadvertently dropped may be irrecoverable or forgotten' (Leavis 1930, 6–7). Leavis attributes such decadence to the rise of the machines of production and dissemination, one that creates a culture of consumption which is numbed and inattentive. In such cultural conditions, Leavis argues, the difference between 'highbrow' and 'lowbrow' becomes more marked and pronounced, and the upholders of desirable culture are pushed to the periphery like never before. Thus, Leavis argues, while *Hamlet*, *Clarissa*, *Paradise Lost*, *Tom Jones*, *Don Juan*, and *The Return of the Native* appealed 'at a number of levels of response, from the top downwards' (ibid., 7), modern literary masterpieces such as *Ulysses*, *The Waste Land*, and *To the Lighthouse* are read only by a select few, a 'very specialized public that are beyond the reach of the vast majority of those who consider themselves educated' (ibid., 17). Implicit in Leavis's study is thus an ontological tension between culture and education, and he readily goes on to state how, in twentieth-century modernity, civilization and culture have become antithetical categories whereby the desire for power and civilization frequently emerge as inimical to culture and cultural values.

Leavis's nostalgia for a pastoral Wordsworthian era of culture stems from an aversion towards twentieth-century semiotic systems of signification and consumption, dominated by what he considers as mindless machines of production and repetition. His essentialist bracketing of earlier literary masterpieces (effacing the fact that *Hamlet* and *Paradise Lost* are separated by several centuries) is romantically reified and reductive. *Mass Civilization and Minority Culture* is particularly pointed in its critique of the consumption of signs, from bad literature (Leavis cites a letter in his notes from the Tarzan creator Edgar Rice Burroughs which admits to satisfying the commercial need to frame fiction whose consumption needs 'minimum mental effort') to bad broadcasting, and, of course, the flat formulaic films produced en masse by the Hollywood cinema industry. In what emerges as a curious approximation and anticipation of Structuralist poetics, Leavis attributes early twentieth-century cultural decline to a hyper-production of signs thus:

> A reader who grew up with Wordsworth moved with a limited set of signals (so to speak): the variety was not overwhelming. So he was able to acquire discrimination as he went along. But the modern is exposed to a concourse of signals so bewildering in their variety and number that, unless he is especially gifted or especially favoured, he can hardly begin to discriminate. Here we have the plight of culture in general. The landmarks have shifted, multiplied, and crowded upon one another, the distinctions and dividing lines have blurred away, the boundaries are gone, and the arts and literatures of different countries have flowed together. (Leavis 1930, 18–19)

Leavis's reading of the decadence of modernity here sounds like Marx's lament of all that is solid melting into thin air, but also implicit in this description is an essentialized version of the past as an uncomplicated and idyllic landscape of time, where culture could flourish without disturbance of *bad signs*. Therefore, Wordsworthian time (which was materially complex and politically volatile) is reduced to a pastoral past, in a deliberately designed contrast to the supposedly ceaseless consumption of signals and signs that mark modernity. Also striking in Leavis's argument here is the unequivocal critique of the mixing of arts and literary idioms of various cultures, which is perceived as contamination that further accounts for the confused consumption.

Leavis's lament about cultural decline due to contamination and his dramatic description of the need to uphold the conservative canon of literature and literary reading is perhaps best exemplified in his discourse on the great canon itself. In his controversial 1948 work, *The Great Tradition*, Leavis offers an elaborate definition of culture from the perspective of literary production whereby culture emerges as a descriptive as well as a diegetic discourse laden with values and moral mappings. Literary greatness, in Leavis's study, is most readily marked by the degree of moral commitment that consolidates and integrates ideology through the fictional frame. Explaining Dickens's absence from his list due to the fact that he sought, as a writer, mostly to entertain, Leavis mentions *Hard Times* as a notable exception in Dickens's oeuvre, as a novel where Dickens's 'distinctive creative genius is controlled throughout by a unifying and organizing significance' (Leavis 1948, 19). Earlier in his book, Leavis had set out to define the benchmarks of belonging to the great tradition by expounding on the combination of innovative formal techniques and, more importantly, 'the moral preoccupations that concern the novelist's peculiar interest in life' (ibid., 9). The great literary work, in Leavis's estimation, must therefore be formally perfect as well as morally profound, and he uses this criterion to include and exclude writers, ending with a list featuring only Jane Austen, George Eliot, Henry James, Joseph Conrad, and D. H. Lawrence. Leavis's exclusion of Joyce from the great tradition, too, is due to his opinion that *Ulysses*, despite its technical brilliance and formal innovations which offer an 'exhaustive rendition of consciousness' and emerges as a new start in 'a cosmopolitan literary world', does not have an 'organic principle' that converts its stylistic structures into one whole and instead appears as a 'pointer to disintegration' (ibid., 25–26). Leavis ends his introduction by restating his rationale and highlighting his choices: 'Jane Austen, George Eliot, Henry James, Conrad, and D. H. Lawrence: the great tradition of the English novel is *there*' (ibid., 27). The final word suggests a closure that precludes possibilities of debate as well as underlining a privileged spatial location that is permanent and unchallengeable. *There* thus dramatically underlines the site of canon production – an unshakeable idea as well as a permanent place – very much in keeping with the Leavisian notion of the organic homogeneity of high culture.

The Great Tradition may be seen as a neat extension of Leavis's understanding of culture as a hygienic wholesome entity which is precious as well as perishable and thus in need of protection and preservation. However, its polemical significance as a blatant advocacy of the conservative tradition in literature is complexly collusive to an idea of culture informed by elitism and exclusivity. As Catherine Belsey argues in her excellent critique of *The Great Tradition*, Leavis's readings reduce the plurality of interpretations and does a disservice to even the texts it selects in the canon by 'confining their meanings within the conventional, the acceptable, the authoritatively "obvious"' (Belsey 1992, 122). Evident throughout Belsey's critique of Leavis is an examination of the latter's unproblematic equation between empiricism and idealism, mediated by classic realism. Literature is thus supposed to showcase human experience, while also instructing how to experience more morally. In the process, what is revealed is Leavis's idea of timeless moral values that great works of literature are supposed to provide through their lifelike and life-affirming characters and situations. Classic realism thus emerges as a potent tool to corroborate and consolidate what are supposedly seamless and universal forms of knowledge through a strategic effacement of their epistemic and narrative unreliability. The great tradition of literature is therefore constituted by works of unifying and edifying values that have no interruptions or fault lines in their moral compass. For Leavis, in literature as in culture, morality and integrative unity are all. Such morality and unity, however, even in a superficial study, emerge as far from being apolitical and are instead invested with white conservative politics of privilege.

Terry Eagleton's views on culture and the politics of literary production may be situated as an interesting obverse to Leavis's, perhaps with some degree of irony because Eagleton may be considered as among the first generation of undergraduates in Anglo-American academia to have emerged from the Leavisian understanding of English as a curriculum-centric canonical discipline. Moving spectacularly away from Leavis's location of literature as a moral compass for grand humanitarian values that unify and integrate, Eagleton instead examines literary production as complexly situated in fields of discursive practices. Indeed, Eagleton's understanding of literature as a special label given to 'certain kinds of writing' within discursive fields is significant in the context of this book in its examination of literature as a complex negotiation with discursivity. Eagleton's direct critique of the Leavisian great tradition may offer interesting light on the politics of literary production and reception which this book seeks to espouse. In his 2012 work titled *The Event of Literature*, Eagleton clearly locates the Leavisian literary morality as a strategic faith system in a post-religious world. Literature to Leavis thus becomes 'an evangelical campaign' (Eagleton 2012, 59) which replaces religion in twentieth-century cultural modernity. It is interesting to situate Eagleton's argument about Leavis in relation to the earlier inference about Arnold in this book, whereby poetry and the novel become the only available grand narratives of faith and morality in white liberal fictional imagination in a post-Darwinian world.

In *The Event of Literature*, Eagleton mentions a series of literary critics and writers espousing this tradition of looking at literature as a grand moral compass. Thus, in the nineteenth century, Arnold, Ruskin, Pater, Wilde, and Henry James shifted the ontology of morality from a set of codes to a value system. Such process was perfected and perpetuated in the twentieth-century English literary imagination and criticism, in Eagleton's opinion, by Leavis, Bakhtin, Trilling, Empson, and Raymond Williams (ibid., 59). Instead of the high morality of Leavis, Eagleton situates literature closer to the project of deconstruction and double inscription, whereby literary texts become 'exemplary' in the Derridean sense, by 'portraying irreducibly specific situations which are at the same time, by the very nature of language, of more general import' (ibid., 83). This dual potential of fiction to connect to the specific event while also retaining an *epistemic elasticity* that allows it to appear as a commentary of other cultural contexts is key to this book, not least as it examines the interface of literary and cultural studies. This connects to the ambivalence associated with the emergence of the literary as an ontological and a representative category, whereby the dual temporality of the fictional frame 'sets up a tension and perhaps a necessary contradiction between the interlocking dimensions of instituted value and reflexive awareness' (Frow 2005, 55–56). In its inconstant location between the temporal orders of historical discursivity and immediate self-reflexivity, literature becomes an act of *narrative emergence* in which culture as an institutional and intersubjective category is uniquely and affectively represented.

In an earlier work titled *The Function of Criticism* (1984), Eagleton historicizes the rise of literary criticism in English and situates its inception in the eighteenth-century bourgeois public sphere. Therefore, literary production and consumption, especially that of the novel in English, was historically and discursively connected to the rise of respectability of the middle classes apropos of a decadent and regressive aristocracy which was to be morally corrected through sermons and satires (Eagleton 1984, 10). In the same book, Eagleton goes on to state how literary criticism in eighteenth-century England was all but a component of and a moral pointer to a larger cultural discourse including, but not limited to, 'attitudes to servants and the rules of gallantry, the status of women and familial affections, the purity of the English language, the character of conjugal love, the psychology of the sentiments and the laws of the toilet' (ibid., 18). It is not difficult to see how this would naturally extend to Arnold's and Eliot's discussion of literature as a special storehouse of conservative culture and as a moderator of moral principles and values. The same strand of vigorous empiricism also informs Leavis's understanding of literary greatness. The coveted *canon* in Leavis's cultural critique is therefore the grand narrative of instructive literature that is designed to disseminate traditional tenets of moral and social greatness. The highly selectionist model of Leavis's desirable literary ontology corresponds closely to the doctrine of culture being the purview of the fit few over and above the commonly consumed. Eagleton's position as a Marxist literary critic is exactly the opposite of this, with its interrogation of presupposed privilege and norms informing literary greatness. This receives its classic corroboration in Eagleton's argument that a culture in the future where Shakespeare is no more important than present-day graffiti may actually emerge from a general sense of 'human enrichment' (Eagleton 1983, 10) rather than bearing signs of decadence.

Eagleton's most direct opposition to Leavis apropos of literature's location in culture lies in his reading of the literary canon as a construct, 'fashioned by particular people for particular reasons at a certain time' (ibid., 10). Implicit in Eagleton's definition is the cognitive and collective biases that inform the canon, which is invested ideologically as well as materially. The construct of the canon is also a pointer to the politics of consumption at a certain time, connecting to the broader definition of culture as an act of construction and consumption that entails effective as well as affective apparatuses. This four-term frame – effective, affective, material, abstract – is key to this book, which seeks to examine culture as an activity and an artefact as well as an organic form of memory and affect. Literature emerges in this examination as a representational activity as well as an affective apparatus. Its location is unique compared to other representational forms such as cinema inasmuch as it is entirely embedded in language construction and consumption. Tracing the growth of literary discourse, its dissemination, and its consumption, Eagleton in *The Function of Criticism* offers a complex understanding of literature's location as a special marginalized presence that is also a privilege, one which reveals as well as conceals the fault lines of late capitalism with which it often colludes even while critiquing. Comparable again to Derrida's notion of the entanglement of revelation and concealment, Eagleton's understanding of literature's play of presence and absence apropos of hegemonic culture is of special significance in this book. The role of *high culture* in relation to capitalism is equally complex as Eagleton argues, for it is 'neither decorative irrelevance nor indispensable ideology, neither structural nor superfluous, but a properly marginal presence, marking the border where that society both encounters and exiles its own disabling absences' (ibid., 92). The marginality of culture and literature had been examined by Arnold and Leavis in a different light, as a glorious as well as a subversive category that aims to situate itself against the hegemony of naturalism and capitalism. Such marginality emerges in Eagleton's reading as a far less innocuous location, for it also becomes a safe haven for capitalism's slippages and absences, where the difference between ideology and its critique is never clear or consistent. This is corroborated above in Arnold's and Eliot's takes on culture, morality, and value formation where any discussion on English imperialism is conspicuously absent.

Eagleton's critique of Leavis has interesting parallels with Pierre Macherey's thesis in *The Theory of Literary Production* (1966), which defines and underlines two kinds of fallacies in criticism: the *empiricist* fallacy and the *normative* fallacy. While the first errs in treating the text as entirely consumable for criticism, as a thing 'isolated for inspection' (Macherey 1966, 13), locating the entire meaning of a text in the manner in which it is received, the second is problematic because it modifies a literary text entirely with the tools of criticism, describing its factual reality (outside of the critical narrative) as 'merely the provisional version of an unfulfilled intention' (ibid., 19). In what appears as an interesting comparison to Derridean deconstruction, Macherey undercuts what he classifies as the *interpretative* fallacy – which he defines as a 'postulate of depth' (ibid., 80) – by advocating a departure from organicist vitalist criticism. Citing Lenin's reading of Tolstoy and connecting that to his own reading of Jules Verne, Macherey argues that the meaning of a literary text lies not in any supposed centre but as a mutable process on the margins. Such a critical perspective, in Macherey's view, eschews any 'false simplicity' (ibid., 79) and instead aspires to arrive at a 'conflict of meaning' (ibid., 79) which is not a sign of its imperfection but rather emerges as an 'inscription of an otherness' (ibid., 79) through which the text connects to its ontological obverse. This corresponds closely to the central philosophical argument in this book, one that examines literature as a production of possibilities, as an articulation of ambivalence whereby commonly consumed cultural codes may be alternately and sometimes simultaneously consolidated and questioned. Macherey is an important theorist in a study to situate literature's interpretative possibilities apropos of a culture's material as well as abstract/affective production principles. More significantly, his accentuation of conflict of meanings and meaningful conflicts render the fictional frame of literature a field of fault lines and fractures where identities are almost always playful and sometimes subversive. In Macherey's reading, the location of literature and literary meanings apropos of culture and cultural valences is also an indicator of the mutable and material quality of values.

Contrary to the Leavisian idea of the ideal literary text as a site of abundant holistic production which throws a healthy moral light on social relations, Macherey describes the complex literary text as not an 'extension of a meaning' (ibid., 80) but rather an incomplete 'incompatibility of several meanings' (ibid., 80) which connects to reality through a 'tense and ever-renewed confrontation' (ibid., 80). More significantly, departing from the Leavisian criterion of literary greatness determined by the text's unifying potential in relation to its contemporary ideology, Macherey concludes the first part of his book by delineating the different fallacies that emerge from conventional literary criticism: the fallacy of depth, the fallacy of the secret, the fallacy of harmony, and the fallacy of rules (ibid., 101). In Macherey's reading, a literary text is informed by what it says as much as by what it refuses to say and what it cannot say. In the process, it is never a closed capsule of its contemporary values and is instead an entanglement of statements and silences which are always open-ended, mutable, and sometimes connected. Similar to Eagleton's examination engaged with above, Macherey proposes a study of literary production where the binary between ideological consolidation and subversion is never neat and consistent. This is corroborated by several texts studied subsequently in this book, from Joseph Conrad's *Heart of Darkness* to George Orwell's *Burmese Days*. Validating Macherey's thesis about interpretative incompatibilities and variations, both texts engage with their contemporary cultural apparatus without a neat binary between consolidation and critique. Both Conrad's and Orwell's takes on imperialism are focalized through a cynical ambivalence that nonetheless retains the racism and complicity of white imperial masculinity. In both texts – as examined subsequently drawing on Macherey's theory of literary production – the unstated and the absences play significant roles in the context of the politics of representation and interpretative possibilities, problematizing the relationship between the centre and the margin, complicity and critique. As Derrida's works on representation, ethics, and politics make clear, any attempt to systematize a stable binary between hegemony and subversion always runs the risk of reduction and reification. This is perhaps most true in the context of literary production, reception, and consumption. It is to Derrida and his lasting impact on the interface of literary and cultural studies that the book directs its attention now.

Jacques Derrida's work on the deferral and difference in signs and the production of possibilities which can also accommodate impossibilities has profound significance for a study that examines matter's relationship with metaphor and memory, at the interface between the cultural and the literary. Derrida seems to be the perfect philosopher for a frame that aims to bring together affect and thing theory within the broad arc of memory studies. More importantly, his study of the politics of production of signs and non-innocence of metaphors brings the literary domain in close and complex proximity to political and cultural landscapes. Shunned by certain cultural theorists for being too theoretical as opposed to being practically and immediately political, Derrida's deconstruction is actually an instrument to examine the politics of production, materialization, and institutionalization that constitutes culture and cultural codes. Derrida's own views on the possibilities of deconstruction as a device corroborate this:

> All that a deconstructive point of view tries to show, is that since convention, institutions and consensus are stabilizations, . . . they are stabilizations of something essentially unstable and chaotic. . . . If there were continual stability, there would be no need for politics, and it is to the extent that stability is not natural, essential or substantial, that politics exists and ethics is possible. Chaos is at once a risk and a chance, and it is here that the possible and the impossible cross each other. (Derrida 1996, 83–84)

What is inherent in Derrida's discourse here is the acceptance of chaos as an ontological and epistemic situation, one which entails the ambivalence of absence and articulation, preclusion and production. This is precisely the point where literature as a representative category emerges apropos of culture and cultural productions. For literature is marked by slippages and structures of stabilization that underline the entanglement of the possible and the fantastic, accommodated in and articulated by the frame of fiction.

Derrida problematizes the possibilities of fiction further by exploring the inexhaustibility of textual interpretations, in the process underlining the textuality of culture and cultural codes. This inexhaustibility is not perceived as hostility but rather hospitality in Derrida's deconstructionist politics. Thus he argues:

> Giving to the other to be read is also a *leaving to be desired*, or a leaving the other room for an intervention by which she will be able to write her own intervention: the other will have to be able to sign in my text. And it is here that the desire not to be understood means, simply, hospitableness to the reading of the other, not the rejection of the other. (Derrida 2001, 32)

Derrida's theorization of the other through the abstruseness of interpretation offers a fascinating frame to examine culture and literary texts alike; whereby the coded constructed quality of both are only incompletely available and interpretable. Highlighting the incompleteness as accommodation rather than rejection, Derrida underlines the plasticity pervading the processes of cultural identity formation and textual production. More importantly, and from the theoretical point of view of this study, Derrida's thesis accentuates the complex combination of materiality and abstraction that constitutes culture and cultural formations, whereby narratives of knowledge as well as its absence become accommodated and articulated. Read in this light, literature and fiction become language games that produce understanding and its slippages as vectors of any given culture. Derrida's deconstruction extends to complex readings of political presences and absences using literary metaphors and analogies, as evinced in his comparison in *Spectres of Marx* of the spectre of communism haunting Europe to the figure of the ghost of Hamlet's father. By mapping the play between presence and absence, and by examining both as productive epistemic categories, Derrida's deconstruction sets the field to study literature as a complex commentary on culture, one that offers an entanglement of information and interpretation. More importantly, Derrida's take on the desirable inexhaustibility and opacity of meanings has interesting bearings on the open-endedness of literary texts, which then emerges as material as well as metaphorical assemblages embedded in cultural narratives, while also offering newer light on the same. Culture and the literary thus enter into representational matrices by depicting how matter may be represented in metaphors, how memory can be remembered by foregrounding the forgotten.

Derrida's critique of *practical political science* that shuns theory and abstraction is also significant in the context of literature and literary theory, for in it he highlights how such practical discourse would 'deck itself out in "realism" just in time to fall short of the thing – and to repeat, repeat, and repeat again, with neither consciousness nor memory of its compulsive droning' (Derrida 1997, 81). Realism as a representative strategy here appears in Derrida's study as a form and a repetitive ritual that produce and perpetuate hegemonic belief systems, in close correspondence to the critique of realism in postmodernist literary and narrative theory. Significant here is also Derrida's examination of the compulsory and compulsive consumption of knowledge that undercuts interpretation and intervention. Culture in its most consolidated and hegemonic form may be seen as such a process of consumption and consolidation, similar to the politics of internalization and interpellation examined by Althusser. Examined in this light, literature may emerge as a further extension of this realism whereby hegemonic practices and power systems are justified and glorified, as in Kipling's imperial fiction and poetry. Equally, literature can emerge as an articulation of ambivalence that undercuts the supposed seamlessness and transparency of realism, as in the fiction of Joseph Conrad and George Orwell, subsequently studied in this book.

Derrida's study of transparency as an ontological and hermeneutic category is important in this context as well, as it connects to his original idea of the desirable *belatedness* and interpretative incompletion of texts. Transparency may also be seen, following Derrida's examination, as dominant cultural consolidation through forms of coercion and consent that efface the fluid fault lines for deconstructive performance. Describing the dangers of such transparent consolidations, Derrida also points out the temporal politics of the same by stating how if 'such transparency of intelligibility were ensured it would destroy the text, it would show that the text has no future, that it does not overflow the present, that it is consumed immediately' (ibid., 32). Noticeable in Derrida's description here is the necessity of the text to survive complete consumption in the *prison house of the present*, whereby absolute transparency and intelligibility are inimical to interpretative possibilities. Therefore, a text can only defy destruction by overflowing the consumption of the present, by foregrounding plasticity instead of fixity. It is interesting to examine how literature and literary productions may be mapped using Derrida's theory here as a play between plasticity and fixity located in language, while also dramatizing how such language can be gainfully used to represent characters and situations in fiction that are reflections of realities as well as productions of possibilities.

Derrida's argument about the *potency* of literature and its exemplary superiority over philosophy and history emerges from his understanding of literature as an activity, one which is based on *iterability* and *condensation* (Derrida 1992, 42–43). While iterability stems from the semantic singularity of literary language, whereby iteration is almost always reiteration, in keeping with the politics of representation, condensation is literature's negotiation with history and historical materiality. The 'economy of exemplary iterability' is for Derrida also an instance of literature's formalization whereby a 'text by Joyce is simultaneously a condensation of a scarcely delimitable history' (ibid., 43). Derrida's definition of literature as a 'counter-institutional institution that is both subversive and conservative' (ibid., 58) fits in perfectly with the theoretical frame of this book which aims to examine literature as simultaneously critical and complicit with its contemporary cultural apparatus. As a sophisticated insider of a culture's sign system, literature is substantive as well as performative in its inconsistent and inconclusive engagements with reality. In the process, it inhabits the seamless surface as well as the fractured fault lines between reality and possibility, producing what Derrida describes as the 'paradoxes of its *economy*' (ibid., 59) that may be alternately phallogocentric and anti-phallogocentric.

Implicit throughout Derrida's discourse on literature is an understanding of the self-sustaining slippages of the literary medium apropos of its cultural consumption, slippages facilitated by deconstruction. Underlining again the element of iterability, Derrida describes how a literary text may be rooted out of its own original location and how, in the process, 'transplantable out of their own context, they continue to have meaning and effectiveness' (ibid., 64). This has immediate relevance for the scope of this book where literature is examined as a variable vector of culture and how cultural valences are materialized, metaphorized, and remembered. In Derrida's reading, the literary text is always already deconstructed (he mentions his reluctance to theorize Beckett due to the close commonality between deconstruction and Beckett's theatre of difference and deferral) and is thus always an inconstant (deferring as well as differing) engagement with reality through (re)iterability. This examination of reality through reiterability (both material and affective) offers an interesting comparison with the works of Slavoj Žižek whose connection with the abstraction-production frame of Louis Althusser has already been mentioned. This introduction will now examine Žižek's work apropos of literature and culture.

Žižek's work on continental philosophy, psychoanalysis, literature, and popular media warrants special attention in a book on cultural and literary studies. The only philosopher to have a peer-reviewed academic journal named after him during his lifetime, Žižek offers a series of frames to examine the entanglement of matter, metaphor, and memory, mixing a critique of culture and literary theory in complex combinations. His own critique of academic cultural studies (as collusive and complicit with capitalism) notwithstanding, Žižek's celebration of theory (over and above the realm of ethnographic and close textual research) is informed by his engagements with Hegel, Marx, and Lacan. While Hegel offers Žižek an epistemological frame to map the dialectical movement of history, Marx's model offers him a materialist vision of the construction and consumption of ideology. Lastly, the Lacanian theory offers Žižek a structure of the subconscious that unpredictably navigates with the historical and ideological realities around the human self. This tripartite model of Žižek's theory, which is largely a critique of capitalism and cultural studies' complicity with it, offers a fine frame to examine the entanglement of materiality and affect. More importantly, this model may be gainfully mapped onto a study of literature's location apropos of cultural production and consumption, which informs the main enquiry of this book.

Examining how it shuttles between Kantian philosophy and vulgar jokes, between Hegel and Hitchcock, Catherine Belsey underlines the exhilaration generated by Žižek's theoretical apparatus (Belsey 2005, 97). Despite their detractors, Žižek's works have pervaded popular culture and academia alike, with its creative combination of several complex theoretical frames. This is most famously eulogized by Terry Eagleton who describes Žižek as the 'most formidably brilliant exponent of psychoanalysis, indeed of cultural theory in general, to have emerged from Europe in some decades' (Eagleton 2003, 200), a description that features in many of Žižek's book covers. In his critique of capitalism, Žižek foregrounds the complex of ideology and psychology, of material reality and the mind, thus dramatizing the play of matter, metaphor, and memory examined in this book. This is immediately evinced in Žižek's reading, in the context of the 9/11 attacks, of Conrad's Kurtz in *Heart of Darkness*, who is examined as a figure who has dangerously over-appropriated the tenets and excesses of imperialism, to the extent that he becomes a problem that imperialism must now get rid of. The Lacanian frame in Žižek's philosophy offers complex readings of the play between the symbolic and the real, with careful attention to the dissemination and appropriation of signs in texts and popular culture alike. More importantly, such Lacanian readings also demonstrate for Žižek the ultimate irreducibility of the human subject to socio-economic conditions, interestingly comparable again to Althusser's notion of relative autonomy examined earlier. This has special significance in the context of this study, as it aims to examine the play between materiality and memory, locating the fictional possibilities offered by literature at the interface of culture and its consumption.

Žižek's issue with compulsory political correctness, which is also his issue with cultural studies as a discipline, has interesting bearings when it comes to the question of literature apropos of culture. Critiquing the disciplinary formalizing of cultural studies and examining how its apparent deterritorialization often emerges as a reaffirmation of capitalist control, Žižek's reading may be mapped onto the productively inconclusive nature of fiction's engagement with reality. This is akin to Derrida's reading of the deconstructive (re)iterability of literary texts whereby the text can be simultaneously subversive and collusive. As in Jane Austen's *Pride and Prejudice*, which may be read as a celebration as well as a scathing satire of the fetish and institutionalization of marriage, or John Fowles's *The French Lieutenant's Woman*, which offers a satire on Victorian morality from an insider as well as an outsider position, literature's negotiation with morality and materiality is mediated by points of view. As stylized representations of reality in language, points of view in literary works are a complex combination of subjective/epistemological and objective/ontological conditions. Such a combination offers alternate possibilities of reality as well as displacing the discourse of the real in symbolic terms, operative at the interface of culture and the literary, through markers of matter, metaphor, and memory. The key issue here is that of *displacement*, which connects the cultural realms of objects and their affect. Literature and literary production may be seen as narratives of this *displacement* in language, whereby the plurality of points of view through several linguistic registers corresponds to several subjective frames. Žižek's notion of the parallax, 'the apparent displacement of an object (the shift of its position against a background) caused by a change in observational position that provides a new line of sight' (Žižek 2011, 244) is particularly pertinent here, offering an entanglement of material reality and affectivity. More importantly, it connects to the theory of literature espoused in this book, a production of possibilities whereby the ontology of the object and its meaning may be mutated according to shifts in subject position and narrative point of view. This has significant bearings on the concept of culture and its critique, as examined in subsequent sections in this study of culture and the literary, through an examination of the interplay of matter, metaphor, and memory.

Žižek would go on to argue that the parallax view in architecture may be mapped onto the experience of reading and storytelling, whereby – Žižek alludes to Claude Lévi-Strauss – time becomes space as in the politics of the production of myth (ibid., 245). The literary landscape apropos of its cultural reality and materiality may be examined as a parallax situation of affectivity and possibility wherein the ontology of reality shifts along with the shifts in subject position. In other words, and in continuation with Žižek's reading of Lévi-Strauss, fiction may be seen as a combination of epistemological and ontological, temporal and spatial orders, offering unique frames of experiential and alternate reality that consolidate as well as question the consumption of culture. The shifting subject positions in fiction – comparable to Žižek's theory of the parallax – may be seen as shifts in space and time that foreground as well as focalize points of view. In the process, literature – especially apropos of culture and cultural production – may be examined as a method of *defamiliarization* whereby ordinary consumable reality is represented in fiction. Such defamiliarization through fictional representation emerges with material as well as affective markers which blur the boundaries between ontological reality and experientiality, sometimes mapping the latter problematically onto the former. This is uniquely pertinent in Joseph Conrad's *Heart of Darkness*, a novel which will be examined in subsequent sections of this book. In Conrad's text, the fictional literary landscape offers an affective, ambient, and ambivalent understanding of the reality of its historical and material setting, making its fictional voices simultaneously critical and complicit with the grand narrative of imperialism. More importantly, the *defamiliarization* and *delayed decoding* in Conrad's novel foreground the stylized representation of reality in cognitive and experiential terms, while also making it politically problematic and racially reductionist.

Žižek's advocacy of fiction ahead of truth (in cinema as well as in narrative prose) has interesting bearings in the politics of representation, especially in an examination of literature's location in culture and cultural materiality. Describing the *effective communication* of fiction in terms of its ontological distinction from truth, Žižek attributes the same to the production of possibilities, which is also the working definition of fiction in this book. In his examination of the *leap of faith* produced by fiction, Žižek argues how such affect becomes effective because it 'cuts the debilitating deadlock of language' by '*presenting what we should strive for as already accomplished*' (Žižek 2006, 52). This description underlines the complex spatiotemporal quality of fiction, whereby possibilities of the present and the real world of culture and materiality appear perfected or problematized in a space-time which approximates the real while also being removed from it. In terms of producing actualized possibilities from the present, fiction thus generates a world which is always already *ahead in time*. In this work on the parallax view produced by fictional representations (in literature as well as in cinema), Žižek theorizes abstraction in literature apropos of cultural consumption in cognitive/epistemic terms, whereby, as in the case of Kafka's fiction, reading 'demands a great effort of abstraction' which entails not 'learning more' but rather of '*unlearning the standard interpretive references*' (ibid., 114). The subversive quality of literature apropos of culture thus often lies in its production and experience of unlearning, whereby the familiar discursive apparatus is defamiliarized. In Kafka's case, as Žižek would go on to argue, the production of *partial objects* and *irresolution* are key to his fiction, where things are either elusively transcendental (the mysterious castle and trial) or grotesquely ridiculous (humans turning into monstrous insects). Such contradictions are meant to be read together, in the true spirit of *jouissance*: that which can never be actually acquired and that which can never be rejected, exemplified in Kafka's genius through an eroticization of bureaucracy (ibid., 115).

Studying the narrative and political potential of fiction in relation to reality, Žižek argues that 'at the most radical level, one can portray the

Real of subjective experience only through the guise of a fiction' (ibid., 30). According to this theory, if the Real represents the ontology of reality that always requires reference points for hermeneutic and experiential engagement, fiction offers the symbolic registers to represent the Real in all its desirability and monstrosity. Žižek's reading here situates literature strategically in relation to meaningful materiality and culture whereby the desirable and the disposable are simultaneously and alternately accommodated and articulated. In such an examination of the desirable and disposable objects as represented in fiction, the culture of consumption and the consumption of culture emerge as connected and axiomatic activities. Such a complex of desirability and disposability may also be connected to the production of a partial understanding of reality and affectivity, most often represented in fiction through the instrument of irony. In that context, Žižek's readings of *partial objects* and *irresolution* in fiction are key to this book, which examines the entanglement of metonymic materiality and affect in relation to literary representation and reception. Undercutting any easy assumption of ontological density and continuity, partial objects in fiction underline the constructed quality of materiality and meaning making in cultural consumption. Likewise, Žižek's study of irresolution offers an insight into the politics of ambivalence, which is a crucial affective and epistemological category in this book, comparable to the category of opacity, which interrupts and interrogates seamless structures of meaning and discourse (Belsey 1980). Žižek's notion of partiality as a privileged epistemic category is comparable with his idea of the privilege of fiction over documented data, as he argues that *'universal truth is accessible only through a partial engaged subject position'* (Žižek 2006, 35), partiality and experiential engagement being the forte of fiction.

Through his combination of dialectical materialism and Lacanian theory, Žižek offers an interface between material engagement theory and affect studies that this book draws on in its attempt to situate literature and literary production apropos of culture, its critique, and its consumption. More importantly, Žižek's study of fantasy as a system of sign production which is also a defence mechanism against the threat of the Real has special resonances in a study of literature's location in an economy of cultural consumption and internalization. As a funny case study, Žižek describes the classic situations from *Tom & Jerry* cartoons where characters get run over by trucks and hammered by heavy machines, turning into grotesque shapes and yet moving on normally in subsequent scenes. Žižek examines those scenes as the fantasy of perversion, which produces the 'universe of pure symbolic order, of the signifiers' game running its course, unencumbered by the Real of human finitude' (Žižek 2001, 84–85). In *Did Someone Say Totalitarianism?*, Žižek offers an excellent example of the entanglement of material production and sentimental abstraction, of conservative consolidation and subversion, apropos of the location of fiction in cultural materiality. Examining Georg Lukács's reading of *One Day in the Life of Ivan Denisovich* by Alexander Solzhenitsyn, Žižek highlights how the socialist work ethic is depicted and almost celebrated in a scene in the novel, despite its dissident narrative that operates at a macro level. The scene in question is set in a Soviet Gulag where the eponymous protagonist rushes back to complete pasting the last bricks on the wall despite sirens from the guards and later ruminates on the finished act with a sense of satisfaction (Žižek 2001, 135–36). That scene may be examined using Macherey's model of mutual incompatibility in fiction as examined above, interestingly comparable to Žižek's theory of irresolution. The solid satisfaction of completing an assigned work even in the repressive Gulag, where one is imprisoned as a dissident, offers an excellent example of abstract (bad) faith amid a hard-core totalitarian political apparatus, whereby 'the specifically Socialist notion of material production as a site of creative fulfilment survived' (ibid., 135).

The survival of such sentiment may be seen as an example of internalization that works almost as motor memory, bringing into play the contradiction of political reality and affectivity, doubly ironical in its situatedness in a coercive site of material production and ideological interpellation. Literature may also be seen, following Žižek's examples, as the production of fiction and fantasy through signs that may reflect as well as represent the Lacanian Real. Such representation may also emerge, drawing on Žižek's study, as cognitive remappings that complicate the relationship between experience and history, event and memory. As studies in cognition and culture through literary representations make clear, literature's embeddedness in language and thought processes makes it a pronounced as well as problematic representation of possibilities that dramatizes cultural identities as well as intersubjectivity.

The theorists and philosophers discussed above are by no means an exhaustive list of thinkers relevant for this line of enquiry. The overarching narrative in this book is an understanding of culture as a coded construct, one which is an instrument as well as an affective activity, and any examination of culture and literature will include a study of their symbiosis and subversion apropos of the politics of power and identity. This book will be particularly directed towards an understanding of how fiction as a production of possibilities may be alternately complicit and subversive towards dominant cultural identities. Through a study of selected theorists and philosophers, this introduction has tried to trace how the hegemonic understanding of culture and literary production has been historically and theoretically consolidated and critiqued, sometimes simultaneously. The fundamental interpretative frame used in this book is deconstructionist, and the main theoretical windows appropriated in this enquiry are memory studies, material engagement theory, and affect studies. Along with the figures discussed in the introduction, the works of several other philosophers – including Michel Foucault, Frantz Fanon, Edward Said, Judith Butler, and Zygmunt Bauman – are examined subsequently across the chapters that follow. This introduction has attempted to examine literature as an affective engagement with culture using the frame of fiction and, in the process, has studied the selected figures in a bid to accentuate the same. Certain figures, especially Arnold, Eliot, and Leavis, have been deliberately selected to critically examine the easy interpellation that can be produced and perpetuated between literature and high culture, underlining the hegemonic quality of both beneath their value-added affective frames. The works of certain other figures in this introduction such as Eagleton and Derrida have been studied as templates of cultural materialism and deconstruction, especially in relation to cultural valences and fiction. The aim has been to examine how literature and literary production may emerge as endorsement as well as subversion of the narratives through which culture and cultural codes are reflected and reinforced. What emerges in the process is the discursive and constructed quality of value and literary merit, which manifests itself as coded categories determined by and invested with affective as well as material markers.

One of the principal points of this introduction, which aims to set the tone for this book, was to examine ambivalence as an experiential and an epistemic category, whereby contradictions and partial meanings may be simultaneously situated and articulated. This is particularly pertinent to highlighting the location of literature apropos of culture and cultural production in terms of studying how matter and metaphor may be described and deconstructed in relation to memory and history. If culture is a complex combination of matter and memory, literature is especially suited to reflect and represent the same with its fictional and sometimes metaphorical engagement with events and eventualities. This deconstructive view of literature and culture is of course aimed towards producing possibilities of reading – which is the working definition of literature in this book – but is more fundamentally situated and suited to study how literature as a response to culture can be simultaneously critical and complicit in its celebration of irony and incompletion. This of course connects to the politics of the canon, the qualities of consolidation and subversion, and how the same literary text can display these differences in their dialogue with their contemporary cultural markers. In their fictional frames of realities and possibilities, literary texts may therefore emerge as affective designs in close and complex correspondences with ideological apparatuses, collective memory, and cultural materiality through an interplay of matter, metaphor, and memory. The chapters that follow aim to offer such study.

REFERENCES

Ahmed, Sara. 2010. 'Happy Objects'. In *The Affect Theory Reader*, edited by Melissa Gregg and Gregory J. Seigworth, 29–51. Durham, NC: Duke University Press.

Althusser, Louis. 2003. 'Three Notes on the Theory of Discourses'. In *The Humanist Controversy and Other Writings*, 33–84. London: Verso.

———. 2010. *For Marx*. London: Verso.

———. 2014. *On the Reproduction of Capitalism: Ideology and Ideological State Apparatuses*. London: Verso.

Appadurai, Arjun. 1986. *The Social Life of Things: Commodities in Cultural Perspective*. Cambridge: Cambridge University Press.

Armstrong, Paul B. 2013. *How Literature Plays with the Brain: The Neuroscience of Reading and Art*. Baltimore, MD: Johns Hopkins University Press.

Arnold, Matthew. 1882. *Culture and Anarchy: An Essay in Political and Social Criticism*. New York: Macmillan.

Belsey, Catherine. 1980. *Critical Practice*. London: Taylor and Francis.

———. 1992. 'Re-reading the Great Tradition'. In *Re-reading English*, edited by Peter Widdowson, 121–35. New York: Routledge.

———. 2005. *Culture and the Real: Theorizing Cultural Criticism*. London: Routledge.

Borges, Jorge Luis. 1982. *Borges at Eighty: Conversations*. Edited by Willis Barnstone. Bloomington: Indiana University Press.

Bruner, Jerome. 2002. *Making Stories: Law, Literature and Life*. Cambridge, MA: Harvard University Press.

———. 2008. 'Culture and Mind: Their Fruitful Incommensurability'. In *Ethos: Journal of the Society for Psychological Anthropology* 36(1): 29–45. https://doi.org/10.1111/j.1548-1352.2008.00002.x.

Butler, Judith. 1993. *Bodies That Matter: On the Discursive Limits of 'Sex'*. London: Routledge.

Carroll, Joseph. 2004. *Literary Darwinism: Evolution, Human Nature, and Literature*. London: Routledge.

Clark, Andy. 1997. *Being There: Putting Brain, Body and World Together Again*. Cambridge, MA: MIT Press.

Derrida, Jacques. 1992. *Acts of Literature*. New York: Routledge.

———. 1996. 'Remarks on Deconstruction and Pragmatism'. In *Deconstruction and Pragmatism*, edited by Simon Critchley and Chantal Mouffe, 77–84. London: Routledge.

———. 1997. *Politics of Friendship*. London: Verso.

———. 2001. 'I Have a Taste for the Secret'. In *Taste for the Secret*, edited by Jacques Derrida and Maurizio Ferraris, 1–93. Cambridge, UK: Polity.

Eagleton, Terry. 1983. *Literary Theory: An Introduction*. Minneapolis: University of Minnesota Press.

———. 1984. *The Function of Criticism*. London: Verso.

———. 2003. *Figures of Dissent: Critical Essays on Fish, Spivak, Žižek and Others*. London: Verso.

———. 2012. *The Event of Literature*. Cornwall: Yale University Press.

Eliot, Thomas Stearns. 1949. *Notes towards the Definition of Culture*. New York: Harcourt, Brace.

Erll, Astrid. 2011. *Memory in Culture*. London: Palgrave Macmillan.
Frow, John. 2002. 'Literature as Regime (Mediations on an Emergence)'. In *The Question of Literature: The Place of the Literary in Contemporary Theory*, edited by Elizabeth Beaumont Bissell, 142–55. Manchester: Manchester University Press.
———. 2005. 'On Literature in Cultural Studies'. In *The Aesthetics of Cultural Studies*, edited by Michael Berube, 44–57. Oxford: Blackwell.
Gregg, Melissa. 2006. *Cultural Studies' Affective Voices*. London: Palgrave Macmillan.
Havholm, Peter. 2008. *Politics and Awe in Rudyard Kipling's Fiction*. Aldershot: Ashgate.
'If, Read by Roger Federer & Rafael Nadal', YouTube video, 1:23, 'Dave Allen', May 10, 2021, https://www.youtube.com/watch?v=is-JCJCUy18.
Iser, Wolfgang. 1996a. *The Fictive and the Imaginary: Charting Literary Anthropology*. Baltimore, MD: Johns Hopkins University Press.
———. 1996b. 'The Play of the Text'. In *Languages of the Unsayable: The Play of Negativity in Literature and Literary Theory*, edited by Sanford Budick and Wolfgang Iser, 325–39. New York: Columbia University Press.
Jones, Rhys Griff. 1996. *The Nation's Favourite Poems*. London: BBC Worldwide Ltd.
Kipling, Rudyard. 1994. *The Works of Rudyard Kipling*. Hertfordshire: Wordsworth Editions.
Leavis, F. R. 1930. *Mass Civilization and Minority Culture*. Cambridge, UK: Minority Press.
———. 1948. *The Great Tradition*. London: Chatto & Windus.
Linde, Charlotte. 2009. *Working the Past: Narrative and Institutional Memory*. Oxford: Oxford University Press.
Macherey, Pierre. 1966. *A Theory of Literary Production*. London: Routledge.
Malafouris, Lambros. 2013. *How Things Shape the Mind: A Theory of Material Engagement*. Cambridge, MA: MIT Press.
Malafouris, Lambros, and Don Ihde. 2019. 'Homo Faber Revisited: Postphenomenology and Material Engagement Theory'. *Philosophy and Technology* 32(2): 195–214.
Mangan, J. A. 1986. *The Games Ethic and Imperialism: Aspects of the Diffusion of an Ideal*. Harmondsworth: Viking.
Orwell, George. 1961. 'Rudyard Kipling'. In *Collected Essays*, edited by Allan Hill, 43–51. London: Secker & Warburg.
Parui, Avishek, and Merin Simi Raj. Forthcoming. 'The COVID-19 Crisis Chronotope: The Pandemic as Matter, Metaphor, and Memory'. *Memory Studies*.
Ricoeur, Paul. 2004. *Memory, History, Forgetting*. Chicago: University of Chicago Press.
———. 2008. *Time and Narrative*. Vol. 2. Translated by Kathleen McLaughlin. Chicago: University of Chicago Press.
Said, Edward. 1994. *Culture and Imperialism*. New York: Vintage.
Terdiman, Richard. 1993. *Present Past: Modernity and the Memory Crisis*. Ithaca, NY: Cornell University Press.

Williams, Raymond. 1985. *Keywords: A Vocabulary of Culture and Society*. Oxford: Oxford University Press.
Žižek, Slavoj. 2001. *Did Somebody Say Totalitarianism? Five Interventions in the (Mis)use of a Notion*. London: Verso.
——. 2006. *The Parallax View*. Cambridge, MA: MIT Press.
——. 2011. *Living in the End Times*. London: Verso.

1

Culture, Commodity, and Colonial Identity

Late nineteenth-century European colonialism may be considered as a systemic process of coercion and consumption that commodified objects and humans alike in its expansionist materiality as well as in its constant production of knowledge and identities. The nature of knowledge in the colonial setting was a complex of instrumentation and abstraction designed to designate human hierarchy and civilizational supremacy through structural and symbolic processes. As a massive and sometimes messy discourse network, imperialism in the late nineteenth century was also, as Elleke Boehmer argues, a 'textual exercise' (Boehmer 1995, 14), including quick construction and consumption of pamphlets, treatises, gazettes, reports, and novels. In its territorial and epistemological expansion, the nineteenth-century discourse network in Western Europe may be broadly conceived as inhabiting the moment, as Michel Foucault contends, when 'the relation between the visible and the invisible – which is necessary to all concrete knowledge – changed its structure, revealing through gaze and language what had previously been below and beyond their domain' (Foucault 1973, xii). This had immediate repercussions in the reification of objects and identities in the imperial setting, often making the entanglement of matter, metaphor, and memory a politically motivated representational strategy.

Foucault's study of the blend of biopolitics and racism in nineteenth-century Western Europe shows how there was a significant shift in the epistemic structure with the pervasive presence and growth of imperialism. The colonial machinery of control also relied on experimentation with meanings whereby familiar metaphors were transplanted onto unfamiliar territories through 'symbolic investments' (Boehmer 1995, 15). The construction and consumption of commodity in colonialism may therefore be examined as being marked by discursive as well as by affective instruments, with identity, its production and processes of othering emerging as key players in the colonial production-consumption frame. This chapter – on Joseph Conrad's *Heart of Darkness* and George Orwell's 'Shooting an Elephant' and *Burmese Days* – corresponds to the ambivalent relationship between literature and culture inflected through commodity and markers of colonial identity. In particular, it studies the representations of melancholic masculinity embodied by the white imperial agents and examines how affect and symbolic objects inform the production and performance of colonial control, as exemplified in Conrad's and Orwell's *misadventure fiction* set in Belgian Congo and British Burma respectively.

Of special significance in this chapter is a study of the colonial commodity (ivory in Congo and teak in Burma) as the marker and manipulator of imperial identity. Most importantly, the chapter will also aim to show that the most vital and compulsory commodity in the colonial space is the culturally constructed white male superiority, which was to be consumed collectively and maintained at all costs for colonial coercion and control. Along with commodification, or reification, the process whereby objects and human subjects are increasingly converted to and characterized by crude use value, *Heart of Darkness*, 'Shooting an Elephant', and *Burmese Days* also describe and dramatize the experience of alienation, whereby the human producer and performer of imperial identity is increasingly removed or alienated from the product of labour. Conrad's and Orwell's writings as studied in this chapter offer complex depictions of the alienation of the white male subject from the compulsory commodity of white male supremacy even as they retain and reinforce the racialized presuppositions and privileges that historically characterized colonialism. In essence, *Heart of Darkness* and *Burmese Days* may be described as examples of politically incorrect fiction, which are ambivalent in their simultaneous critique and consolidation of the colonial classifications that inform their plots and protagonists. Both novels exhibit what Edward Said describes, in his reading of *Heart of Darkness*, as the conversion of the adventurous empire into an order of bureaucratic business which is cynically self-conscious in the knowledge of its hypocrisy and hollowness (Said 1993, 193). While retaining the romance and nostalgia for the empire and an inherent investment in white supremacy, *Heart of Darkness*, 'Shooting an Elephant', and *Burmese Days* also display what Said describes as the knowledge of the limited temporality of the grand idea of imperialism, beyond which it could be conceived only as 'tremendous violence and waste' (Conrad [1899] 1963, 203). It is this conditional and contingent quality of colonialism that appears in Conrad's and Orwell's misadventure fiction as functions of a state of non-synchronicity, whereby the human subject who is also the notional insider of the empire gets increasingly alienated from the machine of colonial control and coercion. The play between insider and outsider gives all three texts a self-conscious quality which eventually transforms into an admission of ambivalence, hollowness, and horror.

The significance of fiction in this study is twofold. On the one hand, at the level of focalization, the psychological interiority and stream of consciousness experienced by Conrad's Marlow and the self-deprecating cynicism suffered by Orwell's Flory foreground ambivalence as an experiential as well as an epistemic category whereby the classifications of colonial culture are interrogated even as they are internalized, in an existential phenomenal frame. The same ambivalence spills over from the order of individual experience and extends to the broader politics of representation and affiliation whereby the very materiality and machinery of imperialism is simultaneously critiqued and consolidated in the fictional frame. Secondly and more generically, the fictionality of the order of representation accentuates the play between knowledge and knowability characterizing colonial literature, which should be studied as a 'metaphoric practice' that sought to convey cultural and geopolitical difference through 'dependable textual conventions' (Boehmer 1995, 15). Such metaphoric practices, which used conventions of a *metropolitan literary culture* such as realism to describe the difference experienced in the *colonial elsewhere*, foreground the function of fiction as a symbolic mapping which is territorial in quality. However, the difference between the realism in Daniel Defoe's *Robinson Crusoe* and that in Conrad's *Heart of Darkness* emerges from the fact that in the latter, realism reaches a crisis point which in turn highlights the defamiliarization and deterritorialization characterizing the complex colonial experience and its representation. Such existential and cognitive de-framing is present in Orwell's *Burmese Days* too, which presents a hollowed-out, scooped self in the character of Flory whose performance anxiety as a white man in the claustrophobic colony combines a crisis in representation as well as in self-fashioning. A similar anxiety of self-fashioning informs the Orwell figure in 'Shooting an Elephant', as an autobiographical essay that may be read as an example of interrupted interpellation followed by a sad surrender of agency in order to preserve and perpetuate the primacy of the colonial commodity. As Elleke Boehmer argues, the '[e]mpire enters the nineteenth century novel chiefly as commodity, in images of riches and trade' (Boehmer 1995, 26), thus highlighting the political and symbolic significance of the colonial commodity consumed in representations in fiction. Conrad's Marlow and Orwell's Flory may both be considered as inadequate controllers of the colonial commodity while also struggling to appropriate and manoeuvre the coveted metaphors in the fictional frame. If colonialism may be described as a 'metaphoric and cartographic undertaking' (ibid., 46), the protagonists in Conrad's and Orwell's novels emerge as spectacular failures in their (mis)navigation through defamiliarized territories and messy metaphors, thus undercutting the conventional 'cartographic and metaphoric authority' ascribed to the colonizer (ibid., 99).

The fictional frame in Conrad and Orwell thus plays the dual role of complexly conveying interiority and ambivalently representing reality, an ability described earlier in the introduction. Interiority and physical materiality appear in *Heart of Darkness* and *Burmese Days* not as ontological opposites but as connected categories whereby human subjects who are imperial agents struggle to situate themselves and navigate across cultural commodities and coveted identities. Such navigations emerge as narrative and performative functions respectively in Conrad's and Orwell's novels, and Marlow and Flory may be considered as examples of an inadequate narrator and a failed performer of colonialism. The misadventure of Marlow and Flory may also be read as the failure of metaphor and memory, with both emerging as inadequate subjects in the metaphoric practices characterizing colonialism, in their failure to be the competent colonial white man and the competent colonial storyteller. In their crisis in controlling matter and metaphor in the colonial space, Marlow and Flory also compromise a colonial activity related to the ability to condense and metaphorize, the *colonial gaze* which included 'investigation, examination, inspection, peeping, poring over, which were accompaniments to the colonial penetrations of a country' (ibid., 68). Therefore, failure in storytelling and self-fashioning in Conrad's and Orwell's novels may be examined as synchronous to the inability to appropriate the colonial gaze that historically and materially mapped and metaphorized the colonial territory. Among other things, therefore, what makes *Heart of Darkness* and *Burmese Days* unique as representations of colonial culture, commodity, and identity is their complex quality of being *fictions about failures*, about aborted actions and interrupted identities, a theme that recurs in 'Shooting an Elephant', which dramatizes how the Orwell-self fails as a human subject in order to perform and perpetuate his role as an empire agent. The three texts studied in this chapter are about failed missions, nervous narrations, and politically inadequate and incorrect perspectives on colonialism, from the point of view of the notionally powerful white male imperial agents. In their incompletions, interruptions, and incorrectness, *Heart of Darkness* and *Burmese Days* exhibit fiction's ability to articulate and combine human unreliability with historical materiality. In the process, they emerge as excellent examples of the entanglement of culture and the literary, through markers of matter, metaphor, and memory.

HEART OF DARKNESS

As a pre-Modernist who is essentially unclassifiable and 'floating uncertainly somewhere in between Proust and Robert Louis Stevenson' (Jameson 1981, 206), Conrad's empire fiction frequently foregrounds existential enigmas and epistemological uncertainties. Conrad had acknowledged his interest in the 'regions of memory' in the human mind that 'know nothing of time' (Conrad 1935, 149), thus offering a model of consciousness in his narratives with its cognitive contingency, flux, and fluidity. Thus, in a typical Conradian narrative, David Lodge contends:

> [t]he gratifications of the conventional adventure story are deliberately frustrated, inverted, problematised, by complex time shifts, shifts of point of view, elaborate framing devices, and a densely written, syntactically complicated, metaphorically rich prose style – all of which together retard and obstruct the delivery of simple narrative excitement. (Lodge 2002, 87)

Lodge's analysis of the convergence between Modernist literature and the discoveries in modern twenty-first century neuroscience carries special relevance to the argument of this chapter which seeks to situate the narrative method of Conrad within the broader realms of scientific and philosophical debates on self and cognition. The political insight articulated in Conrad's stories about imperialist horror emerges out of phenomenal experiences that challenge presuppositions in dominant structures of knowledge. While the crisis of normative European imperial masculinity is most immediately evident in a later text, *Lord Jim* (1900), which emerges as 'a defining tale of doubt which threatened the project of European expansion' (Boehmer 1995, 59) as well as a neo-Gothic narrative about the 'threat of engulfment posed by the feminine' (Mongia 1993, 1), *Heart of Darkness* is possibly Conrad's darkest depiction of the failure of normative imperial masculinity and the consequent crisis in cognition and narration.

Conrad's narrative efforts to make the reader hear, feel, and see, and the corresponding difficulties faced by his narrators to communicate their crises, correspond closely to the larger epistemological uncertainties in his fictional worlds. As David Lodge argues:

> In a world where nothing is certain, in which transcendental belief has been undermined by scientific materialism, and even the objectivity of science is qualified by relativity and uncertainty, the single human voice, telling its own story, can seem the only authentic way of rendering consciousness. (Lodge 2002, 87)

The tension between subjective experience and ontic reality, between private perception and collective experience, and between familiar experiences and defamiliarized expressions runs across the entirety of Conrad's oeuvre. Thus, in Conrad's writing, narration often emerges as a backward process whereby objects are decoded post-perception (Miller 1996, 89–90). Such perspectival positions in the narratives of Conrad rely less on what actually transpires in the physical landscape of change than on how such events impressionistically affect the consciousness of the perceiver. Crucially, the narrative style that Conrad deploys – one that anticipates Modernist experiments of communicating pure human consciousness in language – appears deliberately destabilized as a way of capturing an altered and altering world (Mongia 1992, 174).

Essentially containing the irresolvable conflict between phenomenal experience and logical knowledge, private ambivalence and political presupposition, Conrad's works problematize the narratives of imperial romance that contained the social Darwinist rhetoric of civilizational supremacy used to legitimize imperial territorialization (Dryden 2000, 16–34). More significantly, with its experiments in language that sought to capture human thought processes, Conrad's writing instantiates 'the tensions of a split heritage, divided between the demands of the adventure and the "literary" novel' (Boehmer 1995, 44). The literariness in Conrad's writing emerges as a self-reflexive awareness of its own epistemological process – thus reflecting the ambivalence of the self-reflecting human mind – as well as 'the rhetorical strategy of negation by which Western writing conceives of the Other as absence, emptiness, nothingness, or death' (Spur 1993, 92). But what problematizes the politics of narration further is the manner in which the nothingness and excess that the perceiving mind seeks to project onto the 'other' comes back to consume itself. Such a reversal is enacted through articulation by unsure and nervous narrators, who flag up their failures to negotiate with their narratives in inconclusive tales of guilt and unresolved melancholia.

Such transitions in Conrad's characters inform their existential realm of understanding through the phenomenal experience that also shapes political scepticism. Nervousness in the Conradian narrative – manifested in deceptive appearances and delayed decoding – thus emerges as the panic that merges privately perceived political ambivalence with sensory instability. Such nervousness connects not only to the masculinity crisis in Conrad – whereupon the imperial masculine identity is deconstructed – but also informs the inward turn that opens the subject to an inconclusive existential enigma that may never be fully reported or articulated. The phenomenal quality in Conrad's narration is an extension of the embodied storytelling enacted by his characters, a mode whose 'motivation is existential [as] it is directly connected with his [the narrator's] practical experiences, with the joys and sorrows he has experienced, with his moods and needs' (Stanzel 1986, 93). The embodied nature of Marlow's narration in *Heart of Darkness* – a 'parabolic text' (Miller 1996, 31) that incorporates a process of unveiling – is further heightened by a self-reflexive quality 'firmly constituted by the natural parameter of human consciousness, of experientiality' (Fludernik 1996, 21). This self-reflexive experientiality is a phenomenal and a political process in *Heart of Darkness*, a tale about cognitive unsettling as well as political unlearning.

In a letter to H. G. Wells on 30 November 1903, Conrad commented on his view of writing thus: '[F]or me, writing – *the only possible writing* – is just simply the conversion of nervous forces into phrases' (Bock 2002, 77). Pervasive throughout Conrad's narratives – especially in *Heart of Darkness* – is the manner in which the nervous experience and the traumatic encounter of the human subject are translated into language. As Richard Ambrosini argues, '*Heart of Darkness* is the furthest point in Conrad's attempt to communicate his intended effect through a suggestive language paralleled by an extra-fictional communication' (Ambrosini 1991, 84). Part of the difficulty and density of expressions in Conrad's writing can thus be attributed to the efforts on the part of his narrators to communicate what Virginia Woolf classified as the language of illness which is 'more primitive, more sensual, more obscene', a form of expression in which 'things are said, truths are blurted out' (Woolf 1948, 11, 13). It thus emerges as an example in fiction that depicts how the circuit across matter, metaphor, and memory is essentially incomplete and inconclusive, a quality that also connects to the masculinity and narrative crisis experienced by Conrad's protagonists. Conrad's novels often depict how a metaphorical understanding of lived experience and the messy memory of the same can have permanent primacy over any knowledge of materiality. The delayed decoding suffered by the storytellers in Conrad informs their nervous negotiation with matter which turns to metaphors and then forms episodic memories even before any meaningful materiality is achieved or articulated.

In its ambivalent interpretation of imperialism and its horrors, *Heart of Darkness* also illustrates the inadequacies of late nineteenth-century biopolitical ideologies, while at the same time being awkwardly embedded in the same, in a classic instantiation of fiction's ambivalent frame. As Edward Said argues, Conrad's novel contains an 'uncompromising Eurocentric vision' which paradoxically also constitutes 'the felt tension between what is intolerably there and a symmetrical compulsion to escape from it' (Said 2003, 26). Conrad's empire fiction is characterized by his protagonists' felt ambivalence about agency, which in turn informs the existential dilemma that is caught between the need for selfishness and the desire for self-effacement (Hunter 1983, 13). Ian Watt examines how 'Conrad grew up in the heyday of evolutionary theory; Alfred Wallace was one of his favourite authors; and several aspects of evolutionary thought are present in *Heart of Darkness*' (Watt 1980, 155). 'Impressively well-read in contemporary science' (Greenslade 1994, 106), Conrad's response to his contemporary craniology, degeneration panic, and criminology, although dismissive of their stereotypical excesses, reflects the ambivalence of a creative writer who was sensitive to the scientific theses of his times when 'the borders between criminality, insanity and genius . . . were constantly blurred' (Griffith 1995, 174–75).

Emerging as it did from a culture that contained the pride of imperialist expansion as well the fear of degeneration, increasing territorialization as well as the anxiety of entropy and solar death (Watts 1977, 11–18), *Heart of Darkness* is a complex commentary on commodification, imperialism, and imperial identities at the end of the nineteenth century. Conrad's novel was written at a time marked by international geopolitical conflicts and contradictory notions of imperialism in Africa, a period that witnessed 'the discovery of gold in the Transvaal'; an 'increasing resentment at German imperialism' (the very name of Kurtz in *Heart of Darkness* means 'short' in German, ironically belying his anatomical and imperial excesses); the 'final adoption of an imperialist programme' as 'the leadership of the Liberal party passed from Gladstone to Rosebery in 1894', a move that was accentuated by the Conservative Lord Salisbury's coming into power the next year; the Jameson Raid in 1895; and the Fashoda Incident in 1898 (Watt 1980, 157). The broader backdrop of geopolitical tensions and contradictions is reflected in the misadventures, defamiliarization, and delayed decoding in Conrad's novel which undercuts its own classic-realist narrative frame. The unreliable, nervous narration of Marlow, who is also the incompetent imperial agent in the colonial Congo, corresponds complexly to the crisis of the colonial gaze in *Heart of Darkness*, whereby the white man's gaze is dramatically defamiliarized and deterritorialized through delayed decoding and staggered storytelling.

An excellent example of the entanglement of contemporary cultural and literary codes through a mapping of metaphors, *Heart of Darkness* is also about the masculinity crisis in colonial as well as civilian spaces. The female figures who appear in Conrad's novel are either marginalized or spectralized but often emerge as unnerving presences before the nervous protagonist's eyes. Thus the spectre of soulless science embodied in the image of an automatic knitting machine appears in *Heart of Darkness* in the figures of the symbolic women at the entrance to the office of the ivory company in Brussels, a city that reminds Marlow of a white sepulchre. The whiteness of imperial ivory and the whiteness of Brussels are thus connected through a merging of metaphors in Marlow's imagination. The female figures knit away in an automaton-like manner as Marlow embarks on the corporate rituals and gets grafted into the imperial enterprise that was 'going to run an overseas empire and make no end of coin by trade' (Conrad [1899] 1963, 13). The section is remarkable in the manner in which it juxtaposes the mythical realm with that of the menacingly mechanical:

> Two women, one fat and the other slim, sat on straw-bottomed chairs knitting black wool. The slim one got up and walked straight at me – still knitting with downcast eyes – and only just as I began to think of getting out of her way, as you would for a somnambulist, stood still, and looked up. Her dress was as plain as an umbrella cover, and she turned round without a word and preceded me into a waiting-room. I gave my name and looked about. (ibid., 13)

The protocols of being baptized into the imperialist enterprise are depicted selectively and nervously with the image of the Congo on the map appearing to Marlow's panicky cognition as 'an immense snake uncoiled' (ibid., 12), thus bringing the biblical scene of seduction and its associated connotation of the Fall into a nervous juxtaposition with the imperialist architecture of the unnamed company's office in Brussels. The strategy of selective communication, one that runs throughout the narrative of *Heart of Darkness* and is perhaps most spectacularly evident in Marlow's eventual and dramatic lie to Kurtz's intended at the end of the novel, is anticipated in Marlow's succinct account of his signing of a contract with the company that is never named in the narrative:

> In about forty-five seconds I found myself again in the waiting-room with the compassionate secretary who full of desolation and sympathy made me sign some document. I believe I undertook amongst other things not to disclose any trade secrets. Well, I am not going to. (ibid., 14)

The precision of clock time belies the emotional intensity and movements that are described in the passage. Marlow's withholding of the company's trade secrets (a company that seeks to maximize profit by ivory trade in the Congo) from his European audience that comprises a lawyer and an accountant is not incompatible with his eventual withholding of the truth about the horror of imperialism from the supposedly naive European female in the white metropolis.

Unsurprisingly, on being taken in by the machinery of imperialism, Marlow is subsequently sent to be examined under its medical gaze, one that proceeds by detection and interrogation of hereditary insanity and criminal history. The following scene is delineated through the 'simple formality' of seeing the company's doctor who 'produced a thing like callipers and got the dimensions back and front and every way, taking notes carefully' (ibid., 15). Keen to measure Marlow's cranium for the sake of medical science, the doctor quizzes him on any familial history of madness, asserting that it would be 'interesting for science to watch the mental changes of individuals on the spot' (ibid., 15). Appearing as he does in Marlow's eyes as 'a harmless fool', the facile figure of the doctor confesses that he 'always ask[s] leave, in the interest of science, to measure the crania of those going out there' (ibid., 15), and thus subscribes to the nineteenth-century tradition of measuring men that derived its data from 'a sample of 383 crania from dead criminals, plus general proportions measured for 3,893 among the living' (Gould 1996, 160).

While in the Congo, Marlow tries to comprehend the meaning in the wilderness he sees around him. The passage, in which he describes his equivocal understanding of the surrounding silence and sounds, is evocative in its ambient ambivalence:

> A great silence around and above. Perhaps on some quiet night the tremor of far-off drums, sinking, swelling, a tremor vast, faint; a sound weird, appealing, suggestive, and wild – and perhaps with as profound a meaning as the sound of bells in a Christian country. (Conrad [1899] 1963, 23)

The economy of meanings generated through materials here is interesting as Marlow appears to ascribe some mysterious semantic structure to the sound of drums which is compared to Christian bells. The acoustic alterity of the African drums to the European listener here is equated, for the sake of semantic comparability, to the religious summons in a Christian country. This foregrounds the cognitive and cultural complexity in Conrad's novel whereby materials and their attachment to meanings are seldom stable or in resonance. The nervous narration in *Heart of Darkness* emerges from a fragile economy of matter and metaphor as the narrator attempts to equate familiar and unfamiliar cultural templates, drawing on the memory of his own location. What emerges in the process is an increasing sense of existential dislocation and alienation which informs the melancholia and self-loathing of the storyteller who is painfully aware of the fragile and almost absurd quality of his staggered storytelling. *Heart of Darkness* is thus a dark and complex example of existential and narrative crisis marked by cognitive dissonance and delayed decoding, foregrounding the fault lines of matter, metaphor, and memory. Marlow's narrative thus bears signs of an attempted understanding of the cultural signifiers around him while also betraying the blankness in comprehension as Africa, with its 'stamped-in network of paths spreading over the empty land' (ibid., 23), which changes from a geographical landscape to the 'other' space in Marlow's European imagination. Thus, before long, he too subscribes to the notion that Africa brings out the atavistic nature of the European man and feels that he himself 'was becoming scientifically interesting' (ibid., 24). He travels along the Congo and enters the heart of what he perceives as the African darkness, where the human voices he knows are replaced by sounds and signs he does not understand and incompletely decodes. Thus, later, in the face of a real and immediate physical predicament, the vocabulary of popular degeneration panic returns to the mind that had formerly rejected it as Marlow contemplates the effects that the African wilderness may have had on Kurtz, ostensibly turning him bald. Thus 'it had taken him, loved him, embraced him, got into his veins, consumed his flesh, and sealed his soul to its own by the inconceivable ceremonies of some devilish initiation'(ibid., 49). The language of possession operative here points to an absolute anarchy, which, like the medical context of the novel, appears to appropriate a moral rather than scientific vocabulary.

In his study of Conrad's appropriation as well as deconstruction of the Lombrosian system of criminology, C. T. Watts argues that Kurtz, with his gifted musical attributes and charisma of political potential, represents the 'Pied Piper attribute' (Watts 1977, 227) of the degenerative type: embodying the potential for seduction as well as annihilation with 'the power to charm or frighten rudimentary souls into an aggravated witch-dance in his honour' (Conrad [1899] 1963, 51). Yet Conrad does not characterize Kurtz using any neat discourse of difference that bases itself on contemporary anthropological assumptions. The hysteria at the heart of darkness is as much localized in African otherness as in the finest European attributes, for 'all Europe contributed to the *making* of Kurtz' (ibid., 86). Therefore, making and unmaking, evolutionary progress and regression, are trapped in the same complex of nihilism and enlightenment in Conrad's novel about political and personal panic. The Thames and the Congo ironically and eventually emerge as similar symbols in Marlow's stream of consciousness, both being historical pathways for the traffic of imperialism and places of darkness outside the civilized world at different points in human history (ibid., 9).

Points of view emerge as pivotal in an understanding of the stream of consciousness within *Heart of Darkness*. The novel depicts complex conflations and superimpositions of several points of view: Marlow's on Kurtz's, Marlow's on the various reporters on Kurtz, the inset narrator's on Marlow, and the inset narrator's on Marlow's point of view on his immediate audience which also includes the inset narrator. There is thus a self-reflexive circuit of points of view within the narrative that is a story of repression, entropy, and melancholia, one which operates through an uncertain entanglement of matter and metaphors informing an equally unreliable memory. Such traffic of perspectives brings into play various varieties of reference within the narrative which disturbingly depicts how the subject's objective conception of its environment also constitutes a detached notion of itself as an object in the same cognitive field (Evans 1983, 222–23). An obvious pointer to the existential crisis faced by the masculine subject in a defamiliarized space time, the *delayed decoding* so characteristic of the Conradian narrative emerges as a nervous condition that showcases a slowing down of the cognitive process. This is evinced in *Heart of Darkness* in Marlow's travel up the Congo where the forests around him appear as effects even before their objectivity is cognized by the perceiving mind. A narrative as well as a cognitive condition, delayed decoding depicts the close correspondences between the nervous and the narrative economies that characterize *Heart of Darkness* as Marlow travels through the Congo between various telegraphic stations and famously sees the effect of the shower of arrows on his senses before decoding their meaningful materiality. The passage deserves to be quoted in full to depict the deferral of the cognitive process involved in the act:

> Then I had to look at the river mighty quick because there was a snag in the fairway. Sticks, little sticks, were flying about, thick; they were whizzing before my nose, dropping below me, striking behind me against my pilot-house. All this time the river, the shore, the woods were very quiet – perfectly quiet. I could only hear the heavy splashing thump of the stern-wheel and the patter of these things. We cleared the snag clumsily. Arrows, by Jove! We were being shot at! (Conrad [1899] 1963, 45–46)

The representation of the cognitive process in operation here moves from the effect to the cause, from the unsettled impression of the object to the solid materiality of the same. As the cognitive break between seeing and understanding, the delayed decoding in *Heart of Darkness* emerges as misrecognition as well as a deliberate narrative misrepresentation that retrospectively attempts to transform a subjective moment of cognitive crisis into an intersubjective experience through language.

The politics of narration in *Heart of Darkness* is premised on the effect that is conveyed through 'juxtaposition between a *story* of "what happened" to Marlow and a *tale* of the effect that those events had on him' (Ambrosini 1991, 85). Marlow seeks to secure his original moment of confusion by retaining its real sensation within his narrative frames. The deliberate misrepresentation of objects by retaining the original moment of confusion recurs in *Heart of Darkness* in Marlow's report of his mistaken analysis of the shrunken heads on poles on Kurtz's island, heads that had initially appeared through his binoculars as decorative or totemic balls. As he remedies his earlier misrepresentation, Marlow reports:

> These round knobs were not ornamental but symbolic; they were expressive and puzzling, striking and disturbing – food for thought and also for vul-

tures if there had been any looking down from the sky.... They would have been even more impressive, those heads on the stakes, if their faces had not been turned to the house. (Conrad [1899] 1963, 57)

Marlow's misinterpretation at a point in the past is thus reported in its original temporal structure in the present time to his listeners. In his analysis of Conrad's narrative mode and its delayed decoding, Edward Said suggests that the 'details of reality' in Conrad 'are realized by the recollecting mind' which retraces 'the designs of experience' (Said 1996, 88), foregrounding a complex fault line of matter, metaphor, and memory through fictional narration. The double-helical narrative and the repetition of the same event with different interpretations articulate the panic perceived in the past that lingers into the present. This narrative strategy of communicating nervousness through repetitions thus connects to the broader masculinity panic that Marlow is subjected to in the heart of darkness. Patricia Waugh examines the shrunken heads episode in *Heart of Darkness* and argues that it exemplifies the convergence of cognitive and narrative planes in the novel at a temporal level, a convergence that informs the epistemological enigma in Conrad's story about political unlearning and interrupted storytelling:

> The narrating Marlow, of course, has known all along the identity of the round balls, but has chosen to inhabit the perspective of the experiential character. Reader and listener share his slow approach, with some trepidation and much anticipation, to Kurtz's station, awaiting the first signs of the embodiment of that Voice heard though Marlow's narrative.... Because the reader experiences Marlow's original sensory confusion, his current interpretative problems appear to be simply one more layer of epistemological uncertainty. (Waugh 1992, 97)

Language itself emerges in Conrad's narratives less as a signifier of stable communicative ontology than as an epistemological process that attempts to articulate meanings that lie not embedded inside but perpetually extended outside the narrative, 'enveloping the tale which brought it out only as a glow brings out the haze, in the likeness of one of those misty halos that, sometimes, are made visible by the spectral illuminations of moonshine' (Conrad [1899] 1963, 9). Delayed decoding in Conrad emerges as a unique language of deferral and as a metonymy of (mis) cognition, reversing the normative model of perception located at the site of nervousness and nervous masculinity. This is amply evinced in *Heart of Darkness* in Marlow's admission of his own failure to narrate the complete effect of one of his 'inconclusive experiences' (ibid., 11) to a group of Londoners reposing at the heart of the Thames, enacting a process where 'the telling, rather than the event itself, generates meaning' (Ambrosini 1991, 90). This is strongly suggested by Michael Levenson, who identifies:

> [a] condition that persists all through Conrad's work, a radical disorientation that obliterates any stable relation between the self and the world, and that raises the question of whether there is a world to which the self belongs. The fragility of identity, the barriers to knowledge, the groundlessness of value – these great Conradian (and modern) motifs appear most often in terms of sensory derangement that casts the individual into unarticulated space, a space with no markers and no boundaries, with nothing behind, nothing above, nothing below. (Levenson 1991, 6)

Among the several points of interest in Levenson's analysis is the manner in which language (with its self-reflective knowledge of lack) in Conrad emerges simultaneously with the politics of mappable space and its absence in *Heart of Darkness*, a novel about the loss of agency, whose narrative 'seemed to shape itself without human lips in the heavy night-air of the river' (Conrad [1899] 1963, 30). The crisis of the object in his story – one that relates directly to the masculinity crisis in the real political space (Ahmed 2010, 29–51) – does not allow Marlow to translate his subjective experience into an intersubjective narrative. The lack of *solid objects* in his story – a lack that Marlow is increasingly and painfully aware of – emerges as a failure to trigger 'meaningful construals' that proceed by interpreting 'how the objects and actions depicted in language relate to embodied possibilities' (Gibbs 2005, 200). This foregrounds the fractured fault lines between matter and metaphor in Marlow's memory and narrative economy. Thus Kurtz appears to Marlow as a voice, an all-encompassing senseless voice: 'And I heard – him – it – this voice – other voices – all of them were so little more than voices – and the memory of that time itself lingers around me, impalpable, like a dying vibration of one immense jabber, silly, atrocious, sordid, savage, or simply mean without any kind of sense' (Conrad [1899] 1963, 48–49).

The impalpability of Kurtz is personal and sensory, as well as political and ideological, and Marlow's voice hearing in *Heart of Darkness* is characteristic of what Conrad himself had classified as a condition where the subject loses 'all sense of reality in a kind of nightmare effect produced by existence' (Watts 1977, 114–15). The intangibility and spectrality of Kurtz throughout Marlow's narration is a further pointer to the complexly compromised economy of matter, metaphor, and memory in *Heart of Darkness*, a novel which may best be described as an inconclusive story about an inconclusive experience.

The metonymic construct of Kurtz – he had been 'educated partly in England. . . . His mother was half-English, his father was half-French. All Europe contributed to the making of Kurtz' (Conrad [1899] 1963, 50) – if characteristic of the product perfected and manufactured by the industries and ideologies of European civilization, is also in itself a pointer to the impalpability that Marlow experiences as a narrator attempting to describe Kurtz's presence. The indeterminacy that characterized the construct of Kurtz is rendered more explicit in the end when Marlow receives varying reports on Kurtz's political and personal abilities from his various acquaintances and relatives. Marlow's confusion about Kurtz, who remains more a voice and a spectral presence, is evident as he confesses:

> [t]o this day I am unable to say what was Kurtz's profession, whether he ever had any – which was the greatest of his talents. I had taken him for a painter who wrote for papers, or else a journalist who could paint – but even the cousin (who took snuff during the interview) could not tell me what he had been – exactly. (Conrad [1899] 1963, 71)

As an indeterminable quasi-physical presence that affects his existence, Kurtz emerges as a phantom limb in Marlow's imagination, an amputated part of the past that haunts the lived present (Ramachandran and Blakeslee 1998). In his permanent condition of incompleteness and mystery, Kurtz remains for Marlow what Derrida had classified as an *inaccessible articulation* that instantiates the interstitial play between the spirit and the revenant, between disappearance and repetition. For Derrida, examining the *apparition of the inapparent*:

> For there to be a ghost, there must be a return to the body, but to a body that is more abstract than ever. The spectrogenic process corresponds therefore to a paradoxical *incorporation*. Once ideas or thoughts (*Gedanke*) are detached from their substratum, one engenders some ghost by giving them a body. . . . A more acute specificity belongs to what could be called the 'second' ghost, as incorporation of autonomized spirit, as objectivizing expulsion of interior idea or thought. (Derrida 1994, 126)

Derrida's analysis of hauntology and the Freudian *Unheimlich* as a political as well as a bodily presence – a phenomenal construct that is reconfigured through an abstraction that is also a reification – is particularly pertinent to the figure of Kurtz in *Heart of Darkness* that emerges as an incomplete exorcism of the spectres of imperialist horrors. With his dialectic of the *apparition of the body* (appearing more as a voice than a living body that is always described through abstractions) and the *body of the apparition* (the posthumous voice that constructs its unique body against time), Kurtz appears to embody Derrida's 'second ghost' that is impossible to exorcise but must be mourned forever in a manner that rehearses a process of fetishization (ibid., 5). It is interesting to examine how this process of fetishization operates at a level of abstraction in *Heart of*

Darkness. Kurtz in *Heart of Darkness* embodies what Marlow at the beginning of the narrative had classified as an 'idea', 'something you can set up, and bow down before, and offer a sacrifice to' (Conrad [1899] 1963, 10), that desperate clinging to an abstraction in an attempt to redeem the vulgar materiality of the machinery of imperialism. The abstraction that Marlow had classified at the beginning of the narrative as the sole redeeming quality of imperial territorialization emerges through *Heart of Darkness* as the nemesis that is impossible to exorcise. Such abstraction can also be classified only through a vocabulary of violence and an ideology that is painfully preserved through a system of lies. A symptom born out of the strategy of abstraction that European imperialism required in order to reify its operative system, Kurtz becomes a renegade as well as a revenant at a political as well as an abstract level, ironically through an 'over-identification' with the epistemic (and political) system and by thus turning into an 'excess that the system has to eliminate' (Žižek 2002, 27). Marlow's knowledge of the futility of his own narrative appears as an aporia as well as a privilege born out of an existential awareness of absence. The absence is informed through real material conditions as well as through an emotional imbalance which causes Marlow to feel 'himself separate from the world he is physically part of' (Bohlmann 1991, 32). The otherness of the real physical space appears dialogic with the crisis of cognition that the European imperialist experiences. The crisis is constructed as well as exacerbated by the defamiliarized coordinates that inform Marlow's mis-cognition:

> We were cut off from the comprehension of our surroundings, we glided past like phantoms, wondering and secretly appalled, as sane men would be before an enthusiastic outbreak in a madhouse. We could not understand because we were too far and could not remember because we were travelling in the night of the first ages, of those ages that are gone, leaving hardly a sign – and no memories. . . . The mind of man is capable of anything – because everything is in it, all the past as well as all the future. (Conrad [1899] 1963, 37–38)

Marlow's dislocation from his familiar cognitive culture underpins the defamiliarization that is a prelude to his final existential awakening (Bauman 1991, 57).

As the narrator of *Heart of Darkness*, Marlow is evidently aware of the inconclusive quality of his narration that borders on the absurd and, appropriately enough, juxtaposes his nervousness and his narration in an attempt to account for his imperfect and frustrated articulation:

> 'Absurd!' he cried. 'This is the worst trying to tell. . . . Here you all are each moored with two addresses like a hulk with two anchors, a butcher round

one corner, a policeman round another, excellent appetites, and temperatures normal – hear you – normal from year's end to year's end. And you say, Absurd! Absurd be – exploded! Absurd! My dear boys, what can you expect from a man who out of sheer nervousness had just flung overboard a pair of new shoes?' (Conrad [1899] 1963, 48)

The passage is peremptory as well as loaded with anxiety in its fear of losing the attention of the audience, a fear that accentuates the loss (Derrida 1994, 51) that Marlow is forced to embody through his narrative. As Richard Ambrosini suggests, Marlow's narrative indeterminacy and loss of control 'undermines the white man's language – and consequently, many of the ideological presuppositions which ground his audience's response' (Ambrosini 1991, 93). This corresponds closely to the crisis of colonial control on matter, metaphor, and memory in Marlow's narration in *Heart of Darkness*, one which also undercuts the ontology of the colonial gaze. The absurd quality in Marlow's narration of delayed decoding and cognitive collapse is almost apologetically attributed to the nervousness of the narrator himself while confronting experiential shifts in subjectivity. The 'excellent appetites' and 'temperatures normal' that characterize his listeners are in sharp contrast to the narrator's 'lean appeared face [that] appeared worn, hollow, with withdrawn folds and drooped eyelids with an aspect of concentrated attention' (Conrad [1899] 1963, 48) which emerge as obvious pointers to the hysteric knowledge of the horror that he cannot completely communicate.

In effect, Marlow's failure of narration in *Heart of Darkness* – a text that may be read as a 'melancholic response to crisis' (Ash 2012, 196) – enacts the epistemological enquiry into representation of the lost subject surrounded by slippery objects that undercut the arrogant masculinist colonial gaze. The horror that Marlow cannot communicate in his narrative is as much mimetic as emotional and constitutes 'a psychological confusion between self and other(s) which, in turn, deprives subjects of their full rational presence to selfhood' (Lawtoo 2012, 240). Conrad's novel is a graphic account of such failure of selfhood and its representation, one that converges with a political crisis in a real historical setting. More importantly, the uneasiness that Marlow's tale contains and communicates 'is precisely the effect of the tale's reality which must linger on after the tale is over' (Ambrosini 1991, 115). Conrad's novel highlights such loss in its attempted explication of 'the stillness of an implacable force brooding over an inscrutable intention' (Conrad [1899] 1963, 36). The inscrutability of intention – in an uncanny landscape where a combat warship fires away into a forest ceaselessly and meaninglessly with 'a touch of insanity' (ibid., 17) – ironically informs the loss of intentionality in Marlow's narrative. Thus, instead of an intersubjective experience which may be dialogically imagined and communicated, Marlow is left only with an 'epistemological solipsism' (Vulcan 1991, 95) that extends into the existential enigma of the novel.

The voice of Kurtz and his dying words that never disappear keep consuming Marlow with their hauntological presence – he hears the whispered cry, 'The horror! The horror!' as he stands to wait for Kurtz's intended by a mahogany door. The passage where Marlow lies to Kurtz's intended deserves to be quoted fully in order to understand the drama of deception that operates like a nervous existential experience as well as a strategic telegraphic transmission:

> 'His last word – to live with,' she insisted. 'Don't you understand I loved him – I loved him – I loved him – I loved him.' I pulled myself together and spoke slowly. 'The last word he pronounced was – your name.' I heard a light sigh and then my heart stood still, stopped dead short by an exulting and terrible cry, by the cry of inconceivable triumph and of unspeakable pain. 'I knew it – I was sure!' . . . She knew. She was sure. (Conrad [1899] 1963, 75–76)

The moment of deception is also the moment of containment and consolation as the agent who returns from the heart of the colonial space strategically withholds information from the one who must perpetuate her location in the logic of romance and its strategic structures of faith. The appeal to know the dying word of Kurtz informs the attempt to reconstruct him through the logos that underpinned the ideology informing policy and proportions characterizing nineteenth-century European Christianity as well as imperialism. In the beginning there was the word, and in the end the word must be preserved into perpetuity for the logos to continue. Marlow's role as the imperial agent is thus most fully functional at the precise moment of the death of his human agency. Protecting the naive female in her mourner's role, Marlow embodies the masculine hysteria that may never be explained or articulated in its combination of guilt and shame. This paradoxically informs the existential insight that he attains through his knowledge of loss as his nervous narrative ends at the 'heart of an immense darkness' (Conrad [1899] 1963, 76). Ending as he does 'in the pose of a meditating Buddha' (ibid., 76), Marlow in *Heart of Darkness* becomes less a signifier of spiritual fecundity than a parody of the impotent seer who can pose like a prophet but is unable to articulate his knowledge of loss for 'that would have been too dark – too dark altogether' (ibid., 76).

Conrad's *Heart of Darkness* is a tale of terror that inverts the pleasure principle of imperial romance and instead offers a nervous narration of panic and crisis. A story told by an imperial agent, *Heart of Darkness* is about the death of agency in a landscape of greed and indeterminacy that is 'a wanton smash-up' (ibid., 20), where somebody had dug artificial holes that 'might have been connected with the philanthropic desire of giving the criminals something to do' (ibid., 20). A profoundly political and politically incorrect novel about matter, metaphor, and memory in their inconstant and inconsistent entanglements, *Heart of Darkness* is about an existential and cognitive crisis which turns to a permanent crisis in embodiment. This interrupted embodiment is manifested also in its narrator's nervous attempts at staggered storytelling, foregrounding again how privileged matter and metaphor are connected in the colonial space and how Conrad's misadventure fiction undercuts the ontology of the colonial gaze. In its self-reflexive narrative about unlearning and uncertainty, Conrad's novel situates a feeling and changing mind against a cultural apparatus that must pathologically perpetuate its ideologies through a 'painful entanglement of falsehood and self-contradiction' (Joravsky 2004, 294). In its articulation of failure and its failure of articulation, *Heart of Darkness* undercuts the imperialist arrogance of its times and offers a complex epistemological and existential ambivalence that is increasingly relevant amid the biopolitical uncertainties of the global capitalist world today.

ORWELL AND IMPERIAL MASCULINITY

George Orwell's alienating experience in an intensely class-conscious Edwardian English public school, subsequently informing his experiential accounts of ambivalence and cynicism as a colonial police officer in Burma, offers a complex study of his contemporary colonial masculinity and its anxieties. Like Conrad's *Heart of Darkness*, Orwell's fictional and nonfictional accounts of colonial experiences are often a complexly asymmetric entanglement of matter, metaphor, and memory connecting political and existential realms. Compared to Conrad, Orwell's experience with imperialism was more personal and critical in his capacity as an empire agent stationed in Burma. However, like Conrad, Orwell's fiction about the empire is characterized by a marked ambivalence which undercuts imperial arrogance while also retaining its racial reification and politics of privileged representation. This is reflected in Orwell's empire essays and fiction in the nervous protagonists' existential dilemmas and their inconsistent negotiations with privileged matter, metaphor, and territorial identity characterizing the colonial gaze.

Born in 1903 in Motihari, Bihar, in British India, and having spent considerable time as an anxious colonial officer in Burma, Orwell had described Kipling as 'a jingo imperialist' who is 'morally insensitive and aesthetically disgusting' (Orwell 1961b, 179) while his own works espoused a cynical and ambivalent attitude towards imperialism, drawing heavily on his personal experiences. Orwell's accounts of boyhood narratives in his contemporary culture – most poignantly presented in the autobiographical essay 'Such, Such Were the Joys' ([1952] 1968) – are particularly important for any study of how the imperial masculinist model was cultivated in Edwardian England, a time when 'bully worship and the cult of violence' (Orwell 1961b, 106) emerged as the most popular themes in boys' magazines. Orwell himself studied the popularity of such pulp magazines in England in the early decades of the twentieth century in an essay titled 'Boys' Weeklies' (1940). The weekly magazines containing boy adventures from public schools were readily consumed, and their cult figures such as Billy Bunter ranked, Orwell argues, on the same plane of popularity as Tarzan and Sherlock Holmes, the two brands of masculinity embodying the perfect muscular body and the perfect investigative mind respectively. Playing up the traditional markers of masculinity, the boys' weeklies also exhibited contemporary xenophobia through the circulation of heavily racialized stereotypes. Thus Inky, the Indian boy, 'is the comic babu of the Punch tradition' (Orwell [1940] 1961b, 101), while Wun Lung, the Chinese boy, 'is the nineteenth-century pantomime Chinaman, with saucer-shaped hat, pigtail and pidgin-English' (ibid., 101).

As Christopher Hitchens argues, Orwell's insight into the horrors of empire was informed by his earlier experiences in childhood that showcased models of discrimination, exploitation, and injustice. Such models hypocritically upheld facades of *well-intentioned ideology* and humanitarian objectives that often upheld the *benevolent face* of imperialism. These were particularly operative in more immediately politicized contexts in the contact zones of English imperialism, where structures of privilege and exploitation were strategically concealed beneath a vocabulary of liberal philanthropy (Hitchens 2002, 128). The masculinity manufactured out of Edwardian public schools before the First World War was driven by an attitude of opulence and entitlement that corresponded closely to the self-indulgent imperialist economy that existed at that time. Orwell reports thus in 'Such, Such Were the Joys':

> There never was, I suppose, in the history of the world a time when the sheer vulgar fatness of wealth, without any kind of aristocratic elegance to redeem it, was so obtrusive, as in the years before 1914. . . . From the whole decade before 1914, there seems to breathe forth a smell of the more vulgar, un-grown-up kinds of luxury, a smell of brilliantine and crème de menthe and soft centered chocolates – an atmosphere, as it were, of eating everlasting strawberry ices on green lawns to the tune of the Eton Boating Song. (Orwell [1952] 1968, 409)

The markers of privilege described by Orwell also underline their own hollowness and false sense of everlasting security and supremacy. The passage offers a complex entanglement of matter and metaphors corresponding to entitlement and privilege, delineated in a memory narrative where an older Orwell attempts to reconnect to the confusions of a younger self through a more matured mapping of the processes that informed a certain brand of masculinity formation. The description of decadence emerges as a cultural as well as a personal pointer to the imminent decline of English imperialism, a process which was accelerated after the First World War and which subsequently unsettled the robustness of the Raj. The massive human and economic loss from the First World War saw the carefree conspicuous consumption that prevailed earlier being replaced by a more guarded show of superiority. Orwell states thus: 'After 1918 it was never quite the same again. Snobbishness and expensive habits came back, certainly, but they were self-conscious and on the defensive' (ibid.).

'Such, Such Were the Joys' emerges as an essay that exhibits social Darwinism at work at a boys' school in early twentieth-century England where money, class, and lineage held tickets to progress and privilege. As Gordon Bowker argues in his study of Orwell's experiences at St Cyprian's:

> Later, as a socialist, he saw the place [St. Cyprian's] for what it was – a commercial venture, dedicated to profit, favouring the rich pupils and abusing the poor.... Not only did it embody all the things he came to reject – imperialism, snobbery, the valuing the strong over the weak, the denigrating of his curiosity about the natural world – but helped to distort his normal feelings about sex. (Bowker 2003, 49)

More significantly, Orwell's earlier experiences in shame and segregation helped him see through the overarching ideologies of imperialism that frequently legitimized exploitation using narratives of civilizational superiority. Having been born in colonial India and having grown up feeling like an outsider to a notoriously class-conscious imperial England, Orwell's ambiguous relationship with the Raj offers a complex study of imperial masculinity and its anxieties. This is immediately evinced in his fictional and nonfictional writings based on his life as a colonial officer in Burma.

Imperial Masculinity and Performance Anxiety in 'Shooting an Elephant'

Orwell's essays and fiction set in colonial Burma, most notably depicted in his novel *Burmese Days* (1934), offer a cynical insider's perspective into the dark underbelly of imperialism. As Christopher Hitchens argues, Orwell's gaze into colonialism and his articulation of its human horrors 'are an indissoluble part of his lifelong engagement with the subjects of power and cruelty and force, and the crude yet subtle relationship between the dominator and the dominated' (Hitchens 2002, 25). However, as Orwell's own writing often evinces, especially in his essays on colonial Burma such as 'A Hanging' (1931) and 'Shooting an Elephant' (1936) and his novel *Burmese Days* (1934), the distinctions between the dominator and the dominated were far from stable or straightforward in a cultural climate mapped by aspiration, anxiety, and self-fashioning. The cynicism that emerges from Orwell's autobiographical empire writings may be seen as reflective of the ambivalence between a straightforward critique and the shame in being a complicit agent of the empire. This gives such writings a uniquely liminal quality where the borderlines between critique and complicity are never clear or consistent. In the process, what emerges is a complex entanglement of matter, metaphor, and memory whereby the human subject nervously navigates across materially and discursively determined coordinates.

Set in Lower Burma and offered as a first-hand report of his personal experiences as a colonial officer, the essay 'Shooting an Elephant' starts by stating the collective aversion Orwell was subjected to as an agent of the empire. The essay carefully delineates the dilemma in the mind of a young officer entrusted with executing the mission of imperialism in a colonized space and is a significant study of the repression that informs an imperialist culture of compulsory classifications and control. What emerges in the essay almost immediately is the ambivalence that informs the schism between collective consciousness and individual will. The will appears systematically subjugated by the political unconscious which informs the economy of expectations of the colonizer as well as the colonized. More significantly, the essay also offers a remarkable representation of the classic Marxist ideas of *alienation* and *reification* (Marx's works on these subjects had not yet appeared in English at the time when Orwell wrote this essay) as it dramatizes how the self is coded and commodified into the *pukka sahib* (perfect white man), a culturally and racially reified product from which the human producer is often essentially and existentially alienated.

'Shooting an Elephant' dramatizes a state where the confused colonizer is torn between his personal hatred of individual colonized natives and his ideological aversion towards imperialism. The confusion described by Orwell is connected to the crisis of agency and the purposelessness suffered by the ambivalent individual in the massive machinery of imperialism. The agony of being the object of collective aversion that was too weak to assume political proportion manifested itself in various *sly strategies* of subversion:

> As a police officer I was an obvious target and was baited whenever it seemed safe to do so. When a nimble Burman tripped me up on the football field and

the referee (another Burman) looked the other way, the crowd yelled with hideous laughter. This happened more than once. In the end the sneering yellow faces of young men that met me everywhere, the insults hooted after me when I was at a safe distance, got badly on my nerves. (Orwell 1961b, 15)

The *site of subversion* is significant in Orwell's account here: the football field where the spirit of sport offered a space for retaliation without political penalty and where the subversion would be spectacular as well as safe, where it would be *unmanly* to uphold and seek protection from the notional politics of privilege. The laughter of the Burmese spectators on seeing the *sahib* tripped emerges as a release from repression in an otherwise reified regime of discrimination and difference.

'Shooting an Elephant' is about the no-man's-land between active intervention and passive acceptance, between collective excitement and private nervousness. The political and existential dilemma embodied by the young Orwell torn between his hatred of imperialism and an equal degree of disgust against the Burmese natives is vividly illustrated:

> All I knew was that I was stuck between my hatred of the empire I served and my rage against the evil-spirited little beasts who tried to make my job impossible. With one part of my mind I thought of the English Raj as an unbreakable tyranny, as something clamped down, *in saecula saeculorum*, upon the will of prostrate peoples; with another part I thought that the greatest joy in the world would be to drive a bayonet into a Buddhist priest's guts. (ibid., 16)

With his ideological hatred of imperialism and his private aversion against the colonized natives who are racially reified as yellow faces with revolting attributes, Orwell in 'Shooting an Elephant' articulates the ambivalence characterizing the alienated agent of the empire. Here, and elsewhere in Orwell's oeuvre, one sees the drama of dislocation powerfully at work. The result is a confusion that is political as well as existential in quality, whereby Orwell confessed that he 'could get nothing into perspective' (ibid., 15–16).

'Shooting an Elephant' dramatizes the distinction Michel Foucault makes between the 'universal "left" intellectual' who acknowledges 'the right of speaking in the capacity of master of truth and justice' and the 'specific intellectual' embedded in 'a question of real, material, everyday struggles' (Foucault 1972, 126–27). The resultant confusion informs Orwell's ambivalent attitude towards imperialism and its Burmese subjects. This produces what Slavoj Žižek describes as the misrecognition arising out of the human subject's activity as an agent in an overwhelming political process (Žižek 1989, 2). As a powerless agent of the massive imperial machinery, Orwell, in 'Shooting an Elephant', enacts the annihilation of agency at the heart of the colonial contact zone. With its political and existential complexity, 'Shooting an Elephant' dramatizes a nervous condition that also contains elements of dark humour. Informed about a mad elephant ravaging the local bazaar, Orwell, the colonial superintendent of police, is forced to set out to look for it on a pony with a .44 Winchester rifle, presenting the iconic image of the colonizer expected to control any potential anarchy. The colonizer on horseback with a rifle is not only the signifier of power in the imperial setting but also represents the necessary performance of spectacular imperial masculinity, a mimetic role that Orwell enacts with increasing ambivalence and anxiety. The *neuromimetic performance* of imperial masculinity and its associated performance anxiety give 'Shooting an Elephant' its distinct dark quality, whereby the agency of the notionally powerful white man is increasingly and experientially compromised to conform to the codes that inform the grand narrative of white supremacy in the imperial space.

Appropriately enough, as the *sahib* marches on to shoot the elephant, the Burmese population flock out of their houses to follow him in an image that approximates as well as parodies the Pied Piper signifier even as it produces the possibility of collective excitement in a spectacular sport. The imminent shooting of the elephant becomes a symbolic and spectacular replication as well as a hollow mimicry of the hunting act characterizing colonial white masculinity and its supremacy. The mimetic and performative quality of his imperial identity is exposed before Orwell at the moment in which he is forced to surrender the will of his private self in order to remain 'condemned forever to dance the *danse du pukka sahib*' (Orwell 1961a, 151). The consolidated construct of the *pukka sahib* constitutes perfect pluck as well as unequivocal manliness, one which is not to be compromised by ambivalence or anticlimax in the public space. As Orwell asserts:

> [a] sahib has got to act like a sahib; he has got to appear resolute, to know his own mind and do definite things. To come all that way, rifle in hand, with two thousand people marching at my heels, and then to trail feebly away, having done nothing – no, that was impossible. The crowd would laugh at me. And my whole life, every white man's life in the East, was one long struggle not to be laughed at. (Orwell 1961b, 19)

The white man, the rifle, the elephant, and the crowd all become material as well as metaphorical in this passage that describes the real and the affective production and performance of white privilege in a colonial space. What makes this section and the entire essay political and existential in quality is the construction and consumption of codes of hegemonic white masculinity that exhibits imperial privilege as a compulsory performative category. The passage also problematizes the ontology of agency in the colonial space, and Orwell's insight into his personal helplessness under the collective gaze occupies the epistemic moment when privilege is problematized and the notional colonizer-colonized hierarchy reversed.

The entanglement of the collective gaze and the private gaze in 'Shooting an Elephant' dramatizes the hollowed-out production of power and deserves to be quoted for its full impact:

> I could feel their two thousand wills pressing me forward, irresistibly. And it was at this moment, as I stood there with the rifle in my hands, that I first grasped the hollowness, the futility of the white man's domination in the East. . . . I perceived in this moment that when the white man turns tyrant it is his own freedom that he destroys. He becomes a sort of hollow, posing dummy, the conventionalised figure of a sahib. For it is the condition of his rule that he shall spend his life in trying to impress the 'natives', and so in every crisis he has to do what the 'natives' expect of him. He wears a mask, and his face grows to fit it. (ibid., 19–20)

Orwell's discovery of the hollowness of the white man's privilege occupies an epiphanic moment when experiential awakening mixes insight with existential unlearning. 'Shooting an Elephant' is an essay where the white male subject's action emerges as a nervous mimicry, a *neuromimesis* of the imperial masculinist code, complicating Homi Bhabha's notion of mimicry as an aspirational activity of the colonized native (Bhabha 1984). The anxiety of the white man to appropriate the imperial masculinity that informs white privilege in the colonies emerges as political as the anxiety of the *hyper-civil* native to appropriate the colonizer's code. For in Orwell's essay, it is the colonizer who anxiously attempts to mimic the grand narrative of imperial masculinity in the public space, where the white man is supposedly always the clinical conqueror and the fearless hunter.

In preparing to shoot the elephant despite his conviction of the creature's harmless quality, Orwell enacts the *neuromimesis* of the colonial white man anxious to assert his pre-assigned narrative of supremacist performance:

> A white man mustn't be frightened in front of 'natives'; and so, in general, he isn't frightened. The sole thought in my mind was that if anything went wrong those two thousand Burmans would see me pursued, caught, trampled on and reduced to a grinning corpse like that Indian up that hill. And if that happened it was quite probable that some of them would laugh. (ibid., 21)

The admission of anxiety thus constitutes not the fear of death but the fear of shame as Orwell emerges painfully prepared to prioritize the permanence of the white man's construct over the safety of his human self. This may be seen as an experiential extension of the primacy of shame over fear in the experience of emasculation under the female gaze in 'Such, Such Were the Joys' examined earlier. The episode in 'Shooting an Elephant' corroborates as well as complicates Linda Martin Alcoff's study of *invalidated identities* in heavily racialized spaces, whereby the existential self is infected and increasingly substituted by the notional supremacy of the white man (Alcoff 2006, 206). Orwell's experience in 'Shooting an Elephant' showcases how the self is painfully consumed by the sahib, how the human core is replaced by the discursive construct.

As he shoots the elephant before the Burmese crowd against his human will and sees the animal die slowly and painfully, Orwell essentially enacts the annihilation of his own agency to preserve the purpose of his imperial identity through the performative production of a hunting spectacle. Orwell's painful empathy with the dying elephant is established through his choice of pronouns which humanize the animal and highlight the human as reified, foregrounding the complex matrix of matter and metaphor in an imperially mapped space. This throws light on the colonial climate where everything and everyone could be commodified and where value was determined by the entity's effectiveness in the machinery of production and its codes. Orwell's ambivalence and insight into the horror and hollowness of colonialism thus inhabit a state of interruption in the process of commodification. Equally, his performance anxiety before the act of shooting may be read as the nervousness of the subject before enacting and extending the notional supremacy of the imperial identity, which was the most prized commodity in the colonial space. The value of the most precious colonial commodity and the anxiety to preserve it reappear at the end of 'Shooting an Elephant'. Back at the colonial club, the event triggers a debate between the younger white men, who feel it was shameful to shoot an elephant which costs more than the Indian coolie it had trampled and killed earlier, and the older imperial officers who say Orwell had done the right thing. This episode may be best described as a comparison of colonial commodities, with the younger men's opinion focusing on the priced cost while the more experienced imperialists advocate in favour of the priceless colonial commodity, a spectacle of the white man's superiority, which must be maintained and re-enacted whenever necessary at all costs. 'Shooting an Elephant' ends with the confession mixed with the fear of being found out, as Orwell 'wondered whether any of the others grasped that I had done it solely to avoid looking like a fool' (Orwell 1961b, 23).

Orwell's 'Shooting an Elephant' is an arresting articulation of human hesitation, confusion, and existential hollowness born out of the hegemonic material practices of cultural identity and supremacy. It contains the paradoxical knowledge that the aspiration for privilege and political power can also produce pure human helplessness, that the assertion of privileged masculinity can emerge out of the dissolution of agency. The essay describes the processes of reification and alienation whereby human selves are increasingly coded into commodities that conform to and consolidate hegemonic imperial identities. In situating the confused human mind against the overarching structures of domination and difference, 'Shooting an Elephant' offers a disturbing drama of ambivalence and performance anxiety in an essentially imperialist and masculinist landscape. The human experience in the essay emerges from a production of the paradox that the borderlines between supremacy and vulnerability, between privilege and powerlessness, may become blurred during moments of ideological overdeterminism that result in reified identities. Such an account of the human condition emerges with renewed relevance in the real and virtual discourse networks operative in the post-truth identity politics we increasingly internalize and consume today.

Colonial Masculinity and Its Discontents: A Study of *Burmese Days*

The anxiety born out of inadequate masculinity is a theme that recurs in Orwell's novel *Burmese Days*, whose protagonist John Flory carries his birthmark as a signifier of shame. Like Orwell who saw his school solely as a profit-making enterprise, and like Conrad's Marlow in *Heart of Darkness* who sees the horrors of European imperialism from close quarters as an evil network of lies and exploitation, Flory in *Burmese Days* uses the metaphor of the sick female patient to describe the dying British Empire and asserts unequivocally his disgust at the spurious discourse of the white man's burden:

> I'm here to make money, like everyone else. All I object to is the slimy white man's burden humbug. The pukka sahib pose. It's so boring. Even those bloody fools at the Club might be better company if we weren't all of us living a lie the whole time. (Orwell 1961a, 39)

Evidently positioning itself against the Kiplingesque narrative of imperial adventure and its edificatory duties, Orwell's *Burmese Days* is a remarkable novel about an insider's account of the horrors of colonial domination, hubris, and horrors that consume the dominator as well as the dominated. The nervous tension that constitutes power and its compulsory hierarchies in colonial Burma in *Burmese Days* incorporates issues of race and gender as well as language.

If the characters in *Burmese Days* are less focalized or rounded than those of Forster's *A Passage to India* (1924), Orwell's novel emerges as a more direct depiction of the compulsive qualities of racial law and its perpetuation in the colonial contact zone. This is exemplified by the fictional depiction of the xenophobic imperialist in a character called Ellis in *Burmese Days*, who combines the stereotypes of the crude colonizer with that of incorrigible sense of entitlement. Unsurprisingly, Ellis is immediately threatened when the Indian waiter at the English club retorts in near-perfect English:

> Don't talk like that damn you – 'I find it very difficult!' Have you swallowed a dictionary? 'Please, master, can't keep ice cool' – that's how you ought to talk. We shall have to sack this fellow if he gets to talk English too well. I can't stick servants who talk English. (ibid., 26)

Crucially, the inadequacy of the Indian servant rests precisely at the point where he exhibits an adequate and accurate appropriation of the normative language of the colonizer. The incident immediately instantiates one of the central issues in Orwell's oeuvre on the colonial contact zone: the compulsive construction and circulation of the discourse of difference and its stereotypes. The nervousness of the otherwise arrogant colonizer (embodied in Ellis who never changes throughout the course of the novel from being a megalomaniac imperialist) is located at the point where his assumption of racial superiority is, if only marginally, threatened, not by an actual act of rebellion that can be conveniently punished but by what is perceived as the sly civility of the colonial servant, enacted with an over-appropriation of the colonizer's language.

In his analysis of the sly civility that characterizes the colonial condition of non-reconciliation, Homi Bhabha describes its double inscription. Thus Bhabha states:

> Between the civil address and its colonial signification – each axis displaying a problem of recognition and repetition – shuttles the signifier of authority in search of a strategy of surveillance, subjection, and inscription. . . . Both colonizer and colonized are in a process of miscognition where each point of identification is always a partial and double repetition of the *otherness* of the self – democrat and despot, individual *and* servant, native and child. (Bhabha 1994, 138–39)

The threat that is enacted through hyper-civility is further accentuated through language for Bhabha, as mimicry in the colonial space emerges as a subversive act of spectacular resistance. Thus, for Bhabha, '[w]hen the words of the master become the site of hybridity . . . then we may not only read between the lines but even seek to change the often coercive reality that they so lucidly contain' (Bhabha 1985, 162).

The complex luggage of language and its political performance are depicted again when Ellis 'deliberately exaggerated his Cockney accent, because of the sardonic tone it gave to his words' (Orwell 1961a, 22), while dramatizing his resentment to Macgregor's proposing membership of the club to the natives. Cockney as a social signifier within an English space stands in stark contrast to the standardized English practised at the colonial contact zone, one that is desired and appropriated by the colonized. Language thus emerges in *Burmese Days* as a signifier of both class and race through varying epistemological frames. The political condition depicted in the novel corresponds closely to the class condition in England as the natives in India are frequently equated with the lower classes in Britain. *Burmese Days* thus blends the discourse of degeneration (and its notion of 'bad stock') with that of colonialism through its fictional frame. Thus Mrs Lackersteen, another stereotype of the crude colonizer, laments the loss of authority over the colonized masses by drawing attention to an analogous situation in Britain: 'We seem to have no *authority* over the natives nowadays, with all these dreadful Reforms, and the insolence they learn from the newspapers. In some ways they are getting almost as bad as the lower classes at home' (ibid., 29).

As Mrinalini Sinha asserts in her study of the culture of clubbing during the British Empire, the imperial English club emerged not only as a spatial signifier of the expansive ontology of homosocial white masculinity in the colonial contact zone but also grudgingly granted the right to women to enter the notionally all-male space, for the sole purpose of continued and closely monitored protection from the contaminating presence of the colonized male (Sinha 2001, 515). The club in *Burmese Days* emerges as both a symbol of desire and disgust, along with being the spatial location of hegemonic homosocial masculinity. Thus, while for the Burmese elite males such as the Machiavellian (and perversely pious) gangster Ko Po Kyin and the hyper-Westernized and hyper-servile doctor Veraswami, the White Man's Club at Kyauktada emerges as a sacred shrine of social status that is desired as well as feared; for Flory it represents the crude complacency of imperial English masculinity that is driven by humbug and 'booze as the cement of the empire' (Orwell 1961a, 39). It is this complex location of difference within the masculinist imperialist economy that makes *Burmese Days* a work of original revelation despite its political incorrectness and ultimate appropriation of the vocabulary of imperialism. Sinha's study of the discourse of difference signified by the subscription to imperial clubbability in the colonial contact zone shows how such clubbability 'was always defined in relation to the dependent and the subjected – women, children, servants, employees, slaves, and the colonized' (Sinha 2001, 497). It is interesting to note that such politics of privilege and exclusive systems of admittance are still operative in several clubs in Kolkata (formerly the capital of colonial India) that were originally formed during British imperialism. Also, such clubs still subscribe to strict dress codes that adhere to the grammar of dressing appropriated by imperial British and Anglo-Indian masculinity.

Flory in Orwell's *Burmese Days* (who is considered 'notoriously Bolshie in his opinions') embodies nervous masculinity in the colonies, and like Marlow in *Heart of Darkness*, also realizes the horror of imperialism without being able to articulate or explicate it, except during moments of private hysteria that paradoxically inform his existential insights. Curiously located between his private hatred of imperialism and his discomfort under the collective gaze of the colonized, Flory sees himself and his creed of colonizers as 'condemned forever to dance the *danse du pukka sahib* for the edification of the lower races' (Orwell 1961a, 151), whereby his imagination retains the rhetoric of racism despite his personal hatred of its inherent ideology. The borderlines between the dominator and the dominated are not always clearly demarcated in *Burmese Days*, despite its subscription to the logic of binaries operative in the empire and its colonial space. As the narrative informs the reader, Flory's dislocation and difficulty had begun at the moment of his birth, indeed 'in his mother's womb when chance put the blue birthmark on his cheek' (ibid., 64). The birthmark in the novel does not only emerge as a signifier of social shame but also as a mark of self-loathing and sexual shame (as evinced in Flory's covering his birthmark right after his sexual act with his Burmese mistress Ma Hla May, for he 'always remembered the birthmark when he had done something to be ashamed of' (ibid., 64).

The politics of naming as a strategy of shaming runs throughout *Burmese Days* as evinced in Flory's childhood in school where he was called Blueface and Monekybum in a couplet written by the school poet who had gone on to be a writer for the *Nation*: 'New-tick Flory does look rum, Got a face like a monkey's bum' (ibid., 64). The shame in looking rum and being equated with a monkey (a simile that is loaded with racist connotations) is solely and partially redeemed by Flory's being a 'liar and a good footballer, the two things absolutely necessary for success at school' (ibid., 64). Football and lying thus emerge as two essential criteria for appropriating the model masculinity that is muscular as well as manipulative in what is described by the narrative as the 'formative period' of masculine development, the horrors of which are personally elucidated by Orwell in 'Such, Such Were the Joys'. The formative period had featured again for Flory in a different ontology of imperial masculinity in the colonial contact zone during his first few months in Burma with four other young Englishmen when

> [t]hey swilled whiskey which they privately hated, they stood round the piano bawling songs of inane filthiness and silliness, they squandered rupees

by the hundred on aged Jewish whores with the faces of crocodiles. That too had been a formative period. (ibid., 65)

The two different formative periods delineated here correspond to what Raymond Williams classifies as a 'negative identification', which constitutes an abdication of one's 'initial and formative social experience' in favour of a new horizon of cultural and social hermeneutics (Williams 1971, 20). The formative phase in Burma had thus taught Flory the necessity of withholding private preference in order to superordinate cultural signifiers of performative imperial masculinity, a condition that is manifested by the nervous tensions embodied by Flory at various points in the narrative. The Jewish prostitutes, with faces of crocodiles, embody the stereotype of fallen degenerated human species in the imperial masculine imagination, embedded in highly racialized stereotypes that run throughout Orwell's novel.

A narrative that blends the medical and the political through a mode that locates culture as well as body under the hegemonic gaze that decides discourses, Orwell's *Burmese Days* emerges as a novel that contains the contingencies in the colonial contact zone with its nervous masculinities. Indeed, Flory's discomfiting shame about his birthmark as well as his insight into the horrors of the empire are characterized by a nervous strain that becomes almost hysteric in its compulsive concealment and behaviour: 'He was quite aware of its [the birthmark's] hideousness. And all times, when he was not alone, there was a sidelongness about his movements, as he manoeuvred to keep the birthmark out of sight' (Orwell 1961a, 17). As a signifier of shame, the birthmark also stands for an otherness that Flory appears to be overdetermined by. It eventually contributes towards his failure as a lover as well as an agent in the imperial space. Martha Nussbaum's discursive analysis of shame is particularly pertinent here as a nervous manifestation of inferiority born out of visible physical aberration or cultural deviance. Nussbaum argues thus:

> People who look different from others – people with visible diseases or so-called deformities, the mentally or physically handicapped – wear their shame on their faces. . . . When there is no visible brand, societies have been quick to inflict one, whether by tattooing or branding or by other visible signs of social ostracism or disapproval. (Nussbaum 2004, 174)

Due to the degree of visible social shame that his birthmark carries and contains, Flory's facial maneuvers also correspond to the compulsory neural rituals of concealment and evasion through which such shame is effaced. The medical as well as the social signifiers of shame are contained and corroborated by the facial expressions that Darwin believed represent innate mental patterns (Cornelius 1996, 2). Flory in *Burmese Days* embodies both forms of shaming and segregation examined by Nussbaum, with the conspicuous marker of shame on his face through his crescent-shaped birthmark as well as his private hatred of the ideology of imperialism. Indeed, his Bolshie-ness and birthmark appear together in the vocabulary of tirade used against Flory by the more established imperialist Ellis:

> He's a bit *too* Bolshie for my taste. I can't bear a fellow who pals up with the natives. I shouldn't wonder if he's got a lick of the tarbrush himself. It might explain that black mark on his face. Piebald. And he looks like a yellow-belly, with that black hair, and skin the colour of a lemon. (Orwell 1961a, 34)

The possibility of piebald-ness that Flory carries with his birthmark (which, although actually blue, appears black under Ellis's imperialist gaze) demarcates him from the normative mappings of the imperial homosocial space exemplified by the Englishman's club. More significantly, and in keeping with the discourse of degeneration and denigration in the narratives of imperialism, Flory is equated with effeminacy and homosexuality through his association with the colonized males. This is a further corroboration of the possibility of degeneration that he seems to embody with his piebald skin and black birthmark before Ellis's eyes who calls Flory 'a nigger's Nancy Boy'. The narrative describes the bodily and the ideological transitions by describing Flory's disgust with the empire through the development of his brain:

> For as his brain developed – you cannot stop your brain developing, and it is one of the tragedies of the half-educated that they develop late, when they are already committed to some wrong way of life – he had grasped the truth about the English and their Empire. (ibid., 68)

The development of the brain and the knowledge that comes with the process is both political and neural, and the intersections between anthropology and neuroscience yield rich research into the human mind and how it makes meaning out of matter, how consciousness is informed by culture, corroborating the entanglement of matter, metaphor, and memory examined in this book. This argument is augmented by the anthropologist Clifford Geertz who states that:

> As our central nervous system – and most particularly its crowning curse and glory, the neocortex – grew up in great part in interaction with culture, it is incapable of directing our behaviour or organizing our experience without the guidance provided by the systems of significant symbols. (Geertz 1973, 49)

Geertz's argument upholds the traffic between brain and external matter and analyses how the brain and the body are situated and informed by cultural systems and signifiers. Such a study shows how the self and its cultural location are positioned apropos of each other. Likewise, neuroscientists and psychiatrists have increasingly come to look at the cultural and anthropological determinants that emerge as 'a complex interaction between biological and psychological and social sources of vulnerability' (Kleinmann 1988, 58).

Like Kurtz who discovers the horror of the truth about imperialism in *Heart of Darkness* only when his nerves go wrong, Flory attains the knowledge of the horror only with the transitions in his brain corresponding to experiential transformations and emotional and existential changes. The connection with *Heart of Darkness* as well as with *Nineteen Eighty Four* (1949) is made more direct (albeit at an implicit level in *Burmese Days*) with the depiction of the horror of one who is overdetermined by the power paradigm that he must compulsively inscribe himself into, through a combination of unarticulated hysteria and claustrophobia. This is amply evinced by the narrator's descriptions of the culture of colonial control:

> It is a stifling, stultifying world in which to live. It is a world in which every word and every thought is censored. In England it is hard to imagine such an atmosphere. Everyone is free in England; we sell our souls in public and buy them back in private, among our friends. But even friendship can hardly exist when every white man is a cog in the wheels of despotism. Free speech is unthinkable. All other kinds of freedom are permitted. You are free to be a drunkard, an idler, a coward, a backbiter, a fornicator; but you are not free to think for yourself. Your opinion on every subject of any conceivable importance is dictated for you by the pukka sahib's code. (Orwell 1961a, 69)

The absolute censorship on free speech and freethinking connects the condition immediately with *Nineteen Eighty Four*, with the totalitarian dystopia that punishes thought crime. But *Burmese Days* goes a step further with its complex depiction of the entanglement of law and permissible lawlessness where the insider is also always an outsider who must consummate the compulsory performance of the *pukka sahib*'s code. This is the nervous strain that comes with the compulsory perpetuation of the code manifested in Flory as well as in the Orwellian self in 'Shooting an Elephant'. More significantly, the location of the code is significant inasmuch as it is situated at an epistemic excess in relation to the personal will. As the narrative informs, focalizing itself through the state and voice of Flory, 'You are a creature of the despotism, a pukka sahib, tied tighter than a monk or a savage by an unbearable system of tabus' (ibid., 69).

Burmese Days may be justly criticized for appropriating strategies of imperialist stereotyping and essentialism in its descriptions of 'naked black coolies squabbling over the luggage' (ibid., 71), Burmese women as Dutch dolls, and English-educated Indians as greasy *babus*. Thus Elizabeth asserts her revulsion on seeing the black bodies of the Burmese acrobats who induce disgust in her ingrained ideology of European physiognomic superiority:

> But they have such hideous-shaped heads! Their skulls kind of slope up behind like a tom-cat's. And then the way their foreheads slant back – it makes them look so *wicked*. I remember reading something in a magazine about the shape of people's heads; it said that a person with a sloping forehead is a *criminal type*. (Orwell 1961a, 118–19, emphasis added)

The sloping forehead as a physiognomic signifier of criminal propensities as classified by the criminology of Lombroso continued to exist in the common Western public discourse of disgust well into the twentieth century. Elizabeth with her European past of a Parisian life of white wine and arty cafes subscribes to such discourses of difference. But it is precisely due to its political incorrectness that *Burmese Days*, like *Heart of Darkness*, stands out as a complex text that resists closure even as its narrative moves towards a conventional finale.

One can take up Edward Said's analysis of the politics of representation and assess how anthropology offers representation as a political choice that also constitutes the local and the personal with the inference that 'anthropological representations bear as much on the representer's world as on who or what is represented' (Said 1989, 224). Interestingly enough, in a different yet related work, Said looks at Conrad and examines *Heart of Darkness* as a classic instance of a text that houses the tensions between real political presence and the desire to escape from the same (Said 2003, 26). This reading can be extended to Orwell's *Burmese Days* and accounts for the ambivalence through which it enacts its critique of imperialism while essentially retaining its racist vocabulary. Flory emerges in *Burmese Days* as an ambivalent outsider to the code in a manner which acts as the converse to the fearful otherness that Kurtz comes to embody in Conrad's *Heart of Darkness*. Both their states are eventually connected by an experience (more immediately ostensible in Conrad's novel) of degeneration and decadence, culminating in Orwell's novel in Flory's suicide. Therefore, while Flory's failure is a result of his inadequate appropriation of the masculinist vocabulary specially coded for the colonial contact zone, Kurtz's decline and eventually mysterious death stem from his over-appropriation and over-internalization of the same code. Relevant in both narratives are the issues of location and agency that correspond to the external environment that shapes and re-shapes the constitution of the self. The significance of the surroundings as conditioning the making and unmaking of the self is vividly described in Orwell's novel. Flory's continuous and compulsive envisioning of the perfect future in terms of escaping the corruption of the colonial contact zone and settling down with a 'civilised girl, not a pukka memsahib', is evocative in its escapist zeal and romanticized fecundity:

> They would buy a cottage in the country, surround themselves with friends, books, their children, animals. They would be free forever of the smell of pukka sahibdom. He would forget Burma, the horrible country that had come near ruining him. (Orwell 1961a, 70–71)

The 'cottage in the country' emerges as a utopian metaphor for romantic escape from the horrors of real and reified imperial space where Flory is an insider as well as an outsider. Emerging increasingly in the narrative as an embodiment of nervous masculinity in the colonial contact zone, Flory is also characterized by an inferiority complex that exists in the same plane of shame with the discourses of degeneration and effeminacy in a culture that necessitated compulsory and compulsive performance of imperial masculinity and its ideal body.

With his private ideology of self-disgust and hatred of empire, Flory comes to embody a secrecy that is variously manifested in his clandestine visits to Dr Veraswami for intellectual comfort and his sexual relationships with colonial women, both prohibited by the parameters of the colonizer's law. Like the ivory in Conrad's *Heart of Darkness*, the timber in Orwell's *Burmese Days* emerges as the material as well as the metaphor of the exploitative potential of imperialism driven by a masculinist economy constituting hunting expeditions, horse riding, and excesses of drinking. As Flory's attempts to escape from Burma are frustrated by the sudden death of three men in his firm due to blackwater fever and he is forced to return to his old quarter in Burma, he experiences a sudden and sad insight that transforms him internally. On seeing his Indian servants busy in their usual chores and on being greeted by the same people in a manner akin to the homecoming of a hero, Flory realizes the certainty of his location in colonial Burma and the futility of escaping from the same, a certainty that is also perceived as decadence. The passage, despite its realist frame, is couched in a vocabulary not unlike that of the high-Modernist epiphany:

> Something turned over in Flory's heart. It was one of those moments when one becomes conscious of a vast change and deterioration in one's life. For he had realised, suddenly, that in his heart he was glad to be coming back. This

> country which he hated was now his native country, his home. He had lived here ten years, and every particle of his body was compounded of Burmese soil. Scenes like these – the sallow evening light, the old Indian cropping grass, the creak of the cartwheels ... were more native to him than England. He had sent deep roots, perhaps his deepest, into a foreign country. (Orwell 1961a, 71–72)

The thought processes of Flory here extend into the existential realm, merging matter with metaphor, material with memory, in a changing mind. The phenomenal knowledge and revelation of his location in the colonial contact zone appears as an epistemic moment of change that is internal and private while being directly informed by the external and the material environment. It is a moment that perhaps connects Flory most closely to Orwell, who himself was born in Motihari in Bihar near the Nepal border and had difficulties situating the ontology of *nativeness* throughout his life, appearing as an uncomfortable outsider to the class-conscious patriotism in Britain. More significantly, the figure of Flory appears as characterized by a political determinism (one that makes him painfully aware of his externality to his coveted pure British space) that fixates him like his bodily birthmark. As Keith Alldritt contends in an analysis of the passage describing Flory's recognition of his location, 'If Burma has set its marks on Flory, so also has heredity; though Orwell's use of this element of naturalistic doctrine is such that it has symbolic force rather than meaning in straightforwardly genetic and physiological terms' (Alldritt 1969, 22). Despite being couched in symbolic and cultural terms, the nervous and genetic determinism that is used to characterize Flory in *Burmese Days* is never lost sight of, like his birthmark that continues to stay as a signifier of ineradicable shame.

The association of shame with a mark of bodily aberration, and the inscription of inferiority related to the same, dramatize the complex discourse of difference and discrimination in *Burmese Days*. The homosocial white masculinist space of the English club in Kyauktada is continually threatened in the novel not only by external entities (the election of an Indian as a member of the club and the mob of angry Burmese who gather to attack Ellis) but also by the presence of the uncomfortable Eurasians who notionally belong to the breed of the colonizers. The Eurasians who appear in *Burmese Days* embody the problematic racial hybridity that induces disgust in the *pure white* Europeans in the colonies, most immediately as visible images of sexual and racial degeneration. The Eurasians Francis and Samuel who approach Elizabeth and Flory before they enter the club come to represent the degenerate types in Elizabeth's imagination, with their impure skin and inadequate European-ness. Elizabeth's enquires to Flory carry the rhetoric that informed criminology and degeneration discourses from late nineteenth-century racialized pseudoscience:

> They looked awfully degenerate types, didn't they? So thin and weedy and cringing; and they haven't got at all honest faces. I suppose these Eurasians are very degenerate? I've heard that half-castes always inherit what's worst in both races. Is that true? (Orwell 1961a, 123)

With her earlier assumptions about the inherent criminal propensities of the Burmese men based on the physiognomic feature of their forehead, and with her revulsion on seeing the half-breed Eurasians as degenerates, Elizabeth comes to voice the vocabulary of biopolitical panic that grew out of the popular fin de siècle European imagination with its obsession with hygienic, racial, and bodily order. The collective abhorrence towards the Eurasians Francis and Samuel (who ironically are illegitimate children of colonial clergymen stationed in Burma) constitutes and corroborates the condition which sees racial mixing as a threat to the purity of privileged imperial identity. The progeny of such racial/sexual transgression are characterized by the determinism that informs the retribution of the act, as the Eurasians are termed 'yellow-bellies' (a term used, interestingly enough, by Ellis in his derision for Flory's perceived proximity to the colonized natives) by the British at the colonies and are considered absolute outcasts.

In her work on the politics of disgust, Martha Nussbaum underlines the difference between disgust and anger 'in that its [disgust's] thought-content is typically unreasonable, embodying magical ideas of contamination, and impossible aspirations to purity, immortality and nonanimality'. More significantly, as Nussbaum goes on to contend, 'disgust has been used throughout history to exclude and marginalize groups who come to embody the dominant group's fear and loathing of its own animality and mortality' (Nussbaum 2004, 75). The discursive binary that disgust constructs works by exclusion and segregation, with a structure of sentiments that informs xenophobic and political presuppositions. As an affective economy of material and metaphoric signifiers, disgust operates viscerally by drawing attention to and appearing as a repulsive reminder of the messy corporeality of the body as opposed to the perfect functional frame advocated by the logic of imperialist control. With its threat of contamination and pathological possibilities, disgust often emerges as a nervous and unconditioned reflex response to the non-normative entity and event. Therefore, the Jewish prostitutes in *Burmese Days* carry a biopolitical implication of degeneration in keeping with the popular paranoia and heavily racialized panic at that time.

It is interesting at this point to note the vocabulary that Orwell himself had used while describing anti-Semitism in England. In the essay 'Anti-Semitism in Britain', for instance, Orwell investigates the structure of the sentiment that informed anti-Semitism, offering literary, cultural, and anecdotal accounts while expounding what he considered to be the discursive difference between anti-Semitism and the localized dislike of Jews. Describing anti-Semitism as a 'neurosis . . . [that] . . . has its rationalizations, which are sincerely believed in and are partly true' (Orwell 1961b, 311), Orwell invites an investigation that begins from the self supposedly immune from similar proclivities. The presence of anti-Semitism as a medical condition is reiterated towards the end of the essay as Orwell asserts, 'The point is that something, some psychological vitamin, is lacking in modern civilization, and as a result we are all more or less subject to this lunacy of believing that whole races or nations are mysteriously good or mysteriously evil' (ibid., 314). The embodiments of degeneration in *Burmese Days* appear in the form of the mixed-breed Eurasians who, with their bodily markers of racial miscegenation, emerge as a shameful and almost pathologized presence before Elizabeth who, with her internalized ideas of racial purity, is overwhelmed by revulsion. Such revulsion becomes bewilderment on seeing Flory converse easily with the degenerates and revealing the Eurasians' financial dependence on the natives' charity.

Flory's connection with the degenerates is not just coupled by his shameful birthmark but also by his deviance from the normative imperial ethic in *Burmese Days*. Thus, as he explains to Elizabeth:

> Oh well, I break the rules occasionally. I meant that a pukka sahib probably wouldn't be seen talking to them [the Eurasians]. But you see, I try – just sometimes, when I have the pluck – *not* to be a pukka sahib. (Orwell 1961a, 124)

The discursive domains of the words *pukka* and *pluck* are significant in the context of the passage. The word *pukka* had entered English vocabulary from the colonial contact zone in India and its corresponding linguistic traffic. In common Hindi parlance, the word *pukka* means cemented, strongly ascertained and ascertainable. Most commonly associated with the vocabulary of construction (of building and walls), *pukka* carried a sense of inherent strength against external attacks as well as internal weaknesses. Thus, crucially, *pukka* signified the consummated process of construction that incorporates integration of disparate entities and clinical closure, leading to a final seamless product with no visible loose ends.

It is interesting to read the usage of this metaphor for construction in the vocabulary of colonial masculinity, a discourse that was as characterized by integrated incorporations and closure as the construction of roads and dams. A classic case in point of the merging of the material and the metaphorical, *pukka* became a marker of identity and its strength quotient in the English imperial imagination. Apart from exhibiting the constructed quality of imperial masculinity, *pukka* also carried a sense of immediacy and integration characterizing a code constituted by domination, difference, and reification. The word can also be read as a throwback on the machineries of masculinity in English schools and scout movements that operated along similar constructions of strength and splendour in a cultural climate where 'manhood was an artificial product coaxed by austere training and testing' (Gilmore 1990, 18). Essentially appropriating the vocabulary of road construction, *pukka* thus signified a model of masculinity that would leave no loose ends of its construction process and could thus immediately inform, produce, and perpetuate the ontology of privilege. The seamlessness of imperial masculinity as exhibited in the colonial contact zone may be seen as an instance of what Shannon Sullivan classifies as the surreptitious workings of white privilege that operates precisely where it appears not to operate and is most functional precisely where it appears invisible. The ideologies of racial supremacy, as Sullivan asserts, 'function as if not-existent and actively thwart conscious attempt to pinpoint their existence. This unconscious, invisible mode of operation is what enables white privileged habits to be increasingly effective and pervasive' (Sullivan 2006, 187).

Likewise, the grammar of being the *pukka sahib* worked best when it concealed its constructed quality and instead appeared as an expansive ontology of innate and unquestionable supremacy. The irony that is dramatized in Orwell's *Burmese Days* constitutes the knowledge of the fact that the cemented strength that informs the *pukka* construct of the empire is essentially reliant on alcoholism and mendacity. As Flory asserts this to the non-believing Indian doctor Veraswami who embodies absolute loyalty to the empire:

> It's a tradition to booze together and swap meals and pretend to be friends, though we hate each other like poison.... It's a political necessity. Of course drink is what keeps the machine going. We should all go mad and kill one another in a week if it weren't for that. There's a subject for one of your uplift essayists, doctor. Booze as the cement of empire. (Orwell 1961a, 38–39)

The complexity of *Burmese Days* is enhanced by the private interrogations of ideology as well by the eventual failure of such attempts. The pluck *not* to be *pukka* enacts the private deconstruction of the discursive vocabulary that Flory seeks to subvert through his ambivalence, if only occasionally. The culture associated with the word corresponded closely to the normative masculinity engineered out of the Boy Scouts and public schools with its bravado and stoic indifference to feminine sentimentality (attributes embodied extremely and perfectly by Verrall in *Burmese Days* whose comradeship with his horses is stronger than his emotional bonds with any human beings). But in the context in which Flory uses it before Elizabeth, it required real pluck to break the discourse of pluckiness that informed normative masculinity in the colonial contact zone, a pluckiness that emerges only as a sporadic sentiment and an eventually ineffectual attribute in the nervous protagonist in Orwell's fictional account of colonial Burma.

Unsurprisingly, Elizabeth, who embodies essentialized European-ness in the colonial contact zone, consumes and hero-worships the model of imperial masculinity that thrives in hunting, shooting, and exhibiting normative masculine machismo. Therefore, when Flory describes his hunting adventures, her immediate interest incorporates a nervous unconditioned reflex response:

> Elizabeth wriggled her shoulder-blades against the chair. It was a movement that she made sometimes when she was deeply pleased. She loved Flory, really loved him, when he talked like this. The most trivial scrap of information about shooting thrilled her. If only he would always talk about shooting, instead of about books and Art and that mucky poetry! In a sudden burst of admiration she decided that Flory was really quite a handsome man, in is way. . . . He was standing with his birth-marked cheek away from her. She pressed him to go on talking. (Orwell 1961a, 161–62)

The passage is remarkable in the manner in which it incorporates the nervous behaviour of the two individuals: Elizabeth's wriggling emerging as an almost unconditioned reflex reaction that manifests her erotic excitement, and Flory's manoeuvre of hiding away his birthmark at the moment of high affirmation as a conditioned nervous reflex ingrained into his system with time. Elizabeth as well as Flory exhibit what Horacio Fabrega classifies as the motor behaviour of human nerves, a term that is used 'to denote patterns of muscular responses which are viewed in psychical terms' (Fabrega 1977, 443).

Fabrega's enquiry on the neural behaviour of a particular human being exposed to a unique environment as breaking off from the original genetic narrative is particularly significant in the case of Flory in *Burmese Days* whose sense of shame with his birthmark and his corresponding nervous behaviour may be seen particularly accentuated by the cultural code of the colonial contact zone that operates with the notional binaries of masculine/feminine, white/black, civilized/uncivilized, and, most significantly, powerful/powerless, in an affective economy where matter, metaphor, and memory mix in complex combinations. Therefore, while his birthmark stands as a signifier of genetic determinism, Flory's continuous and almost unconditioned manoeuvre to conceal the same during moments of assertion emerges as nervous reflex naturalized by habit. Struggling to inscribe himself into the hegemonic white masculinist code in the imperial space, Flory keeps looking back at Britain as the lost paradise he cannot return to, the space where freedom of thoughts and action runs undeterred, thus assuming a gaze that is essentializing as well as nostalgic. Meanwhile, in real time, the masculinity of Flory emerges before the imagination of Elizabeth as metonymically constructed by the hunting narrative that operates in all effect as a strategy of seduction.

As John Mackenzie asserts in his analysis of imperial masculinity and hunting narratives, with the turn of the twentieth century, hunting shifted from a mode of survival and preservation to an imperial masculinist ritual that increasingly reified its class and cultural codes (Mackenzie 1987, 184). By the 1920s more and more women were participating in the hunting process and partaking of its elitist and heavily coded culture. Flory's interest in books, art, and poetry are an anathema to the normative masculinity Elizabeth subscribes to and consumes with erotic excitement. Flory's subsequent and almost reluctant shift to a more normative masculinist code in order to impress Elizabeth is premised on a strategy of seduction. In it, Flory performs imperial masculinity with his hunting trips with Elizabeth as well as with his anecdotes about personal hunting machismo exhibited earlier:

> Flory told it all perfunctorily enough – did not the proverbial Anglo-Indian bore always talk about tiger-shooting? – but Elizabeth wriggled her shoulders delightedly once more. He did not realize how such talk as this reassured her and made up for all the times when he had bored her and disquieted her. (Orwell 1961a, 162)

The recurrence of the word *bore* is significant in the passage as it relates to two mutually contradictory orders of boredom that are politically located as well as gendered in quality. The first arises from the ritual repetition of the masculinist narrative to a male audience already always expected to perform it. The second mode of boredom is perceived by a female interlocutor freshly introduced to the machinery of masculinity in the empire. Elizabeth's boredom thus results when she is denied the typical masculinist narratives of imperial heroism. The passage is significant inasmuch as it situates storytelling as an imperial activity and Flory as an inadequate storyteller offering the undesirable narratives about art and poetry in the colonial space, before a female listener keen to consume the hegemonic codes of white male supremacy through stories about shooting, hunting, and horse riding. Like Marlow in *Heart of Darkness*, Flory in *Burmese Days* emerges as a failed storyteller with an incomplete and inconsistent control of privileged metaphors in the colonial territory. This crisis in storytelling informs their larger anxiety in performative embodiment in the imperial space, immediately instantiated by their neurotic dispositions and inadequate appropriations.

As Nalin Jayasena argues, Flory 'realizes too well the role he is expected to play, but he fails to disavow this peculiarly imperial invention for fear of disappointing Elizabeth' (Jayasena 2007, 136). The discursive correlation between 'Shooting an Elephant' and *Burmese Days* situates Elizabeth as well as the Burmese natives in similar planes as consumers of the white man's machismo. Flory's hesitation and private deconstruction of the ideology of imperialism characterize him in a similar manner as his reluctance to perform the normative imperial masculinity, and they highlight his eventual failure to retain the prerogatives of his private self. Flory's betrayal of Veraswami emerges as discursively similar to his betrayal of his private conscience in favour of a forced appropriation of the ethic of heroic masculinity before Elizabeth. Flory's attempts to appropriate stereotypical imperial masculinity results in a spectacular and pathetic failure as he embarks on tent pegging after Verrall in a bid to impress the approaching Elizabeth. In her naive consumption of narratives of imperial heroism, Elizabeth may be compared with Kurtz's intended in *Heart of Darkness* who would only receive a report on Kurtz that is overly couched in romanticized masculine glory. Both Elizabeth's and Kurtz's intended appear as perfect performers in the established economy of eulogy and mourning in the imperialist narrative, which is also heavily gendered in quality. Likewise, both Marlow and Flory appear as discomfited agents of imperialism who must forego their human ambivalence and agency and perpetuate the politics of pseudo-glory in the masculinist imperial space. The burden of masculinity experienced by Marlow and Flory thus appears as an overarching construct that consumes their independent intentionality and free will. In depicting the schism between the human subject and the imperial agent, Marlow and Flory depict the painful ambivalence that may never be respectfully articulated. This constriction of will and agency directly informs their public cynicism and moments of private hysteria.

Unsurprisingly, the libidinal and masculinist economy in the narrative of *Burmese Days* is reconfigured dramatically with the arrival of the military officer Verrall who with his 'aura of horsemanship and soldiering' seduces Elizabeth immediately as the latter sees in Verrall 'the splendid panache of a cavalryman's life' (Orwell 1961a, 214). As the narrative informs the reader, Flory is reduced in Elizabeth's imagination at this point only to his birthmark, and her bond with Verrall is exacerbated by their mutual hatred for highbrow culture. In effect, Verrall embodies in the novel the hard-core military masculinity that had emerged out of the Boy

Scouts and public school, and his extravagant callousness towards people as well as property is a complex combination of abstinence and indulgence. Seen in a more discursive light, Verrall embodies the stereotype of the sporting boy as extolled by the *Empire Annual for Boys* at the turn of the twentieth century. Thus the first volume of the *Empire Annual* in 1909 contained a celebration of the sporting masculinity that was put on the same pedestal as nationalist triumph: 'The bond of sport is one of the strongest and most far-reaching in the British race . . . accepted as almost the hallmark of uprightness. "To play the game" is constantly quoted as the supreme standard of excellence' (quoted in Kanitkar 2017, 187).

Crucially, Verrall's brand of masculinity is characterized not just by the perfect nervous and muscular condition advocated by the boys' manuals – 'He exercised himself ceaselessly and brutally, rationed his drink and his cigarettes, slept on a camp bed (in silk pyjamas) and bathed in cold water in the bitterest winter' (Orwell 1961a, 203) – but also by manipulative and excessive egotism: 'Up and down India wherever he was stationed, he left behind him a trail of insulted people, neglected duties and unpaid bills' (ibid., 203). The perfect comfort and command that Verrall managed to achieve and enjoy in the colonial space is based on his perfect appropriation of the dominant and desirable code of imperial military masculinity, its associated heroism, and its non-emotional constitution. In effect, Verrall embodies in *Burmese Days* the perfectly clinical and almost automatically functioning body that Nussbaum studies as the desirable construct of imperial and xenophobic masculinity that saw fluidity and messy mutability of the body as filthy and subversive signifiers associated with women and racial 'others' (Nussbaum 2004, 111–12). Verrall's easy and almost constant disgust with all around him, including the other Europeans in the colony, stems from his knowledge of his own bodily and masculinist superiority over others and differs discursively from the uneasy and self-loathing disgust that Flory carries within him with the existential knowledge of the horror and hollowness of the ideology he is forced to embody. Therefore, Verrall's interest in Elizabeth is purely bodily and erotic without any personal emotional attachment:

> He had no intention of mixing himself up with all the petty *sahiblog* of the district. He knew the society of those small Burma stations – a nasty, poodle-faking, horseless riffraff. He despised them. (Orwell 1961a, 202)

The politics of disgust that Flory and Verrall embody with their strands of masculinity differ dramatically and constitutionally, and although Flory emerges as the real hero (he rescues the Europeans from the mob attack of the Burmese by swimming to the nearest police station, whereas Verrall is nowhere to be seen) while Verrall is simply the model of one, even Flory is intimidated in his anxiety to appropriate the model that Verrall so elegantly embodies with his showy horsemanship and military demeanour. In effect, Flory emerges as a pathetic mimic man trying to incorporate the hegemonic discourse of masculinity, and it is here that Orwell's novel becomes most political, in its depiction of the stratified realms of power and difference even within the seemingly homogenous territory of the colonizers' laws. Flory's failure to be sufficiently masculine before Elizabeth thus emerges as pathetic as Veraswami's inability to speak English except in stilted phrases and his ultimate failure in becoming a member of the Europeans' club in Kyauktada. The tension between Flory and Verrall around Elizabeth thus emerges as a conflict between real human emotions and a model of masculinity, with the latter overshadowing and overwhelming the former in the discursive space of the imperial Europeans in Burma with its preset codes of conduct. Flory's life thus emerges from as well as ends with his anxiety and inability to be sufficiently mimetic, what with his discomfited dislocation from the imperial ideology in the colonial contact zone or with his attempted and failed representation of the model of masculinity that would seduce Elizabeth. The failure to be appropriately and adequately mimetic is corroborated by political as well as nervous conditions in a cultural climate where, '[w]hen one does get credit in this life, it is usually for something that one has not done' (ibid., 85).

Ironically, what finishes Flory ultimately and makes him an immediate and permanent *pariah* in the colonizers' community in Kyauktada is a mimetic act of hysteria that is strategically performed by his former Burmese mistress Ma Hla May. She makes a spectacle of Flory's shame (as instructed by the Machiavellian gangster U Po Kyin who seeks to ostracize Flory in order to socially destroy Flory's Burmese friend Veraswami) during 'the six-weekly church service [that] was the great social event of their [the Englishmen in Burma] lives' (ibid., 269). Barging into the service, Ma Hla May performs the spectacular and stereotypical act of female hysteria, being immediately intimidating yet credible in its disconcerting as well as familiar excesses, as she demands the money Flory had supposedly promised her for her sexual services:

> She was screaming like a maniac. The people gaped at her too astounded to move or speak. Her face was grey with powder, her greasy hair was tumbling down, her *longyi* was ragged at the bottom, she looked like a screaming hag of the bazaar. Flory's bowels seemed to have turned to ice. . . . The wretched woman was yelling out a detailed account of what Flory had done to her. (ibid., 273)

The hysteric intrusion into the church service enacted by Ma Hla is as performative as the elegant mourning enacted by Kurtz's innocent European fiancée in the domestic space in *Heart of Darkness*. Both episodes arrest the males – Marlow and Flory – in a state of real repression due to their inability to explicate or articulate agency in the rigid imperial narrative where masculinity is reified through inflexible structures of shame and glory. With her carefully engineered hysteric appearance – her powdered face and greased hair – and dramatic disruption of the sacred social space of the white colonizer, Ma Hla manages to induce the intended disgust and visceral shudder that shocks with its sudden violation of white social normalcy.

The pseudo-hysteric mimetic act that is politically strategized as well as bodily performed emerges immediately as the obverse of the private unarticulated nervousness of Flory who sits 'staring fixedly at the altar, his face so rigid and so bloodless that the birthmark seemed to glow upon it like a streak of blue paint' (ibid., 274). The episode is significant in a number of aspects, apart from depicting the obvious dramatic contrast between sanctioned spectacular female hysteria and forbidden masculine nervousness, strategic mimesis and failed appropriation. On a more discursive level, the episode also dramatizes the blurring borderlines between the notionally powerful and powerless in *Burmese Days*. Thus the scheming Burmese gangster U Po Kyin wields absolute control by pitting the doubly marginalized Burmese woman against the British imperial officer in a deliberate drama of disgust that can transcend the codes of notional imperial hierarchy. The episode also highlights the difference in mimetic performances that characterizes Flory and Ma Hla, between the latter's successful appropriation of spectacular feminine hysteria and the former's failed mimesis of the white man's masculinity in the colonies.

Crucially, what emasculates Flory socially and casts him out of the white community in Kyauktada is not the illegality of his action but the disgust born of it, a disgust that is operative outside the notional parameters of imperial law. This disgust is focalized through the physiognomy of Flory that appears in the eyes of Elizabeth as an objective correlative of ugliness:

> She had not understood a word of what Ma Hla was saying, but the meaning of the scene was perfectly clear. The thought that he had been the lover of that grey-faced, maniacal creature made her shudder in her bones. But worse than that, worse than anything was his ugliness at this moment. His face appalled her, it was so ghastly, rigid and old. It was like a skull. Only the birthmark seemed alive in it. She hated him now for his birthmark. She had never known till this moment how dishonouring, how unforgivable a thing it was. (ibid., 274)

The vocabulary of hysteria that Ma Hla performs through her body requires no narrative in the form of understandable language to signify the scandal it seeks to communicate. The signifiers through which Flory's ugliness travel to Elizabeth are his skull and his birthmark, both carrying pseudoscientific suggestions of degeneration and disgust in the imperial European imagination in the early twentieth century. The animated birthmark flickers with Flory's shame and disfigures him permanently in Elizabeth's eyes after Ma Hla's hysteric act. The theme of genetic determination is returned to here, and as the narrative informs the reader, 'It was, finally, the birthmark that had damned him' (ibid., 278), bringing into play the combination of matter and metaphor in Orwell's novel where everything stands for something else in a racially and imperially overdetermined map of meanings.

The mark that had informed Flory's inferiority complex all his life suddenly and permanently deforms and decimates him as he realizes the impossibility of attaining the mythical piano in his imagined landscape of an ideal future. The final moment of rupture is narrated in a vocabulary that is symbolic in a high-Modernist manner:

> Like a hallucination, painfully clear, he saw again their home as he had imagined it, he saw their garden, and Elizabeth feeding Nero and the pigeons on the drive . . . and the bookshelves, and the black piano. The impossible, mythical piano – symbol of everything that that futile accident had wrecked! 'You should have a piano,' he said despairingly. 'I don't play the piano'. He let her go. It was no use continuing. (ibid., 278)

The mythical piano in Flory's oneiric landscape beams up as a final reminder of his hopeless vision and its destruction. As the narrative hurries towards closure with Flory's suicide and Elizabeth's quick conversion into a *burra memsahib* (dominating and irritable white woman) through her marriage to Mr. Macgregor, *Burmese Days* reveals the rewards of adherence to the imperial code of the white man in the colonies and the retribution for deviance from the same. Flory's death is as unheroic as his life had been, and he perpetuates his failure to inscribe himself into the masculinist discourse through his suicide. The marker of shame that had characterized Flory disappears with his death – 'With death, the birthmark had faded immediately, so that it was no more than a faint grey stain' (ibid., 282) – and his posthumous ignominy is partially resisted by the doctor Veraswami who spuriously certifies that Flory had died accidentally while cleaning his revolver.

While Marlowe's spurious report of Kurtz's death in *Heart of Darkness* retains him as a romantic masculinist hero in the European imagination within the European space, Flory's death is too direct not to be derided in the real colonial contact zone where imperialism as a masculinist misadventure emerges as 'not a pretty thing when you look into it too much' (Conrad [1899] 1963, 10). Therefore, his failure to appropriate the privileged metaphor, to mime the desirable discourse of masculinity, haunts Flory even after his death as he is reduced to a local legend and a signifier of shame, a 'dark chap with a birthmark' a 'bloody fool' who shot himself in Kyauktada in 1926 over a girl (Orwell 1961a, 283). Although his physical birthmark had disappeared with his bodily death, Flory's shame continues to circulate among the Anglo-Indians and colonial officers in Burma in their drunken discourses in homosocial spaces. Orwell's *Burmese Days* is a novel, like Conrad's *Heart of Darkness*, about the complexities of power, performance, and privilege that characterize as well as problematize the self in the colonial contact zone, the political space where the machinery of imperialism operates with perfectly reducible and replaceable human beings. If Kurtz in *Heart of Darkness* becomes a threat to the machinery of imperialism due to his over-identification with the imperial economy of power and privilege, Flory in *Burmese Days* dramatizes the discomfort due to his insufficient identification with the same system. More significantly, like *Heart of Darkness*, Orwell's narrative is about the nervousness at the heart of the empire and the conflict between private hesitation and public performance within the phenomenal frame of existential awakening.

As the background of this chapter sought to illustrate, masculinity as a construct of nerves and narratives emerged less as a homogenous structure of suppositions and more 'as a historical phenomenon that responded to the economic, political, and cultural shifts in the imperial social formation in the late nineteenth century' (Sinha 2001, 184). Although ostensibly less medical than Conrad's *Heart of Darkness*, *Burmese Days* exhibits medico-cultural myths on degeneration, criminology, and inferiority in a more racialized space of epistemic exchange, despite its flawed narrative space where the subaltern never speaks except as a stereotype. Elleke Boehmer argues thus:

> *Burmese Days* is distinguished from earlier colonial writing by its knowingness – its anti-adventure cynicism, its penetrating insights into the less than honourable mechanisms of empire. Flory the anti-hero, the little man of modernism transplanted to the colonial town, bears the painful self-consciousness of one aware of imperial wrong-doing yet impotent against it. (Boehmer 1995, 155)

The knowledge of ambivalence that Flory carries without articulation marks him as a uniquely dislocated figure who informs the narrative about nervous conditions in the imperialist space. More ironically, located in a notional position of power, Flory illustrates with his failure the curious and complex convergence of structured forms of privilege – medical, cultural, and political – and their strategic politics of presuppositions. Like Septimus Smith in Woolf's *Mrs. Dalloway*, Flory's suicide emerges not so much as an act of escape as one of the ultimate assertion of the self's impotence under a hegemonic gaze characterized by compulsive classification, love of proportions, and strategic shaming.

This chapter has attempted to examine how matter, metaphor, and memory entangle in an economy of imperial identities which are material, political, and affective in quality. In examining nervous narrations about colonial conditions by white imperial agents, this study also foregrounds the fault lines in hegemonic imperial mappings, manifested in insufficient embodiment and inconsistent storytelling. It showcases the performative quality of imperial identities and reads the selected fiction and nonfiction as examples of how objects and their web of affect inform political as well as existential experiences. Conrad's *Heart of Darkness*, Orwell's 'Shooting an Elephant', and *Burmese Days* have been read in this chapter as examples in fiction and nonfiction of how white male privilege in the imperial and racially reified space can existentially and paradoxically generate guilt, cynicism, shame, and melancholia, experientially undercutting the ontology of power in the colonial space. In examining the historical realities and their literary representations apropos of each other, this chapter underscores the primary aim of this book, which is to show how cultural identity as a process of production, reproduction, and consumption requires complex narrative, material, and metaphoric investments, which in turn produce, de-produce, and determine acts of remembrance.

REFERENCES

Ahmed, Sara. 2010. 'Happy Objects'. In *The Affect Theory Reader*, edited by Melissa Gregg and Gregory J. Seigworth, 29–51. Durham, NC: Duke University Press.

Alcoff, Linda Martin. 2006. *Visible Identities: Race, Gender and the Self*. Oxford: Oxford University Press.

Alldritt, Keith. 1969. *The Making of George Orwell: An Essay in Literary History*. London: Edward Arnold.

Ambrosini, Richard. 1991. *Conrad's Fiction as Critical Discourse*. Cambridge: Cambridge University Press.

Ash, Beth S. 2012. 'The Horror of Trauma: Mourning of Melancholia in Heart of Darkness?' In *Conrad's Heart of Darkness and Contemporary Thought: Revisiting Horror with Lacoue-Labarthe*, edited by Nidesh Lawtoo, 181–200. London: Bloomsbury.

Bauman, Zygmunt. 1991. *Modernity and Ambivalence*. New York: Cornell University Press.

Bhabha, Homi. 1984. 'Representation and the Colonial Text: A Critical Exploration of Some Forms of Mimeticism'. In *The Theory of Reading*, edited by Frank Gloversmith, 93–122. Sussex: Harvester Press.

———. 1985. 'Signs Taken for Wonders'. *Critical Inquiry* 12(1): 144–65.

———. 1994. *The Location of Culture*. London: Routledge.
Bock, Martin. 2002. *Joseph Conrad and Psychological Medicine*. Lubbock: Texas Tech University Press.
Boehmer, Elleke. 1995. *Colonial and Postcolonial Literature: Migrant Metaphors*. Oxford: Oxford University Press.
Bohlmann, Otto. 1991. *Conrad's Existentialism*. New York: St. Martin's.
Bowker, Gordon. 2003. *George Orwell*. London: Little, Brown.
Conrad, Joseph. (1899) 1963. *Heart of Darkness*. New York: Norton.
———. 1935. *The Nigger of the 'Narcissus': A Tale of the Sea*. New York: Doubleday.
———. 2008. *Notes on Life and Letters*. Middlesex: Echo Library.
Cornelius, Randolph R. 1996. *Science of Emotion: Research and Tradition in the Psychology of Emotions*. Upper Saddle River, NJ: Prentice Hall.
Derrida, Jacques. 1994. *Spectres of Marx: The State of the Debt, the Work of Mourning & the New International*. Translated by Peggy Kamuf. New York: Routledge.
Dryden, Linda. 2000. *Joseph Conrad and the Imperial Romance*. Basingstoke: Palgrave Macmillan.
Evans, Gareth. 1983. *The Varieties of Reference*. Oxford: Clarendon.
Fabrega, Horacio. 1977. 'Culture, Behaviour and the Nervous System'. *Annual Review of Anthropology* 6:419–55.
Fludernik, Monika. 1996. *Towards a Natural Narratology*. London: Routledge.
Foucault, Michel. 1972. *The Archaeology of Knowledge*. Translated by A. M. Sheridan. London: Tavistock.
———. 1973. *The Birth of the Clinic*. Translated by A. M. Sheridan. London: Routledge.
Geertz, Clifford. 1973. *The Interpretation of Cultures*. New York: Basic Books.
Gibbs, Raymond W. 2005. *Embodiment and Cognitive Science*. Cambridge: Cambridge University Press.
Gilmore, David. 1990. *Manhood in the Making: Cultural Concepts of Masculinity*. New Haven, CT: Yale University Press.
Gould, Stephen Jay. 1996. *The Mismeasure of Man*. London: Penguin.
Greenslade, William. 1994. *Degeneration Culture and the Novel, 1880–1940*. Cambridge: Cambridge University Press.
Griffith, John W. 1995. *Joseph Conrad and the Anthropological Dilemma*. Oxford: Clarendon.
Hitchens, Christopher. 2002. *Orwell's Victory*. London: Penguin.
Hunter, Allan. 1983. *Joseph Conrad and the Ethics of Darwinism: The Challenges of Science*. London: Routledge.
Jameson, Frederick. 1981. *The Political Unconscious: Narrative as a Socially Symbolic Act*. London: Methuen.
Jayasena, Nalin. 2007. *Contested Masculinities: Crises in Colonial Male Identity from Joseph Conrad to Satyajit Ray*. New York: Routledge.
Joravsky, David. 2004. 'Between Science and Act: Freud versus Shnitzler, Kafka, and Musil'. In *The Mind of Modernism: Medicine, Psychology and the Cultural Arts in Europe and America, 1880–1940*, edited by Mark S. Micale. Stanford, CA: Stanford University Press.

Kanitkar, Helen. 2017. 'Real True Boys: Moulding the Cadets of Imperialism'. In *Dislocating Masculinity: Comparative Ethnographies*, edited by Andrea Cornwall and Nancy Lindisfarne, 173–84. London: Routledge.

Kleinmann, Arthur. 1988. *Rethinking Psychiatry: From Cultural Category to Personal Experience*. New York: Free Press.

Lawtoo, Nidesh, ed. 2012. *Conrad's Heart of Darkness and Contemporary Thought: Revisiting Horror with Lacoue-Labarthe*. London: Bloomsbury.

Levenson, Michael. 1991. *Modernism and the Fate of Individuality: Character and Novelists from Conrad to Woolf*. Cambridge: Cambridge University Press.

Lodge, David. 2002. *Consciousness and the Novel: Connected Essays*. London: Secker and Warburg.

Mackenzie, John. 1987. 'The Imperial Pioneer and Hunter and the British Masculine Stereotype in Late Victorian and Edwardian Times'. In *Manliness and Morality: Middle-Class Masculinity in Britain and America, 1800–1940*, edited by J. A. Mangan and James Walvin, 176–98. Oxford: Manchester University Press.

Miller, Christopher L. 1996. 'The Discoursing Heart: Conrad's *Heart of Darkness*'. In *Joseph Conrad*, edited by Elaine Jordan, 87–102. London: Macmillan.

Mongia, Padmini. 1992. 'Narrative Strategy and Imperialism in Conrad's *Lord Jim*'. *Studies in the Novel* 24(2): 173–86.

———. 1993. '"Ghosts of the Gothic": Spectral Women and Colonized Spaces in *Lord Jim*'. *The Conradian* 17(2): 1–16.

Nussbaum, Martha C. 2004. *Hiding from Humanity: Disgust, Shame and the Law*. Princeton, NJ: Princeton University Press.

Orwell, George. (1952) 1968. *Such, Such Were the Joys*. New York: Harcourt, Brace.

———. 1961a. *Burmese Days*. London: Secker & Warburg.

———. 1961b. *Collected Essays*. Edited by Alan Hill. London: Mercury Books.

Ramachandran, V. S., and Sandra Blakeslee. 1998. *Phantoms in the Brain: Human Nature and the Architecture of the Mind*. London: Fourth Estate.

Said, Edward. 1989. 'Representing the Colonized: Anthropology's Interlocutors'. In *Critical Inquiry* 15:205–25.

———. 1993. *Culture and Imperialism*. London: Chatto & Windus.

———. 1996. *Joseph Conrad and the Fiction of Autobiography*. Cambridge, MA: Harvard University Press.

———. 2003. *Freud and the Non-European*. London: Verso.

Sinha, Mrinalini. 2001. 'Britishness, Clubbability, and the Colonial Public Sphere: The Genealogy of an Imperial Institution in Colonial India'. *Journal of British Studies* 40(4): 489–521.

Spur, David. 1993. *The Rhetoric of Empire: Colonial Discourse in Journalism, Travel Writing and Imperial Administration*. Durham, NC: Duke University Press.

Sullivan, Shannon. 2006. *Revealing Whiteness: The Unconscious Habits of Racial Privilege*. Bloomington: Indiana University Press.

Stanzel, Franz K. 1986. *A Theory of Narrative*. Translated by Charlotte Goedsche. Cambridge: Cambridge University Press.

Vulcan, Daphna Erdinast. 1991. *Joseph Conrad and the Modern Temper*. Oxford: Clarendon Press.

Watt, Ian. 1980. *Conrad in the Nineteenth Century*. London: Chatto & Windus.

Watts, C. T. 1977. *Conrad's Heart of Darkness: A Critical and Contextual Discussion*. Milano: Mursia International.
Waugh, Patricia. 1992. *Practising Postmodernism, Reading Modernism*. London: Edward Arnold.
Williams, Raymond. 1971. *George Orwell*. Glasgow: Collins.
Woolf, Virginia. 1948. 'On Being Ill'. In *The Moment and Other Essays*, edited by Leonard Woolf. New York: Harcourt Brace Jovanovich.
Žižek, Slavoj. 1989. *The Sublime Object of Ideology*. London: Verso.
———. 2002. *Welcome to the Desert of the Real! Five Essays on September 11 and Related Dates*. London: Verso.

2

Culture, History, Memory, and Forgetting

The relevance of remembering and forgetting in cultural narratives and their associated production and consumption of identities is significant and complex. If culture may be read as a contagious and controlled economy of codes which are furthered by effective as well as by affective instruments, the role of remembering becomes key in the processes of production and preservation. Equally, forgetting frequently emerges as an agentic activity informed by political and discursive investments. Therefore, what gets remembered and what gets forgotten in cultural narratives and identity politics are often reflective of particular predilections and biases unique to that point of historical time. Examined in this light, culture, memory, and history emerge as complexly intertwined processes containing affective as well as material markers, informing individual lives as well as collective identities. Memory studies offers an epistemic framework through which the micro and macro narratives of remembering and forgetting are examined with their malleability and mutability, as well as in their episodic and collective qualities. Drawing on discursive conditions as well as affective networks, memory studies offers an interdisciplinary interpretative method which situates literature and fictional frameworks apropos of the historical materiality of political and cultural changes. This chapter maps memory studies in all its complexity in its attempt to offer a reading of literature's location in volatile and mutably material and political points of time.

The role of fiction in narratives of remembering and forgetting apropos of historical materialist conditions needs to be studied in some detail before moving on to the texts selected for this chapter. If fiction is the liminal landscape between reality and fantasy, between actuality and possibility, it offers a unique platform to examine and experience the entanglement of remembering and forgetting, between what really happened and what gets left behind. More importantly, fiction produces narratives that intersect between what took place historically and what could have or may have happened existentially. As a production of possibilities, and as a complex combination of perspectives and points of view, fiction merges moments of historical and existential changes, foregrounding imagination, intersubjectivity, and empathy as cognitive categories. The ambivalent quality of fiction – whereby multiple and sometimes contradictory values and possibilities may be accommodated and articulated simultaneously – offers a fluid framework for representing experiences of remembering and forgetting. If memory as a process of reconstruction has unreliability, cognitive bias, and incompleteness embedded in it, fiction is perhaps the most suitable form to represent the same in real as well as in imagined networks of time. Hence philosophy of mind and time play key roles in an understanding of memory as represented in fiction, in terms of examining how the mind remembers even as it forgets, or rather remembers and un-remembers simultaneously. More importantly, such study situates memory and its loss as informing a complex order of subjectivity, one which is always mutable and moving in its negotiation with political, historical, and material realities. In their representations of human subjects with shifting memories of their existential experiences, literary texts offer a unique understanding of recall and re-formations, connecting cognitive and existential orders with cultural and political ones. In the process, they underline the primary philosophy of this book, which studies matter, metaphor, and memory as narrative as well as cognitive categories, while examining literature as a special function of culture.

Memory and political change often involve a series of subjective shifts, cutting across different orders of space and time while also connecting to crucial components affecting material markers informing citizenship, rights, agency, and identity. Mapping memory studies and literary studies in an examination of political changes and their existential extensions, this chapter will underline how culture as a constant process of coding, construction, and reconstruction draws on as well as informs an economy of remembering and forgetting. As *cognitive instruments* to make sense of the world, narratives may be seen as capsules of meaning production, preservation, and dissemination in cultural systems (Assmann and Shortt 2012, 174). Likewise, if remembering and forgetting may be considered as narrative categories, memory and oblivion in the political sphere emerge as complexes of what Frederic Bartlett defines as *schema* or patterns underlining psychological processes and *textual functions* as classified by the narratologist Vladimir Propp (Assmann and Shortt, 174). This brings the psychological and political processes of remembering and forgetting into a complex combination whereby the neural and the textual qualities of memory and erasure are highlighted as connected categories. As the American psychologist Howard Eichenbaum – famous for his neuroscientific research on the hippocampus – states, the function of human remembering entails 'encoding complex information that contributes to our memory for personal experiences', constituting what are classified as episodic memories. More significantly, such episodic memories formed out of that encoding are subsequently synthesized into 'our body of world knowledge, fact or semantic memory' (Eichenbaum 2012, 148). Thus, if memory requires encoding and semanticization at a neural level, the same is functionally replicated in the cultural and social sphere where traces of events and experiences are encoded and represented at a textual level through monuments, documents, anecdotes, and storytelling. The *narrative templates* or semantic structures used to map specific episodic events onto collective imagination play a crucial role here in ways through which personal and collective experiences in complex political conditions are replicated, retold, and remembered through processes of storytelling. Such narrative templates may be used in the political collective, as James V. Wertsch argues, in productive as well as in provocative ways, sometimes simultaneously, generating 'mnemonic standoffs and sealed narratives that contribute to human conflicts' (Wertsch 2012, 184). This in turn creates *mnemonic communities* which remember events through metaphors and other cognitive codes, producing private narratives of memory which may or may not align with hegemonic historical narratives. Acts of remembering are thus cognitively connected to the issue of agency at a personal existential as well as at a political collective level in terms of the choice of memory and forgetting. Memory as a representational activity can thus be hegemonic as well as subversive, situated across a spectrum of institutions and individuals connected to complex questions around political will, affect, and agency. Therefore, at a fundamental functional level, remembering relies on templates of representation, making literature as a narrative category crucial in mapping memory through an asymmetry of fact and fabulation. Equally, forgetting emerges not necessarily as a passive marker of loss and lamentation or as a neat ontological opposite of remembering but as an active agentic decision enacted by an individual or a community in relation to reconstruction or preservation of identity.

As Italo Calvino argues in *The Uses of Literature*, literature and literary narratives are particularly suited to articulate absences in traumatic memory and conditions of political violence, experienced existentially as well as collectively. This takes place largely due to literature's ability to give a 'name to what has no name, especially to what the language of politics excludes'. As 'one of a society's instruments of self-awareness' connected to 'the origins of various types of knowledge, various codes, various forms of critical thought' (Calvino 1986, 97), literary forms of representation emerge as nodal points through which memory and its loss can be stated and stylized. The simultaneously embedded and extended quality of literature – whereby literary narratives can be inward looking in their representations of human thought processes as well as being reflective of the extended material discursive world where subjects navigate with intersubjective intertwinements – is uniquely suited to represent memories that lie outside the official records of recollection. If the literary text may be seen as an act of reconstruction which can also be simultaneously self-reflexive, offering plural points of view in its privileged fictional frame, it bears structural as well as functional similarities with the act of remembering, which, as the cultural philosopher Ernst Cassirer stated in his 1944 work *An Essay on Man*, is a creative and constructive process which requires recollection, organization, synthesis, and assemblage (Cassirer 1994, 51). More recent research in neuroscience also reveals that remembering as reconstruction is crucial for the subject's sense of continuity in space time as well as for cultures to transmit and continue with their coded quality. Joseph LeDoux's work on memory as an act of reconsolidation is particularly pertinent here. A globally acclaimed neuroscientist famous for his research on synapses and synaptic plasticity, LeDoux proffers a model for memory as reconsolidation which states that each time a subject retrieves a memory, it does so not from some original unchanged template bearing neural traces of the event but from the last remembered version of the same (LeDoux, 2016). In his famous work on the synaptic self, LeDoux uses the concept of chunks and chunking to define the ways human minds process, preserve, and replay remembered information, whereby large pieces of memory are condensed together in language, 'which exponentially increases our ability to categorise information, to chunk,' in ways by which an entire culture 'can be implied by a name' (LeDoux 2014, 177). This bears remarkable parallels to the works of cognitive narratologists working on memory such as Andy Clark and David Herman, the latter, in *Storytelling and the Sciences of the Mind*, using the same metaphor of chunking while arguing that segments of information and experiences in the human mind are saved as chunks or 'units that are bounded, classifiable, and thus more readily recognizable and remembered' (Herman 2017, 233).

The concept of chunking, whereby storytelling and remembering both operate through mechanisms of coding and condensation, also entails cognitive bias and imaginative insertion as crucial components in memory and forgetting. This is corroborated strongly by scientists working on the human brain such as Eric Kandel who states in *Memory: From Mind to Molecules* that the act of reconstruction also includes 'creative errors, deleting some parts of the story, fabricating other parts, and generally trying to reconstruct information in a way that makes sense' (Kandel and Squire 2009, 85). The creative errors, fabrications, and sense-making mechanism underscoring the process of reconstruction correspond closely to what the cognitive narratologists define as narrative chunks, the 'manipulable structures' (Herman 2017, 233) that offer a spatiotemporal sequence through which stories form from encoded experience. Memory may thus also be defined as the stories saved in the brain which inform the self's sense of continuity in space and time, emerging from experience. The narrative structure of memory thus contains condensation (through metaphors and symbols), focalization (through privileged points of view), and cognitive bias (through which the more convenient meanings are produced and preserved). This connection between remembering and storytelling corroborates the materiality of memory and consciousness, whereby the act of remembering becomes experiential and cognitive as well as extended and enactive. As the 'intersection of material, experiential, and sociocultural forces', memory has been examined by psychologists such as Sidonie A. Smith as a narrative category that produces 'situational meaning' that 'rematerialize the embodied subject of narration' (Smith 2003, 108). In the same essay, Smith draws on the concept of a quantum self that underlines the fluid subjectivity as well as the materiality of consciousness that emerges as a distributive phenomenon. As a 'materially activated and materially enacted' category, memory becomes a marker of the self which in turn emerges as an activity 'in process, configuring and reconfiguring in constant mobility – of quanta, of genomic combinations, of neural nets and connections'. What emerges at the end of such study is a realization of 'how malleable, how plastic, how responsive the material of our bodies might be to our lived experience in the world' (ibid., 92).

The concept of quantum self with its fluidity, malleability, and distributive quality offers a perspective which bears interesting parallels to the postmodern representation of experientiality which is essentially metonymic, inconstant, and unreliable in quality. The liminality of literary representation, whereby, as Milan Kundera puts it, 'the concreteness of the present as a phenomenon to consider' (Kundera 2015, 127) is impossible to hold on to or reconstruct, appears compatible to the notion of the quantum self which is a play between indeterminacy and tangible materiality. In her remarkable work on *The Quantum Self*, Danah Zohar offers an excellent analogy between the behaviour of electrons and human minds in terms of their materiality and malleability and then goes on to extend the analogy further in an elegant and complex model of individual and collective behaviour. In an interesting analysis, Zohar argues thus:

> In fact, this tension between particles and waves at the quantum level does seem to mirror in an interesting way the similar tension between individuals and groups in human society, raising the whole question of the meaning and nature of individual and group identity as we experience them, and whether the roots of each might lie in the quantum mechanical nature of consciousness. (Zohar 1989, 106)

This view of human mind, memory, and consciousness from the perspective of quantum mechanics offers an original and robust reading of the entanglement of remembering and forgetting. Most immediately, it corroborates one of the central theses of the research on the interface of literary studies and neuroscience, which argues that 'telling stories' is a 'brain obsession', empirically establishing the idea that 'the brain's persuasive "aboutness" is rooted in the brain's storytelling attitude' (Damasio 2000, 189) while also acknowledging that the 'narrative nature of consciousness' is a 'narrative full of lacunae' (Lodge 2002, 31). This acknowledgement of ambivalence about narrativity and inconstancy is significant for a study of memory and history from the perspective espoused in this chapter and in the book at large. If memory and history are both narrative categories, like literature, they also incorporate an intertwining of materiality and ephemerality which makes them fluid as well as discursive in quality. The fluidity emerges as a cognitive as well as an epistemic category, attracting more attention to the interpretation involved in the act of remembering than to the passive processing of information.

The focus on interpretation rather than information in the memory system in the mind has received substantial support from some of the leading neuroscientists in the world today. Michael Gazzaniga, one of the most globally respected scientists doing research on split-brain patients, describes the process of memory as reconstruction thus:

> The interpreter, the last device in the information chain in our brain, reconstructs the brain events and in doing so makes telling errors of perception, memory, and judgement. The clue to how we are built is buried not just in our marvellously robust capacity for these [neural] functions, but also in the errors that are frequently made during reconstruction. Biography is fiction. Autobiography is hopelessly inventive. (Gazzaniga 2005, 2)

Gazzaniga's thesis on the crucial presence and function of errors during reconstruction is an acknowledgement as well as a celebration of unreliability, which makes its presence felt consistently in postmodern narrativity and autobiography. A famous case in point is Roland Barthes's

Roland Barthes by Roland Barthes — an imaginative autobiographical text that deliberately deconstructs its own narrative politics — which explicitly acknowledges in its opening page that it should be considered as a work of fiction. More significantly, Gazzaniga's thesis on reconstruction as an error-riddled process, with the errors informing experientiality and the extended self, places a high premium on interpretation, the play between presence and absence, between fact and fabulation, which is the domain of fiction. Gazzaniga would go on to make the connection between cognition and fiction more compelling by associating the issue of agency with it. Thus he argues that cognition and remembering incorporate fictional processes, creating in their wake a sense of the self which is an extension of this fiction; as a result, we 'don't feel like zombies; we feel like in-charge, conscious entities' (ibid., 172). This feeling of being in charge due to the fictional world created by our interpretative brain serves, Gazzaniga would go on to argue, 'the glue that unifies our story and creates our sense of being a whole, rational agent' (ibid., 174). Thus rationality, as we experience it, is a complex of fiction and interpretation, the cognitive glue that connects us to the world around and generates an illusion of seamless continuity in space and time. This finds resonance in the definition and cognitive function of fiction as theorized by David Lodge who studies how narrative literature 'creates fictional models of what it is like to be a human being, moving through time and space' (Lodge 2002), experiencing as well as articulating ambivalence. Ambivalence as an experiential as well as a cognitive category is crucial to the process of remembering, which is also simultaneously a process of forgetting. This is corroborated by Daniel Schachter in *Searching for Memory*, which advocates a move away from the dualistic understanding of memory as it argues that 'memories do not exist in one of two states — either true or false' (Schachter 1997, 277). This understanding of memory as an accommodation and articulation of ambivalence is philosophically akin to the notion of *narrative truth* that becomes a major marker in personal and collective memories alike.

The ontology of *narrative truth* may be connected to the experience of *narrative time*, the play of temporality which inhabits the place between *chronos* and *kairos*, between simple succession and psychological condensation which is the territory of fiction. Frank Kermode's *The Sense of an Ending* offers one of the earliest examples in literary criticism of the play between clock time and narrative time in fiction. In his study, Kermode defines the time of the novelist as 'a transformation of mere successiveness' to 'the experience of love, the erotic consciousness' (Kermode 1967, 46). This metamorphosis of sequential clock time into an experiential order of time achieved in fiction is akin to, as Kermode would argue in the same section, the 'bundling together perception of the past, memory of the present, and expectation of the future' whereby 'that which was conceived of as simply successive becomes charged with past and future' (ibid., 46). Memory thus emerges, in Kermode's study of the temporality in fiction, as an activity of becoming, un-becoming, and re-becoming of the remembering subject whereby the order of time transforms from the mere sequential to the entangled experiential which blurs the borderlines between fact and fantasy. Kermode's notion of *forward memory*, emerging from the 'mind working on an expected future' (ibid., 53), is of special significance in fiction, mixing complexly with what Kermode defines as the memory of that we fail to absorb immediately but which is only available belatedly upon retrospection. The narrative time is thus often outside of the chronological order, inhabiting 'that here and now in which memory, fantasy, anticipation of the future may intrude, though without sharp differentiation' (ibid., 20). As we know from major neuroscientists such as Joseph LeDoux, Eric Kandel, and Daniel Schachter today, the neural processes of encoding and decoding often operate through a complex of memory and fantasy, whereby what is remembered is frequently far from the actual event and closer to the subject's subjective understanding and interpretation of the same. Moreover, as Howard Eichenbaum argues in his study of encoding and retrieval in the remembering process, the cognitive quality in information integration and memory organization involves a 'working-with-memory', 'the manipulation of information that is not memory per se, but handles our memory processing' (Eichenbaum 2012, 311). This closely connects to Kermode's notion of remembering as a cognitive process which incorporates information of the present through a process of integration as well as interpretation, whereby the *memory of memory* connects the past with the expectation of a future.

In his philosophical treatise *Time and Narrative*, Paul Ricoeur underlines the importance of metaphors of movements in memory as examined in the philosophy of Augustine, in terms of how chosen figures of speech condense experiences and the process of their remembrance spatiotemporally. Studying the affect and intent in the remembering process, Ricoeur foregrounds how those combine through the 'progressive dynamization of the metaphor of the spaces traversed by expectation, attention and memory'. Defining the *good metaphor* and the *living metaphor* as processes of 'passing away' or 'ceasing' and that of 'passing through' or 'relegating', Ricoeur argues that the 'metaphor of the transit of events through the present seems unsurpassable' (Ricoeur 1984, 21). In a related study, *The Rule of Metaphor*, Ricoeur draws on Humboldt's thesis on discourse as a combination of infinite uses of finite means as underlined by the 'extended function' (Ricoeur 2004, 72) of the figure trope (the metaphor) in memory, while also foregrounding the generative potential to 'give colour, to astonish and surprise through new and unexpected combinations' (ibid., 73). This dual potential to condense experience as well as to generate astonishment through imagination renders to metaphor a key role in memory studies today. Metaphor may thus be seen as a representative narrative instrument through which the complex of information and interpretation so crucial to memory plays out in space and time in the human mind. Through their dual coding of verbal and visual information, whereby meanings operate at linguistic as well as pictorial levels, metaphors play a key role in remembering, as corroborated by works in psychology as well as in philosophy of mind. The Dutch psychologist Douwe Draaisma examines this connection in his remarkable work *Metaphors of Memory* where he delineates three key functions of metaphors in the remembering process. First, the verbal-visual bind offered by metaphors generates a 'dual coding' that emerges as a 'cognitive investment which pays off in the reproduction phase'. Secondly, the image offered by the metaphor also plays the role of 'an integrated package or "chunk" and can also be reproduced again as a coherent whole'. The *chunking* of information mediated by memory connects remembering and representations in storytelling, as examined by psychologists and narratologists such as LeDoux and Herman. Lastly, the vehicle of the metaphor can serve as what Draaisma defines as a *'conceptual peg* on which more abstract terms can be hung', thus corroborating the extended quality metaphors can contribute towards the cognitive and remembering processes. The threefold function of metaphors in memory plays a key role in the information, interpretation, and preservation of images and experiences through a complex mechanism of abstractions and attachments, which are embedded as well as enactive and extended in quality. Thus Draaisma says: 'Metaphor enables the memory function to fish with several hooks at once' (Draaisma 2001, 17). Likewise, the analogy Draaisma makes between the attrition of a metaphor due to wearing down – culminating in the product of the dead metaphor – and the loss of memory due to depletion also underlines the narrative quality of remembering and forgetting.

In a different yet related work, Ricoeur offers an equation between the discourse of memory and forgetting and that of guilt and forgiveness (Ricoeur 2004, 92), mapping the same with a study of representational matrices. Ricoeur would go on to underscore the ontology of forgetting not as an effacement of traces or depletion of memory but rather as a cognitive extension of memory inasmuch as it 'designates the *unperceived* character of the perseverance of memories, their removal from the vigilance of consciousness' (ibid., 440). Seen in this light, forgetting emerges as a playful activity as well as a subliminal storehouse of memory, one which is not guarded by consciousness or rituals of remembering. This playfulness becomes an act of production, akin to the production of possibilities in fiction, whereby what takes *place* (underlining the innate spatial quality of memory), as well as what does not, merge with modes of representation. One of the most fruitful ways in which memory studies can operate as an interpretative method is to examine the interfaces between the individual and collective modes of remembering. Forgetting as an institutional or collective activity carries special cultural connotations apropos of agency and identity. In the equation Ricoeur makes between forgetting and forgiving, whereby the boundary between the two is 'crossed surreptitiously, to the extent that these two dispositions have to do with judicial proceedings and with handing down a sentence' (ibid., 453), the narrative and discursive quality of forgetting gets foregrounded, a theme which recurs in Milan Kundera's *The Book of Laughter and Forgetting*, studied subsequently in this chapter. Ricoeur's *Time and Narrative*, vol. 2, ends with an equation between historical representation and fictional forms which share 'the same configurating operation' of emplotment (Ricoeur 1986, 156). In other words, collective history and fictional narratives both require and rely on politics of positioning and sequencing which operate with their internal structures of privilege rather than any objective unchanging order. By producing the 'privileged place for the intersection of an imaginary world and an actual one' (Ricoeur 1986, 160), fiction offers a unique perspective into the play of memory and forgetting, creating worlds which are or were actually there along with the ones which never were or could have been. This brings memory studies closer to the scope of cognitive narratology which examines fiction and cultural narratives alike in their coded, enactive, and fabulatory forms.

In his work on storytelling and cognitive science, David Herman highlights the research in recent studies that examines the 'dynamic interplay between embodied intelligent agents and their broader environments for actions and interactions' (Herman 2017, 47). Crucial to Herman's work – like that of the scholars in critical neuroscience – is the constant enactive entanglement of the inside and the outside, between the phenomenal self and the material environment in which that self is situated. In a similar vein, current research on embodiment examines the mind as 'an activity of an essentially *situated* brain: a brain at home in its proper bodily, cultural, and environmental niche' (Clark 1998, 257). Such *situationality* is uniquely represented in literary fiction, with its enactive frames that play between reality and possibility, offering complex cognitive mappings that combine cultural codes with affect and experientiality. In her work on Kafka's cognitive realism, Emily Troscianko underlines the enactive process of representation and cognition in Kafka's fiction, which has interesting parallels with the embodied and distributive model of memory studied by psychologists such as Antonio Damasio and Joseph LeDoux. In a compelling argument, Troscianko highlights how the nonrealist minimalism in Kafka 'taps into the fundamentally non-linear, non-pictorial processes of perception, precisely by evoking the fictional world through the perceptual enaction of it, which directly stimulates the reader's imagination' (Troscianko 2014, 159). The non-linearity of Kafka is precisely what makes it authentically enactive as well as cognitively realistic in Troscianko's study, moving away from the classic realist representations in fiction which appropriate 'totalizing processes of retrospective narrativization' (ibid., 165). Instead, it offers representations of experiences which are episodic and incomplete in quality, corresponding closely to the cognitive process in the human brain with its complex of recollection, simulation, and imagination.

Burke and Troscianko's 2017 edited work titled *Cognitive Literary Science: Dialogues between Literature and Cognition* is an excellent collection of essays on the enactive model of memory and cognitive processes offered by fiction. In particular, Merja Polvinen's essay 'Cognitive Science and the Double Vision of Fiction' examines the ways in which fiction offers an embedded immersive as well as an enactive performative loop uniquely suited to represent remembering and cognition. It does so, as Polvinen puts it, through a foregrounding of the fictional frame which operates with an 'enactive actualization of the cognitive process' (Polvinen 2017, 143). The idea of the fictional frame as a cognitive instrument recurs in Patrick Colm Hogan's essay in the same volume which studies simulation in fiction as a special form of representation of emotional memory. If simulation relies on imagination and performative action, fiction appears, in Hogan's study, as an affective device through which simulation may be stated as well as stylized. Examining literature as a 'matter of intensification', 'cognitive particularity', and 'emotional consequence' (Hogan 2017, 114), Hogan upholds one of the central philosophies espoused in this book, which is fiction as an interplay of matter, metaphor, and memory. Hogan's study of simulation and fiction is particularly pertinent for a broader understanding of fictionality as an extended form of empathy, whereby the experience of reading fiction generates a sense of cognitive connectedness through an interplay of reality and fantasy. More specifically, this offers a more nuanced understanding of history and collective memory as an affective narrative, one that 'crucially includes simulation guided by exemplars from emotional memory' (ibid., 129). Emotional memory emerges, at the end of Hogan's reading here, as a narrative structure with its unique causal code, which is simulative and probabilistic rather than law-like or objective in quality. Significantly, such reading reveals that a subject's emotional response to an event is not necessarily tied to the moment or context of that event alone but extends to an experiential order incorporating 'responding to the current situation as organized and re-simulated by tacit references to narratively structured emotional memories' (ibid., 131). The concept of re-simulation is crucial here, particularly in this study of literature and literary fiction as an affective and narrative reordering of remembered events which are historical as well as experiential in quality. As an embedded as well as an extended cognitive category, re-simulation incorporates intersubjective and intertextual experiences whereby the self emerges as a subject as well as a text, matter as well as metaphor, in an endless play of representation and remembering. In terms of its cognitive embeddedness and social enactive extensions, re-simulation bears structural as well as functional parallels with fiction.

Alan Palmer's concept of the *fictional mind* as an amalgam of evaluations, beliefs, skills, knowledge, tendencies of thought, memories, desires, and imagination (Palmer 2004, 81) is crucial in terms of connecting the micro psychological components and the macro cultural components of remembrance. Drawing on Mikhail Bakhtin's concept of dialogic imagination, Palmer examines the interface of fictional and social minds and argues that a 'postclassical perspective on the construction of fictional minds should be concerned with this complex relationship between the inaccessibility to others of a character's thoughts and the extent to which the same thought is publicly available to others in the storyworld' (ibid., 174). This interplay between the inaccessible interiority of thoughts and the publicly accessible world of beliefs and knowledge which inform the same private thought processes is crucial to a study of fiction, forgetting, and remembered identities as examined in this chapter. More broadly, it connects to the coded quality of material and metaphoric markers of culture and memory, and literature's location in the same, which is the principal enquiry of this book as a whole. If culture as an economy of codes is embedded, extended, enacted, and embodied by various cognitive constructs, fiction as studied by Palmer offers an excellent instrument to condense the same in complex combinations. This complexity is accommodated and articulated in literary novels which combine omniscient third-person and unreliable first-person narratives to draw on and enact the same story worlds. If, as the neuroscientist V. S. Ramachandran argues, the ability to combine the first- and third-person perspectives is the single biggest challenge in current cognitive neuroscience (cited in Lodge 2002), the fictional novel offers a structure of the same with its combinations of monologic and dialogic orders of narration and imagination. The *social mind*, as examined by Palmer, is a complex of 'situated cognition, cognitive artifacts, and distributed cognitive systems' (Palmer 2004, 164) and is thus a moving and mutable process that incorporates a constant merging of the phenomenal sentient self and the socially extended and enactive self. As Palmer would put it, culture as a process of coding and consumption entails that the 'individual and social dimensions of cognition begin to shade into each other' and that the human subject who embodies and enacts the same is 'to a large extent constituted by this process' (ibid., 165). The metaphor of shading as used by Palmer connects closely to the central philosophy espoused in this study, which examines literature as a process of shading, a liminal landscape where private and public spaces, historical materiality and story worlds, meet and merge in asymmetric entanglements of fact and fiction.

Cultural memory as a broad category of recollections and representations draws on a range of production and preservation techniques which are pragmatic as well as cognitive in quality. If literary fiction offers a unique perspective to examine the episodic quality of human recall and forgetting, it also presents a fluid framework to mark cultural memory in all its inclusions and elisions. As a 'depragmaticized medium' (Neumann 2008, 334), literature can operate apropos of the pragmatic productions of cultural memory as a consolidation as well as a counterpoint, generating its 'own memory worlds with specific literary techniques' (ibid., 334). If the depragmaticization as studied by Neumann enables literature to produce possibilities between historical materiality and existential interiority, the ambivalent frame of fiction offers an order that can accommodate as well as articulate the discursive and diachronic processes through which cultural memory is coded and consumed. Neumann's notion of *fictions of memory* in this context, like Kermode's concept of fiction and *future memory*, is significant for a nuanced understanding of collective and cultural history. Examining how such fictions can accommodate as well as creatively construct conflicting narratives of how collective and cultural memories are remembered and relived, Neumann equates literary productions with a 'laboratory in which we can experiment with the possibilities for culturally admissible constructions of the past' (ibid., 342). This metaphor of an experimental space of semanticization is significant for the broad understanding of culture and literature undertaken in this book, especially in the context of fiction, remembering, and forgetting. If remembering and forgetting may both be studied as acts of production that operate privately as well as culturally, *fictions of memory* foreground the fabulatory qualities in the same whereby the processes as well as the products of memory and oblivion may be uniquely described as well as deconstructed.

Yuri Lotman's concept of cultural memory is uniquely relevant in the study undertaken in this book, one which aims to examine literary representations apropos of cultural codes and their consumption. Studying the semiotics of cultural memory, Lotman highlights the textual transmission and constancy of codes in a shared culture. The *dialectic of memory* in Lotman's cultural studies' take on the same examines the internal mutations of 'local semantics' (Tamm 2019, 134) which determine broader narratives of remembering and forgetting. Thus the two types of memory, *informa-*

tive memory and *creative memory*, as described by Lotman highlight the passively sequential and phenomenally non-sequential orders of remembering respectively. This is particularly relevant in a study of cultural events and literary representations of the same. For literature may be seen as a production of possibilities which combines the present and the past in asymmetric combinations. In this, the idea of creative memory in collective imagination, whereby events, figures, and works are remembered and dismembered periodically, emerges with renewed relevance. Defining memory 'as not a passive storehouse for culture but a constitutive part of its text generating mechanism' (ibid., 137), Lotman's study of collective remembering underlines its mutable material processes invested in the production as well as in the revision of consumed codes of meaning. Thus the semiotic aspect of culture reveals that the 'past is not destroyed or relegated to oblivion but rather undergoes selection and a complex coding process by which it is placed in storage so that under certain conditions it may resurface' (ibid., 140). If memory as a cognitive process of coding and retrieval is the function of the recollecting brain which remembers and forgets simultaneously, cultural memory also incorporates similar coding and retrieval mechanisms through semiotic systems informed by and invested with material and discursive conditions. More importantly, the mutable materiality of cultural memory makes it episodic in quality whereby relegations and retrievals take place through spasms and triggers that may be profoundly political in quality. This is clearly evident in Manto's short fiction on Partition and Kundera's *The Book of Laughter and Forgetting*, which flag up the episodic and spasmodic quality of retrieval and relegation in collective memory and imagination, while also situating the similarities and contrasts between how a subject remembers and how a collective recollects. Fiction's unique location in the episodic and unreliable nature of recall and forgetting is highlighted by narrative devices such as focalization and condensation, whereby the complexities of cultural events and the human experience of the same converge in political and phenomenal frames.

MANTO AND THE FICTION OF VIOLENT REMEMBERING

The 1947 India-Pakistan Partition, which forms the broad backdrop of Saadat Hasan Manto's short fiction, may be seen as a violent watershed moment in human history and political identity in the subcontinent. More importantly, it is also an event which interrupted the collective and existential realities of millions of people with extreme experiences of alienation and trauma. Quite literally a collective experience of dislocation and disorientation, the 1947 Partition is a story of massive human suffering at social and existential levels, where millions were uprooted and mutilated due to conveniently conceived political and bureaucratic decisions. The ad hoc bureaucratization of borders and identity spaces during the Partition was accompanied by mass exodus and spectacles of suffering, and in the nine months following the independence from colonial rule, 'at least sixteen million people – Hindus, Sikhs, and Muslims – were forced to flee their homes and became refugees; at least two million were killed in ethnic violence' (Daiya 2008, 6). A spectacular scene of violent remapping at a cartographic as well as an epistemic level, the 1947 Partition forged two hastily manufactured nation narratives along with a crudely categorized identity politics using the communal tension of religion. As Ayesha Jalal argues in her book on Manto and Partition, the 'cataclysmic events of partition, civil war, and balkanization' which characterized the end of the British Empire at various geopolitical zones was largely due to the hasty decisions to quit 'in the absence of any agreement on power sharing arrangements' (Jalal 2013, 2). The British policy to quit and forego their Indian empire was executed with a blunt bureaucracy that emerged out of the desperate desire to leave a bad business that was not yielding profit anymore. In a malevolent self-serving logic, the imperial bureaucracy in India, headed by the ad hoc viceroy Lord Mountbatten, decided to declare the final territorial map of the two divided nation-states *after* the declaration of independence. Thus the official declaration of divided territories and their final national locations was made by Mountbatten in a radio speech on 16 August 1947 (Daiya 2008, 6). The idea was not to interfere with the euphoria of independence celebrations and to use it as a convenient shield to seal and draw the dividing lines that would unleash unprecedented violence and trauma in the subcontinent subsequently. Thus Hindus and Muslims on either side of the hurriedly drawn divide were forced to migrate to their politically correct destinations – Hindus to India and Muslims to Pakistan – due to the cartographically categorized locations. This produced the spectacle of one of the most massive migrations in human history whereby millions of subjects were forced to flee their homes, possessions, extended families, and the associated affective entanglements for uncertain and dangerous destinations (Sarkar 1983).

As a cultural and political event that affected the lives of millions and became a complex and contingent marker of the memory and the postmemory economy in the subcontinent, the 1947 Partition may be read as a symbolic shadow line of trauma, materiality, and spectrality, with a complex entanglement of matter, metaphor, and memory. Such theatre of human emotions and experiences of shock and loss often underline the metaphoric quality of events in a collective memory, especially in the manner in which such events are remembered and represented in oral narratives as well as in stylized forms such as literature and cinema.

As Shahid Amin argues in a similar study of the metaphoric quality of memory of another political event in India's colonial struggle – the Chauri Chaura incident in 1922 – the official documented record of the event often becomes secondary in comparison to the affective replaying of the same in popular imagination. In such instances, 'exaggeration, conflation, repetition, redundancy' complexly 'condense to delineate the ambiguities and tensions of an officious record', underlining in the process the knowledge that incongruence with officially known facts is not a 'lapse of memory' but rather 'a necessary element in the stitching together of a story' (Amin 1995, 197). This highlights the fabulatory and focalized quality of storytelling apropos of memory and history as important epistemic categories, with the textuality of *stitching together of stories* as examined by Amin bearing close parallels with the concept of *chunking* as theorized by neuroscientists and cognitive narratologists alike. A 'dramatic instance of postwar decolonization based on arbitrary redrawing of boundaries' (Jalal 2013, 3), the 1947 Partition emerged as a politically and bureaucratically constructed catastrophe that highlighted the common man's absolute absence of agency. The abrupt production and experience of homelessness, which also caused unimaginable human horrors and brutalities, may be read as a massive spectacle of the uncanny, the *outside-of-home* or homeless state which is political, spatial, and spectral in quality.

The uncanny quality in Manto's fiction is an intertwining of material reality and existential experience, depicting how millions of human subjects were abruptly alienated, violated, and interrupted from their daily discourses of normalcy and identity. As a writer in Urdu whose works have seen a massive revival in readership and critical acclaim with a series of English translations, Manto's fiction may be examined as literary experiments in form and narrative style that 'illuminate the everydayness – the banality of evil – that inhabited Partition, that lies beyond the pale of documentary, historical writing' (Daiya 2008, 55). Such representations of the daily experience and consumption of trauma and loss also underline the gendered nature of the violence of Partition where the female body often emerged as the site of the male fantasy of desire, destruction, and territorialization. The metaphoric and metonymic representation of the violated female body in Manto's fiction is also testimony to the abrupt blurring of the borderlines between private and public spaces, neighbour and enemy, homely and the unhomely, during moments of extreme violence which are corporeal as well as epistemic in quality. More importantly, Manto's fiction inhabits the interstitial space between information and affective experience, with a merging of different narrative registers, undercutting the official historian's account of the Partition as a 'new constitutional/political arrangement' and instead focalizing the survivor's account which experienced the event as a 'radical reconstitution of community and history' (Pandey 2002, 6). The short staccato representational style of Manto's Partition stories illustrates the episodic slice that crystallizes complex experiences of violence, trauma, and loss into cognitive states which stay unprocessed and unnarrated. This chapter reads Manto's fiction as a moving representation of the complex entanglement of materiality, spatiality, and spectrality that characterized the 1947 Partition, which witnessed mass mutilation and the execution of human bodies as well as experiences of traumatic triggers and memories which complicate narrative orders and storytelling. The study also examines how embodiment, memory, and storytelling are connected categories, especially in times of political and social violence and how the same violence operates at inter-corporeal as well as inter-epistemic levels.

The relationship between traumatic memory, embodiment, and storytelling is a recursive theme in Manto's fiction about Partition. This chapter studies four stories specifically – 'Khol Do' (Open It), 'Thanda Gosht' (Cold Meat), 'Mishtake', and 'Toba Tek Singh' – while examining the experiences of trauma, interrupted embodiment, motor memory, and forgetting in each. Manto's representations of Partition may be examined complexly from the perspective of memory studies in terms of offering alternative readings from statist narratives of decolonization and nation formation. What makes Manto's writings unique in this context, as Ayesha Jalal argues, is the 'remembrance of things past located just across the spatial and temporal threshold of 1947' which 'enables a new way of envisaging and writing the history of friendship that survived or transcended the moment of rupture' (Jalal 2013, 14). Thus, by focusing on and foregrounding micro memories of intimacy, shudder, and numbness due to shock, Manto's fiction offers an experiential and affective understanding of Partition which undercuts and deconstructs the dominant discourses of religious divisions and nation formations. Such an order of representation in fiction highlights how the shocked human mind processes matter and metaphors during experiences of extreme violence and how the same enters the realm of remembering and storytelling. In a close reading of selected short stories, this chapter examines the categories of embodiment, remembering, and forgetting at the interface of the political and existential orders. In close correspondence to the central thesis in this book, the relationship between matter, metaphor, and memory as represented in Manto's fiction is studied as complexly reflective of the interface of political and historical events and the human existential experience of the same. Manto's short stories are often entirely about one traumatic trigger – as evinced in 'Khol Do' and 'Thanda Gosht' – which never finds narrative or experiential closure and instead highlights shattered subjects in numbed shock or cognitive suspension. The complexity of such fiction often lies in the focal points selected for traumatic experiences which often inhabit extreme ends in Manto's stories. Thus, while 'Khol Do' depicts the motor memory of a multiply mutilated female body which proceeds passively to untie itself only to suffer yet another act of sexual violence, 'Thanda Gosht' depicts the traumatic memory of a perpetrator of such violence. Such experiential encounters bring the materiality of political change and violence in close proximity to the psychic traces of the same in the experiencing subject. In the process, it condenses the trauma and alienation often found in spatiotemporal metaphors which emerge as chronotopes, capsules of space-time which the shattered subject desperately desires to cling to, as represented in 'Toba Tek Singh', perhaps the most famous short story on the 1947 Partition. Along with the trauma of Partition, Manto's stories also convey the 'complexities of Hindu-Muslim relations in cities such as Bombay' (Jalal 2013, 13), depicting the dark cosmopolitan quality of late colonial decadence and exhaustion, a writerly trait which also informed Manto's writing for another medium, cinema.

Perhaps what makes Manto's short fiction so uniquely suitable to contain and convey the trauma of violent encounters and incomplete recalls is the narrative technique used therein, which inhabits the registers between episodic existential intensity and journalistic reportage. Thus Manto's stories deploy narrative voices which appear detached, even indifferent, to the experience of trauma, lending the entire episode of violence and cognitive unsettling clinically cold in quality. This apparent lack of empathy exhibited in the narrative tone becomes a marker in Manto's fiction of the crude corporeality of Partition violence whereby emotional responses to shock dwindle into motor and muscle memory of passive and repeated suffering. This corresponds closely to what modern neuroscientists such as Antonio Damasio describe as the lack of the feeling of what happens, the depletion of the overarching order of sentience and emotion which informs the subject's agency and autobiographical identity, along with a sense of the self which is seamless and continuous. The interruption in continuity produces what Damasio describes as 'transient impoverishment' of the 'autobiographical self' which remembers and reconnects to reality (Damasio 2000, 207). This receives reflection in representations of the fractured and flattened self in fiction, which becomes a grotesque reflection of the existential suspension characterizing the India-Pakistan Partition. Thus the hollowness and lack of interiority in Manto's short fiction are also indicators of the repetitive quality of traumatic encounters at physical as well as psychological levels, whereby the mind and the body are numbed by the experience of violence which takes place ad infinitum. This numbness extends to a crisis of embodiment whereby the subject's ownership on their own body apropos of the material reality around them is shattered due to an endless consumption of shock and shudder. Seen in this light, the 1947 Partition emerges with an extended understanding of alienation, mutilation, and epistemic violence. Manto's writing often depicts how experiences of shock and shudder in fiction, especially in a political context of repeated violence, find fractured narratives which do not cohere to any sustained experience of self. As the matter or material markers of violence appear metonymically, they also assume similar metaphoric status in the collective imaginary before entering the realm of memory. More importantly, Manto's short stories are often dark parodies of the grand narratives of new nation formations, with their hollowed-out and emotionless voices emerging as structural and functional parallels with the agency-less suffering subjects. Again, this corroborates Damasio's thesis of the strong and organic connection between emotion and cognition, with characters who have tragically lost their ability to emote and feel due to repeated violence and trauma, resulting in a compromise in their embodied, enactive, and extended orders of cognition.

Before moving on to a detailed study of Manto's selected fiction, it is worth unpacking the flatness and detached tone of the stories' narration and how it connects to the cognitive crisis characterizing the violence of the 1947 Partition. For if Conrad's suffering subject in *Heart of Darkness* offers a focal point which is inward looking with an interiorized existential voice that informs the storytelling, Manto's narrators are detached omniscient observers who often assume a panoramic godlike gaze on the spectacle of suffering caused by the Partition. Significantly, the spatial borderlines in Manto's stories are often blurred as the homely and the unhomely, the intimate and the public spaces of violence, merge metaphorically as well as functionally in the fiction, corroborated dramatically in 'Thanda Gosht', a story about 'sexual sadism, necrophilia, and the politics of "saving" women' (Bhalla 2001, 27), which also foregrounds the close proximity of desire and death in a violent space. The seemingly non-empathetic journalistic quality in Manto's fiction, whereby the observer-narrator just watches and reports, often assumes ironic and sarcastic undertones, as evinced most spectacularly in 'Toba Tek Singh' which is set in a madhouse in Lahore. This uninvolved narrative voice – in complete contrast to Conrad's angst-ridden, over-involved neurotic narrators who articulate their frustration in not being competent or complete storytellers – lends a special and spectral quality to the narrative gaze in Manto's fiction, the spectrality being a compound of alienation, emptiness, and indifference. In such clinical gaze, the objectivity of objects and the materiality of memory merge in an alienating economy of cognitive dissonance and trauma. If the affect and objects of memory in Manto's stories appear most fully during moments of loss, what further accentuates the darkness of the cognitive and episodic experiences are the moments of revelation that stun the subjects and act as traumatic triggers later. The *state of staying stunned* in Manto's fiction is conveyed through a voice which defamiliarizes with its detachment, offering an entirely different mode of readerly defamiliarization compared to Conrad's fiction, the latter being overly rich in its complex cognitive and narrative layers. The minimalism in Manto's fiction instead generates a *cognitive flatness* with its *narrative austerity* which offers sharp contrasts to the sudden experiential encounters containing intense episodes of violence and shock. The matter-of-fact quality with which extreme experiences of trauma and alienation appear in Manto's stories underline the earthly, vulgar, and visceral violence of Partition. There is no effort on the part of the narrative voice to aestheticize, interiorize, and engage with the rationale of such violence. Instead, Manto's fiction foregrounds the supreme and spectacular randomness of the brutalities perpetrated during Partition, also exhibiting how materials become markers and metaphors of mindlessness, trauma, and loss. More significantly, the staccato sentences in Manto which describe the encoding of incomplete information also underline the construction of confused collective as well as private phenomenal memory, where the embodiment of trauma often emerges as an incomplete cognitive process and passive motor movement.

The quasi-journalistic quality in Manto's fiction on Partition comes from his location in his contemporary news media apparatus as a reporter-writer. This dual method of reporting and describing gives a unique blend to Manto's narrative voice as argued above. As Ayesha Jalal underlines, 'Manto's Partition stories were based on information gleaned from visits to refugee camps and what he learnt about the plight of fleeing humanity as he sat in newspaper offices, coffee houses, and smoke-filled bars' (Jalal 2013, 3). The access to experience was thus first-hand as well as imaginative in Manto's writing, lending a uniquely liminal quality to his representation of human violence, brutality, and loss. More importantly, this makes the relationship between matter, metaphor, and memory complex and contingent in Manto's writing where the borderlines between reportage, fiction, and focalization are never constant or consistent. His stories are thus uniquely suitable for the study in this book which aims to examine the location of literature in a broader analysis of the material apparatus informing the production and consumption of cultural codes with their markers, metaphors, and memory. Relying on techniques such as anticlimax and inversions that ironically undercut any stable sentiment of representation, Manto's fiction foregrounds the mindless mayhem of Partition that was clinical, almost surgical, in quality, exemplified in the seven-sentence short story titled 'Mishtake'. More importantly, the sudden shudder at the end of Manto's stories often represents a 'dislocating force' that 'affectively rehearses the loss of footing', extending to an experience of deterritorialization that 'reveals the precariousness of claims to the certitudes of religious identities' (Menon 2012, 149). What emerges therefore in Manto's fiction is a centreless world of violence where social as well as intimate identities blend and fall together against an anarchic tide of trauma and deterritorialization. The home and the world both become violated spaces in such stories, highlighting the trauma of losing the original home and what Hannah Arendt describes in her study of human displacement as the loss of the 'social texture' associated with the same, which determines the subject's 'distinct place in the world' (Arendt 1973, 293). The unprecedented quality in the Partition violence lay experientially in the impossibility of finding a new home after the loss of the original one and the permanent states of homelessness and unhomeliness generated by the same. Inhabiting such an interstitial location of the uncanny between absolute destruction and impossibility of recovery, Manto's Partition fiction articulates what Veena Das defines as the 'register of the imaginary' which gives shape to 'the passion of those who occupied this unspeakable and unhearable zone' of shock and loss (Das 1996, 87). As the stories studied here reveal, the voices in such fiction emerge as powerfully moving renditions of the trauma of dislocation and the impossibility of completely processing or articulating it. Such stories blend the affective and informative registers of representations to underline the emotional as well as the emotionless quality of traumatic memory caused by violent historical events in ways which official records of history cannot accommodate or articulate.

'Mishtake' is a small piece of seven sentences which has no plot or character development except for a brutal communal murder followed by the regretful realization of having killed the wrong man (hence the deliberately misspelt title). The story or the narrative snippet (it is also considered a poem by certain readers and scholars) is remarkable for its episodic intensity which underscores the absurd and random quality of the Partition violence. The 'randomness of terror' (Bhalla 2001, 22) that characterizes Manto's fiction often rests on an unsettling mixture of matter and metaphor whereby structures of suffering are determined by small signs which become metaphors of identities during communal violence. The matter-metaphor compound in 'Mishtake' is the circumcised male genital organ which becomes the most embodied marker of masculine religious identity in the context of Partition. This also foregrounds the unsettled spatial politics during the time of communal violence when the private-public divide dissolves and the most private part of the human body becomes the most public identity. The circumcised skin as matter and metaphor in Manto's story about Partition violence highlights how the body is marked and materialized in high-conflict zones where the notional understanding of the inside and the outside, private organ and public identity, becomes contingent and abruptly deterritorialized. 'Mishtake' is about one swift movement, one slice of the knife, followed by a slower slice to ascertain the religious identity of the dead body. The mistake at the end of the episode concerns the knowledge of killing the wrong man, attacking the wrong genital organ. The religious locations of the perpetrator and the sufferer of violence are never clearly spelt out except for the reference to the *kalma-i-taassuf* associated with the killer when he realizes he had murdered a man with the wrong genital organ, the wrong identity marker. *Kalma* as the holy Muslim book for acknowledging the unquestionable authority of God and his messenger becomes a marker of fundamentalist religious identity here, while also offering the template for forgiveness for wrongdoing. Therefore, its presence in the context of the story becomes a metaphor for rigid religious identity devoid of any spiritual essence, as the realization of the wrong murder at the end of the story as the killer stares at the circumcised skin of the murdered man does not emerge from any deep remorse, but rather 'the staccato conclusion at the end suggests his irritation at his inefficiency' (Menon 2012, 148). The 'ritual repetition of holy words' (Bhalla 2001, 27) from the *Kalma* to save the subject from an act of sin is removed from any empathetic or spiritual connection to humanity, exhibiting how communal sentiments were fanned by fundamentalist appropriation of religion on either side during the Partition. This underscores again the indiscriminate quality of the Partition violence where the biggest casualties were human emotions and empathy, a fact foregrounded by the flatness in Manto's fiction which is also characterized by narrative austerity.

As Alok Bhalla argues, the knife in Manto's 'Mishtake' emerges as a mindless machine which is also a metaphor 'for the partition as an annihilating event' (Bhalla 2001, 24), highlighting how matter and metaphor mix in experiences of extreme unrest and traumatic memory. By making the knife almost a central character in the story where the murderer and the murdered are both unnamed, Manto emphasizes how the instrument of torture makes little difference between the belly which is sliced open and the pyjama string which is untied subsequently. The slicing of the belly is depicted with almost surgical precision and motor movement, devoid of any dilemma or human hesitation. The clinical quality of the murder in 'Mishtake', followed by a ritual apology emerging from irritation rather than remorse, exhibits the production of the unhomely characterizing the violence of Partition, whereby the human self, ambivalence, and agency become less important than the mechanical repetition of religious texts and the clinical control of cold killing objects. The knife and the circumcised penis both acquire metaphoric qualities in this story, becoming signifiers of brutality and public identity respectively, in an anarchically violent world where one's metonymic marker of religious identity determined the difference between life and death. Likewise, the intestines and pyjama strings which are sequentially slit open by the knife reveal the messy and blurred borderlines between the organic and the inorganic, the living and the dead, in Manto's fiction. This is dramatically exemplified by the short story 'Thanda Gosht' or 'Cold Meat'.

Jisha Menon examines how Manto's stories often crystallize into a moment of shudder which reverses all expectations built by the climax, 'peeling away the reader's horizon of expectations' (Menon 2012, 149) and producing in its wake a sudden and startling glimpse into the human horrors of Partition. This takes place not through an over-engagement with the sufferers' psyche in a bid to reveal the workings of the shuddered mind but through a paradoxical narrative detachment which is reflective of the absence of empathy in the narrative landscape. Instead of the interiority of the mind, what gets foregrounded in Manto's fiction is the violent and violated corporeality of the *mindless body*, whereby the messiness and mutilation of Partition are exhibited by motor movements which are devoid of mindfulness or thoughtful agency. The movements of mindless bodies in Manto's stories depict an intercorporeal economy where the difference between desire and death, between lust and lifelessness, is unclearly mapped, with contrasting experiential and affective bodily states blending into each other. As examined in 'Mishtake', mindless motor movements of violence in Manto's fiction often reveal unsettling post-mortem knowledge that generates regret. 'Cold Meat' depicts an episodic encounter of bodies during extreme violence of the sexual kind, following which the perpetrator's body experiences the same coldness of the female subject he had wanted to brutally rape. A story about inadvertent necrophilia where a rioting man desires to sexually consume his looted female trophy without realizing she is dead already, 'Cold Meat' is about the metaphoric meat gone awry, depicted by the hypermasculine figure's failure to consummate a sexual act following his unsettling experience with a cold corpse.

Valentine Daniel's anthropological study of communal violence in Sri Lanka affirms the paradox of cultural recognition in times of religious wars whereby the victory of one religious group over the other 'is the recognition of a corpse, which is no recognition at all' (Daniel 1996, 69). The recognition of spectrality in such experiences of violence emerges not from an effacement of the body but from a foregrounding of the same in mutilated corpses. The recognition in the form of nothingness as examined by Daniel incorporates corpse count as well as the anarchic absurdity of attack in times of such communal violence where dead bodies or vessels of nothingness become perverse trophies of triumph as well as markers of posthumous public identities. This phenomenon of the production of nothingness becomes a recursive theme in Manto's stories, often through intercorporeal encounters which blur the borderlines between desire and death, fantasy and fear, in moments of extreme violence.

Priyamvada Gopal studies how Manto's fiction frequently foregrounds the woman's body as a 'type of shorthand for the "real", functioning both as metaphor for her own degraded condition and for the lamentable state of society' (Gopal 2002, 245). Connected to this is the hypermasculine body perpetrating the violence as well as suffering from the same in moments of extreme neurosis, shock, and trauma, highlighting the self-reflexive quality of Partition violence as foregrounded in Manto's fiction, 'which brought into articulation psyche and history, emotion and morality, individual and society' (ibid., 247).

What emerges in this complex interplay of matter, metaphor, and memory in Manto's fiction on the Partition is a representation of the event as an anarchic spectacle of mindless violence where bodies attack and consume other bodies, forgetting and foregoing 'that civic ethos, that moral bond with each other, without which human community is impossible' (Ahmad 1992, 119). This accounts for the empathy-less and indifferent narrative tone espoused by Manto, as examined above, to foreground the fractured human condition in the time of Partition. What also emerges in such fiction is the moment of shudder and dramatic deterritorialization, when the mindlessness of the violence is interrupted only for the subject to acknowledge and articulate the horror of their own making. As evinced in 'Cold Meat', that shudder also entails a crisis in embodiment for the male subject who is otherwise hypermasculine and hyper-heterosexual, resulting in a moment of frozenness which is clinically cold in its death-like state. That moment of shudder resurfaces from a traumatic memory which incorporates the corporeality of a corpse as well as the spectrality of its lifeless state, a lifelessness which is also a paradoxical production of permanence in the traumatized perpetrator's mind.

Peter Bradbury's examination of sexuality and male violence highlights what is often understudied in Left-feminist discourses on the subject, which is the location of the male body in the violence perpetrated by patriarchy. In his study of male self-reflexivity in overt as well as covert orders of violence, Bradbury particularly investigates 'what it is to be violent; and what that violence means for our existence as men' (Bradbury 1992, 156). Manto's 'Cold Meat', a story about violence, intended rape, and near necrophilia culminating in the sexual frozenness of the perpetrator, presents Ishwar Singh, a hypermasculine Sikh man coupled with his hypersexualized lover Kulwant Kaur. The story, which courted controversy as well as a year-long legal dispute, may be read as an example of perpetrator trauma which firmly locates the otherwise strong and agentic male subject in an emasculated and paralytic state in the end, corroborating what Philip Mellor and Chris Schilling had classified as 're-forming the body' (Mellor and Schilling, 1997). At the beginning, the readers receive graphic descriptions of communal unrest followed by looting and murders. The story mixes the erotic and violent registers seamlessly even as it blurs the borders between public and intimate spaces, underscoring 'the organic connections that Manto emphasizes here between mind, body, and morality' (Gopal 2002, 254). Ishwar Singh's failure to consummate his sexual act with his amorous lover emerges from the traumatic memory of trying to rape a young woman who had already died in the hands of his fellow rioters. In essence, Ishwar's confrontation with the corpse of the young girl he is about to rape becomes what Valentine Daniel defines as *recognition of nothing*. The symbolic emasculation and impotence of Ishwar, which infuriate his hypersexualized lover Kulwant who renders him a death blow with his own dagger, become complete as he dies tasting his own blood. This also produces a paradoxical self-reflexivity in the erstwhile violent man which resonates with what Daniel defines as the 'transcendence of narcissistic particularity' (Daniel 1996, 68).

The dagger in 'Cold Meat', like the knife in 'Mishtake', becomes a metaphor of motor movements of violence, while also dramatizing the self-reflexivity of the process whereby the perpetrator becomes the consumed. The title of the story conveys a cannibalistic quality of violence whereby bodies consume other bodies in mindless moments, but problematizes it further with the association of frozenness which extends to an interruption of the consumption process. The meat gone cold points to the cold corpse of the female subject who was intended to be sexually violated post-riot. It also underlines the paralysed penis of the perpetrator of violence who cannot enact his *trump card* or final sexual arousal anymore, despite his hypermasculine efforts and frame. Manto's story is set in a riot-torn city which is described as strange and spectral, whose human and civic machinery is defamiliarized, where the intimate space is informed and designed by looted jewels from the outside, underscoring the blurred borderlines between public and private space in times of extreme communal violence. Thus Ishwar Singh decks his lover Kulwant with gold brought as spoils from the pillage and disappears again for days. The story starts with Ishwar returning after a hiatus and being interrogated by Kulwant who suspects his sexual involvement with another woman. Ishwar's response that he had been with and had a sexual relationship with *nobody* is ironically true in the context, as he had spent time with a female who was a cold corpse, underlining again the complex of spectrality and materiality – matter, metaphor, and memory – in Manto's fiction. The metonymic markers of masculinity and femininity in this story assume blunt physiognomic descriptions, and the private space of the lovers is informed as well as invaded by the violence from the outside.

The libidinal intercorporeal space in the lovers' room is marked also by violence, as Ishwar Singh's foreplay with Kulwant involves bodily hurt and aggression. The violence from the riot-torn city thus enters the intimate space, and the female body continues to serve as the consumable entity and trophy object to the hungry and violent male. The crude and vulgar descriptions of lovemaking – as Ishwar continues to hurt Kulwant with his moves and manoeuvres – are accompanied by graphic details of the lovers' hypersexualized bodies, corroborating the corporeality in Manto's depictions of Partition violence. In essence, Ishwar and Kulwant emerge as the male and the female body in heat in 'Cold Meat', the brutal quality of lust and possessiveness ascending with the climactic rise of foreplay, along with the cruelty caused to the sexualized and objectified female body. The cruel quality of foreplay enacted by Ishwar may be read as an extension of the cruelty and mutilation of the female in public space during Partition, which becomes a sanctioned and even desirable masculine behaviour in intimate/libidinal as well as communal/public space. Manto's choice of metaphor for the sexual act is interesting as well as complex – the *pack of cards* that is shuffled and reshuffled but never delivered – becoming a marker of hypermasculine playfully hypersexual cruelty as well as eventually emerging as a metaphor for emasculation from libidinal freezing. Kulwant's plea to Ishwar to throw the *trump card* meets a failed and frustrated end as he cannot consummate the sexual act due to his frozenness, and his entire *deck of cards* collapses in one fell swoop. The series of negatives in Ishwar's responses to an increasingly suspicious Kulwant – that he had been *nowhere*, had been with *nobody* – becomes ironically and psychologically true in the context of the story as he proceeds to narrate his traumatic experience. The flashback narration of near necrophilia and cold fear appears after Ishwar is stabbed in the neck by the fiercely jealous and jilted Kulwant with the very dagger he had used to commit communal killings in the violent and volatile public space. The violence of the dagger, like that of the knife in 'Mishtake', assumes almost a machinic mindless quality, invading public as well as private intimate spaces indiscriminately. Thus Ishwar confesses to murdering six people with the same dagger that kills him eventually, corroborating how the instrument and instrumentality of violence symbolically as well as functionally override the logic of human agency in moments of mindless destruction.

The story's switch from brutal bodily sexuality and corporeal violence to a de-corporealized melancholia has a complex cognitive quality, as the dying Ishwar proceeds to tell his story. As the tone and tempo slow down and the spent and dying Ishwar muses philosophically on the absurdity of human desire and existence, he narrates the story of cold fear from the necropolis of Partition. From the hypermasculine Sikh full of vigour and virility, Ishwar is converted into a lump of cold meat that merges into death. His bodily paralysis, emerging from his erstwhile sexual frozenness, receives its backstory which he narrates even as he lies dying. The reader gets to know, along with Kulwant Kaur, that Ishwar had gone looting like most men as riots broke out in the city. He had brought in jewels and other spoils from the looting for his lover but had withheld one crucial piece of information. After murdering six people and looting a house, Ishwar saw a beautiful girl whom he wanted to consume sexually before killing. The metaphors of corporeal consumption return here as Ishwar offers a rationale behind his motive; the fact that he consumes Kulwant every day makes him want to *taste a different fruit*, corroborating the consumable quality of the female body in a hypermasculine hypersexual space informed by anarchic yet perversely sanctioned violence. As he carries his coveted female body on his shoulders, throws her on a bush, and proceeds to throw his *trump card*, he realizes she had already been dead, that he had been carrying and was on the verge of sexually consuming a corpse. The politics of gaze gets reversed here as the violent male who had been objectifying the female body for his consumption is frozen into a stone as the female corpse stares back at him. The knowledge of his necrophilia freezes Ishwar, invading his erstwhile virile male body, and he carries this trauma back to the intimate space with his lover who had been receiving and using the jewels that may have belonged to the dead woman. As he confesses his sexual violence and trauma to his lover, Ishwar describes his experience of cold meat, the cold corpse of the female he had intended to sexually violate. The story ends with an experience of tactility as Kulwant Kaur touches Ishwar's hand only to discover it is colder than ice, the skeletal coldness of corpse-touch highlighting and reiterating the absence of human life and humanity in times of violence when mindless bodies cannibalistically consume each other.

Manto's 'Cold Meat' may be read through the lenses of gender studies whereby the two female figures become counterpoints as well as agentic extensions apropos of each other. Thus the passive and unnamed female who gets brutally killed in a communal riot and almost raped posthumously stays as a spectral presence but eventually emasculates the hypermasculine violent man at the high point of his libidinal lust. In contrast to that coldness, the named Kulwant Kaur is the aggressive assertive woman in heat who flaunts her proud Sikh lineage and avenges her lover's infidelity by killing him with his very own murder weapon. Thus, while the violent man murders and mutilates the female in the public space during the Partition pogrom, he is symbolically avenged by the female(s) in the private intimate space following his emasculation and sexual fear. Manto's story is remarkable in its depiction of the self-reflexivity of sexual violence whereby the perpetrator's body is paralysed by the dead violated woman who assumes a Medusa-like stony stare posthumously which symbolically castrates and eventually kills the erstwhile violent male. The traumatic memory in 'Cold Meat' mixes matter and metaphor, dramatizing a shift from crude corporeality to the absence of body and life. At a symbolic and psychological level, Manto's story is about the production, experience, and articulation of absence, whose existential darkness and spectrality lie beneath the deceptive and superficial show of sexual strength and hypermasculinity. The coldness of matter and body eventually becomes a metaphor for fear and trauma in Manto's story about violence and the grotesque, causing an interruption in embodiment and engagement with lived experience at a cognitive and corporeal level. Depicting an intense episodic experience of violence and perpetrator trauma with the 1947 India-Pakistan Partition as backdrop, Manto's 'Cold Meat' is especially and uniquely significant for the scope of this book, which aims to examine the complex entanglement of matter and metaphor, spectrality and corporeality, in literary representations of human lives with the backdrop of cultural codes and political shifts.

'Khol Do' or 'Open It' is another short story about the motor memory of trauma, depicting what the body remembers through repetitive acts of violence on it. The site of sexual abuse is again the female body, and the setting is the riot-infested city of Mughalpura filled with refugee camps and a hospital meant to treat victims of communal violence. 'Khol Do' opens with a typically Mantoesque description of horror and brutality rendered through an almost detached, indifferent tone. The iconic image of Partition violence, that of the corpse-filled train cutting across the newly designed borders, appears at the outset, underlining the rituals and randomness of mass killings across stations which are located in the different newly formed nation-states. The train as a vehicle of violence as well as mass migration during Partition has assumed a totemic quality in the collective memory of the event, with statistical records showing that 'as many as 673 refugee trains moved approximately 2,800,000 refugees within India and across the border' (Kaur 2011, 948). The movement of trains with refugees as well as corpses became a recurrent symbol of relocation as well as brutal violence in the memory of Partition. Thus the third-person narrator in the opening sentence informs how the 'special train left Amritsar and reached Mughalpura' eight hours ago, also stating that '[m]any people were killed en route, many injured; some went astray' (Tasheer 2010, 25). The reader is introduced to the protagonist of the story, Sirajuddin, who finds himself in a refugee camp, in search of his daughter Sakina, after having seen his wife killed brutally in a communal riot. The sensory experience of numbness due to repetitive trauma is a recursive theme in Manto's Partition fiction, and in 'Khol Do' Sirajuddin is described as having a vacant look, unable to hear anything anymore, 'as if his eyes were blocked' (ibid., 25). Similarly, and in keeping with the constant consumption of trauma that affects normal neural functioning, Sirajuddin's 'nerves were frayed' and 'he felt as if he were floating in a void' (ibid., 25), the cognitive blankness and existential emptiness emerging from an endless experience of extreme violence. The crisis in embodiment suffered by Sirajuddin is informed by the traumatic memory of having seen his wife's 'intestines spilled out' (ibid., 25) in the riot which killed her, a recursive image in his mind which blocks his thought processes and instead fixes him at the moment of horror.

The fundamental premise of the story is about the father searching for his lost daughter, whose missing *dupatta* he carries across refugee camps with the hope of finding her. The loss of *dupatta* becomes the primary marker of Sakina, becoming a metaphor of her unclothing which anticipates the sexual violence she is subjected to by unnamed men who move in groups and travel in trucks across borders. Sirajuddin's disconnected cognitive sensory states are exemplified in the story in his inability to recollect anything after the train stopped on the way and the rioters appeared aboard, and also by his impulse to cry but his physical inability to do so. The cognitive crisis suffered by Sirajuddin thus becomes a marker of violence operating at a corporeal as well as a fundamental epistemic level, whereby the subject's sense of self and location in the extended environment becomes fragile and fractured. This results in an extreme form of deterritorialization common in Manto's fiction on the Partition, where the human agent is dislocated from any stable sense of space, time, memory, and identity. The final recognition scene in the story, where Sirajuddin gets to see his daughter on a stretcher inside a refugee hospital after she was found unconscious by some railway tracks, is evocative of the order of the uncanny typical of Manto's writing. Sakina is identified by the beauty spot on her right cheek, a marker which appears with intense irony in the context of the grotesquely violent setting of the story. As Sirajuddin rushes to his daughter and calls her by her name, an irritated doctor checks her pulse and instructs him to open the window of the room. The sound and order of opening it ('Khol Do') triggers a motor memory in Sakina's corpse-like body as her limbs proceed to untie her salwar and lower it, generating happiness in Sirajuddin at the sign of life and fear in the doctor who is 'drenched from head to toe in sweat' (ibid., 26). Manto mixes emotions at the end of the story to further underline the anarchic and morbid quality of violence in the Partition where the borders between life, death, and desire were constantly redrawn and re-territorialized.

'Khol Do' may be read as a complex example of cognitive deterritorialization whereby motor and muscle memory become markers of the constant consumption of trauma and violence which is increasingly naturalized. The human self and agent become almost entirely represented and recognizable by the bloodied and brutalized corporeal frame, exemplified by the torn-out intestines of Sirajuddin's wife which assume the same symbolic status as the circumcised penis in 'Mishtake'. Again, the inside-outside, public-private divides are grotesquely inverted in Manto's story, the innards of the female body becoming a marker of publicly brutalized identity, with violence becoming the most recursively enacted social and public performance. The men who appear and move in 'Khol Do', like the bunch of rioters in 'Cold Meat', are faceless and anonymized, rendering a spectral quality to the spectacle of violence and fear in the story. Like 'Cold Meat', the corporeality of the suffering body is foregrounded in 'Khol Do', whereby the embodiment and enactment of death become the most visible corporeal movement, generating in its wake further fear and numbness. More interestingly, there is a sinister quality in 'Khol Do' whereby the difference between men who help find lost girls and men who rape and torture them is never fully demarcated or mapped out. Interestingly and ironically, the location of the doctor in 'Khol Do' and that of the perpetrator of violence in 'Cold Meat' apropos of the violated female body are quite similar in their experiential encounter with the uncanny. As two men who cause and cure respectively the violence on women during Partition, the murderer and the doctor share the same cognitive frame of fear and unsettling, eventually appearing paralytic and drenched in cold sweat. This corroborates the blurred borderlines between the coercive and curative agents and spaces during Partition, between the men who hurt and the ones who are supposed to heal, a theme which is dramatized fully and spectacularly in Manto's most famous short story on the absurdity of the two-nation divide, 'Toba Tek Singh'.

A tale of two nations presented through the prism of madmen, 'Toba Tek Singh' is also a sharp satire of the mindless bureaucracy which was instrumental in enacting the 1947 Partition. The story starts with the typically Mantoesque voice which is detached from the drama it narrates, rendering the experience of loss and its absurdity more clinical in quality. In an almost journalistic tone, the reader is informed that two years after Partition, it suddenly 'occurred to the respective governments of India and Pakistan that inmates of lunatic asylums, like prisoners, should also be exchanged' (Manto 2008, 9) based on their religion. The governments' decision to move the madmen surfaces, the narrator informs, not due to any empathetic understanding of their alienation but due to a crudely curated mathematical and statistical divide that completely overrides any human sentiment or agency. Manto continues to underline the absurdity of the process with a tone that borders on dry humour as the narrator confesses, 'Whether this was a reasonable or an unreasonable idea is difficult to say' (ibid., 9), following that with further information about many high-level conferences which were undertaken to arrive at the most politically correct decision. The decision to exchange madmen across the borders – the non-Muslim lunatics from Pakistan to India and their Muslim counterparts in India with relatives in Pakistan to Pakistan – makes perfect sense in bureaucratic discourse but is absolutely absurd in terms of human sentiment and agency. The story then quickly cuts into the Lahore lunatic asylum where it is set, where the inmates are suddenly informed of the two new nations and of their imminent migration, with one of them declaring Pakistan as the place in India where cut-throat razors are made. This is followed by a scene of one inmate climbing a tree and deciding to stay atop it rather than going to India or Pakistan, and another one undressing and running down the garden entirely naked. The debate and confusion about the precise locations of India and Pakistan – how come what was India is now suddenly Pakistan? and if they are in Pakistan, how come this was India earlier? – continue in the asylum followed by a series of other insane activities which border on the carnivalesque and the grotesquely comic. Manto's story gradually underlines the inversion of the rational-irrational binary, with the inmates of an asylum asking more humanely rational questions and behaving with more honest emotions than the cold clinical bureaucracy designed to impose and enact order.

The protagonist of the story – Bishen Singh – is introduced as a silent and harmless madman from a village called Toba Tek Singh, with inordinately swollen feet, who neither sits nor sleeps. The aberrated embodiment and corporeal frame – his sleepless state and swollen legs fixating Bishen Singh to his original moment of madness and loss – has a temporal quality in Manto's story, the swollenness of his feet becoming a signifier of the phantom limb of forgotten time gathered in the body. This corporealization of time becomes a major marker of memory in Manto's story as Bishen Singh is shown suffering from what is currently classified as retrograde amnesia whereby the subject retains memories of much earlier events while failing to encode new experiences into neural patterns which may become memories. This gives the story a chronotope-like quality as, in being fixated to his memory of the village Toba Tek Singh which does not exist in the new cartographic constructs or nationalist narratives anymore, Bishen Singh symbolically morphs into Toba Tek Singh, with the memory of his forgotten space becoming his only marker of identity. This is symbolically and spectacularly demonstrated in the conclusion of the story, when in his refusal to move to either India or Pakistan and in his insistence on returning to his native village, Bishen Singh collapses and dies in the no-man's-land between the two nation-states. As the narrator informs, the 'bit of earth, which had no name' (ibid., 15) becomes Toba Tek Singh, symbolically situated between the barbed wires of the classified territories of India and Pakistan. In close correspondence to the central enquiry in this book, Manto's story foregrounds an entanglement of matter, metaphor, and memory, while also depicting a literary representation of a profoundly political event. Thus, if the forgotten village

Toba Tek Singh becomes a metaphor of the space and time which must be dematerialized and dismembered from the new narratives of memory and history exemplified by the abruptly manufactured nation-states, it also exhibits the phantom limb which never quite disappears entirely from embodied memory, existing instead as the liminal territory between remembering and forgetting, materiality and spectrality, best focalized in the fluid frame of fiction.

Bishen Singh's constant refrain, on knowing about the Partition and the government decision to migrate madmen across the borders based on their religion, makes an absurd comment on the deteriorating quality of lentil and the indifference of gods towards the same. The metaphor of lentil as the rottenness of basic food and source of sustenance is significant in the context of the story, as is the constant complaint of divine indifference which has an obvious political ring to it. Manto's narrator further flags up the absurdity of Partition and the epistemic violence and anxiety it generates as the madmen speculate whether Lahore, which had hitherto been in Pakistan, would slide to India any moment and whether both India and Pakistan might entirely disappear from the world map altogether. What is dramatized in the madmen's debates is the mutability of the markers of spatiality and identity and how they had earlier existentially informed each other but now exist in a state of cognitive dissonance, which forms the fundamental fabric of the story. The same cognitive dissonance is dramatized in the story in Bishen Singh's conversation with Fazal Din, a Muslim friend from his village, which also articulates the ambivalence of assurance and disappearance one finds in 'Khol Do', the site of violence and loss being the lived land as well as the female body. On being asked where Toba Tek Singh was, Fazal Din first responds by stating that is where it always had been, revealing the natural and sentimental association with a place and its memory. When Bishen Singh presses further by asking if it is in India or in Pakistan, a flustered Fazal Din responds with both nation names. The more sinister response comes when Bishen Singh enquires about his daughter Roop Kaur and Fazal responds – after a hesitation – that she 'is safe too . . . in India' (ibid., 13). The moment of hesitation in reporting on the absent woman is also the moment when the possibility of violence is concealed as well as articulated covertly, corroborating the corporeal as well as the epistemic quality of Partition violence in Manto's fiction. As in 'Cold Sweat' and 'Khol Do', the articulation of absence becomes a major marker of memory in 'Toba Tek Singh', as the village which disappears from the newly constructed cartographic imaginary continues to exist as the sole memory device in a madman's amnesiac mind.

Manto's choice of setting in this story is symbolic as well as political. Situated outside of the decision-making, meaning-making mechanism of the state apparatus, the asylum in Lahore exemplifies the agency-less aberrative space inhabited by madmen where cure and coercion appropriate similar strategies. Ironically and yet unsurprisingly, the madmen ask the most rational questions in 'Toba Tek Singh', with their partitioned minds, memories, and sense of self in the micro cognitive plane uniquely suitable to subvert the logic of the grand narrative of Partition at the macro political level. There is a complex spatiotemporal quality in Manto's story whereby the madmen are located in a pre-Partition space-time from where they refuse to move, physically as well as existentially. This refusal – which receives an extreme and tragic embodiment at the end of the story – emerges as a desperate and eventually ineffectual act of agency directed against the cold and clinical bureaucracy which divides destinies by making and remaking maps. The two orders of time and memory in Manto's story – the private existential order and the public nationalist ones – offer a complex incongruence between statist structures of matter, metaphor, and memory and the phenomenal ones, whereby what the subject remembers and aspires to reconnect itself to is painfully incompatible with the new narratives of memory and materiality exemplified by the Partition and subsequent formation of two new nation-states. This dramatizes the 'difference in emplotment' (Anderson 1983, 205) between private and national narratives as examined by Benedict Anderson whereby the narrative quality of memory through a strategic sequence of matter and metaphor works uniquely for a national history in order to generate its seamless quality. In sharp contrast to that sense of seamlessness, the madmen's memories in Manto's story are deeply defined by a before and an abrupt after, the after-experience of the accident marked by 'wounds that have the power to cause a metamorphosis which destroys individual history, that cannot be reintegrated into a normal course of a life or a destiny' (Malabou 2012, 53). In the context of 'Toba Tek Singh', the wound of madness as experienced and embodied by Bishen Singh and the schism caused due to Partition undercut each other, generating in their wake an extreme example of spatiotemporal alienation whose fixity also paradoxically produces an order of agency. In presenting a sleepless madman who is a symbolic guardian of lost time, standing endlessly with swollen feet, and one who stubbornly wants to go only to his own pre-Partition village, Manto's story depicts a subject who 'refuses to remember and forget in ways that would facilitate the seamless moving on of the newly formed national narratives' (Parui 2015, 63).

The final setting in the story is also symbolic in the ways it merges matter, metaphor, and memory. The narrator describes the blunt bureaucracy that oversees the transfer of madmen across the dividing line between the two new nation-states, where '[s]enior officials from the two sides in charge of the exchange arrangement met, signed documents and the transfer got under way' (Manto 2008, 14). Against this cold and clinical system of exchange, the madmen from either side 'run pell-mell in every direction' (ibid., 14), weeping bitterly and refusing to leave, as they 'simply could not understand why they were being forcibly removed, thrown into buses and driven to this strange place' (ibid., 14). In its images of confusion and consternation, Manto's story also shows the production of the uncanny, the unhomeliness or outside-of-home status experienced by madmen who appear like zombies before the officials and bureaucrats. When Bishen Singh is pushed towards a table with an official for the paperwork before being sent off, he enquires about the location of Toba Tek Singh one last time, whereupon the indifferent officer rudely responds that it is in Pakistan, the new nation-state from where he is being sent off. That fixates him further in his location as he resists all physical force to push him across the border, Manto's story symbolically converting him into a giant monument of lost time which refuses to budge against the new orders of nationalist imaginary. Thus he 'stood in no-man's-land on his swollen legs like a colossus' (ibid., 14), occupying a liminal territory, between memory and forgetting, the fault line between two newly forged land masses with his rejection and refusal to move on and merge in either, symbolically becoming Toba Tek Singh as he collapses and dies at the end of the night, with guards and officials rushing to his corpse from either side. The final image in Manto's story, whereby the stretch of land which had no name, located between barbed wires, becomes the twilight territory that cannot be classified, foregrounds an existential entanglement of memory, space, and identity, with a complexity that undercuts as well as parodies the precision of bureaucratic cartography.

Marc Augé's concepts of oblivion and *non-place* are particularly pertinent and mappable in Manto's story in terms of how the liminality between being and becoming, the sentient subject and the citizen, between classified and unclassified identities, is dramatized. In his celebrated essay titled 'Oblivion', Augé examines memory and forgetting as dialectically connected categories, with both activities informed by processes of fiction (Augé 2004, 22–23). Augé's enquiry, a major scholarship in memory studies research, foregrounds the cognitive connection between memory, forgetting, and spatiality in the subject's engagement to create location and meaningful identity. The no-man's-land in which Bishen Singh collapses, converting himself into a fallen human monument, also exemplifies the ontology of the *non-place*, a liminal conveyor belt between stable and meaningful masses, where the subject establishes a contractual relation with the material vectors around (Augé 1995, 82). But Manto's story problematizes this further by underlining the fixity of the non-place as the final act and assertion of agency, merging the matter, metaphor, and memory of the dying subject who is symbolically as well as literally pulled by the forces of the new nation-states. The mad human subject in 'Toba Tek Singh' emerges as an embodiment of a space-time which has been deterritorialized in the normative narratives of nation-states, while also making a desperate attempt to re-territorialize the same with extreme forms of corporeality. In becoming a human monument of a place which is conveniently forgotten by the new nation narratives, Bishen Singh enacts what Michael Rothberg defines as 'anachronistic metonymy' as well as 'postmemorial agency' in the multidirectional vectors of remembering and forgetting (Rothberg 2009, 305). The metonymic anachronism is amply evident in Manto's story in the madman's partial and fragmented remembering of home and homeliness against abrupt changes in the classified geopolitical landscapes. The partiality and metonymic process of remembering emerge as the post-memorial agency in a complex spatiotemporal sense as Bishen Singh rejects and resists relocation to the new narratives of memory and history and instead embodies a posthumous monument of forgotten space and time in the borders between the two new nation-states. In its depiction of a madman's extreme embodiment and existential alienation through a desperate fixation on an order of space and time increasingly incompatible with the emerging nation narratives, 'Toba Tek Singh' dramatizes the 'belated psychological after effects of the rupture of Partition' (Saint 2012, 53). The violent outburst and dying scream of Bishen Singh after years of silence, stillness, and sleeplessness emerge as a telling testimony to this belated articulation of absence and loss. Ironically written after Manto's own sojourn at Lahore's mental asylum for alcohol-related ailments (Jalal 2013, 184), 'Toba Tek Singh' is generally considered the best work of fiction on the 1947 Partition.

Manto's fiction foregrounds extreme violence and trauma which deterritorialize the suffering subject's embodiment, identity, and agency against the backdrop of a major political shift of structures of power. The human movements in Manto are often minimalist in their perpetration and consumption of violence which is visceral and epistemic in quality. This minimalism manifests itself in the cognitive flatness and narrative austerity in Manto's fiction where the characters are often numbed by the constant consumption of trauma and where the narrator appears detached in their objective god gaze on human violence and suffering. In the process it mixes matter with metaphor even as it depicts and dramatizes failed acts of remembering and forgetting. The impossibility of remembering and forgetting in Manto's story operates at private motor levels as well as in the collective imaginary, with materials of destruction and damaged bodies and organs assuming affective markers in a spectral landscape of loss. The contagious quality of violence and loss forms the backdrop in Manto's fiction, against which human existential isolation and interruption are dramatized, epistemically as well as in the order of embodiment. The fiction here appears as a complex medium which combines the lived historical reality of the trauma of Partition with human cognitive and existential engagements with the same. It thus underlines the unique form of representation offered by fiction apropos of culture, with its material, metaphorical, and memory markers. In its stylized and affective engagement with extreme political conditions which arouse emotional experience of loss, Manto's short stories on Partition as studied here highlight the epistemic and corporeal quality of trauma corroborated by modern neuroscience. The fictional frame of Manto often mixes materiality and spectrality, foregrounding the human subjects' incomplete and unprocessed understanding and consumption of the traumatic reality of the 1947 Partition and its violent territoriality. It also offers a complex perspective on the fault lines between hegemonic collective memory and private experiences of imaginative reconstruction, a theme which receives an almost dark-humorous treatment despite its grim political setting in Milan Kundera's *The Book of Laughter and Forgetting*, examined in the section which follows in this chapter.

KUNDERA AND THE POLITICS OF FORGETTING

Milan Kundera's work – especially the *Book of Laughter and Forgetting* examined in this chapter – often situates the interplay of fiction and forgetting as affective instruments against political and cultural totalitarianism and censorship. What makes it more complex is Kundera's use of humour and laughter as subversive strategies informing human negotiations with structures of coercion and control. Drawing on irony, self-reflexivity, and unreliable narrativity, Kundera's writing frequently emerges as an entanglement of fact and fabulation, the latter often appearing as an activity in agency in subjects otherwise denied dignity and the fundamental rights of selfhood and citizenship. This entanglement is of special significance for the scope of this book, examining as it does the connection between culture and the literary, informed by an economy of matter, metaphors, and memory. As Ellen Pifer argues, the 'reliance of human and cultural identity upon language, and of language upon memory, is a central theme in *The Book of Laughter and Forgetting*' (Pifer 1992, 87). Remembering is a complex cognitive and cultural activity in Kundera's writing, often foregrounding forgetting as a key quality in the remembering mind and collective. Therefore, such descriptions of political and existential identities emerge as metonymic, inconstant, and incomplete in Kundera's fiction, where the boundaries between historical events and fictional eventualities are always blurry and mutable. Unsurprisingly, silences and absences play major roles in the cultural-literary entanglements in Kundera's writing on fiction and forgetting, whereby what is not remembered or not articulated becomes existentially as well as politically significant. Such structural and functional interplay of silence and censorship lends a liminal quality to Kundera's fiction, drawing on complex chronotopes which dramatize as well as deconstruct shared and sometimes coercive orders of space, security, memory, and identity. This foregrounds the textuality and materiality of memory as informing a mutable activity of becoming and un-becoming that corresponds to existential as well as political orders.

In his essay on Kafka's sole statue in Prague – the city of his birth – Alfred Thomas examines the dialectic of remembering and forgetting through material and metonymic processes of reconstruction. Immediately evident in such memory settings is the interplay of the politics of remembering and the remembrance of politics, and how certain figures move from being marginalized to centralized signifiers in mutable narratives of memory, informed by political predilections as well as by ideological impulses. Thus, Thomas argues, Kafka's reception and resurrection as a major literary icon in post-socialist Prague reveal the 'interplay between remembering and forgetting that has characterized key moments – and key religious and cultural figures – in the history of the city'. Such an interplay appropriates a range of material and political factors representing a 'history of constant reinvention in which political-cultural self-fashioning and economic calculation have all played – and continue to play – an integral role' (Thomas 2015, 157–69). Thomas's study of Kafka's presence in Prague points to some of the key qualities in Kundera's depiction of the same city in *The Book of Laughter and Forgetting*, transitioning from the communist to the post-communist era through a complex range of rituals and materials moving from memory to oblivion. More importantly, Kundera's writings on Prague – like Thomas's reading of Kafka's statue – also depicts and dramatizes the self-fashioning informing remembered cultural, political, and existential identities. Such self-fashioning underlines the performative quality of memory as a collective and individual activity, consolidating as well as sometimes subverting dominant modes of remembering.

Kafka appears in Kundera's *The Book of Laughter and Forgetting* as a forgotten figure who had ascended the same stairs which later witnessed a major moment in communist history in Czechoslovakia featuring the leaders Gottwald and Clementis. The forgetting of Kafka and the selective remembering of the communist leaders (Clementis is killed and erased from all photos subsequently) appear synchronously and symbolically through encoding and re-encoding of architecture and monuments in *The Book of Laughter and Forgetting*. Thus the palace from the

Austria-Hungarian Empire which had been a German school where Kafka went in his time had become a communist political building later with iconic status, the balcony of which becomes the setting for the opening of *The Book of Laughter and Forgetting*. The same building, Kundera's narrator informs, had also housed the shop of Hermann Kafka, father of Franz, whose shop sign was one of a jackdaw, symbolizing the word *kafka*, which meant jackdaw in Czech. Kundera's novel dramatizes the disjunction and play of historical time and *fictional time* (the latter incorporating deliberate anachronisms as well as imaginative insertions), describing how Kafka *had been aware of how he would be forgotten* by the political figures in his own city. This highlights the play of liminality and liquidation in *The Book of Laughter and Forgetting*, which shows a world where 'the future devours the present relentlessly in the sequential time Europe has preserved into its senility, when only timelessness is real' (Banerjee 1990, 66). The literary production of Kafka, in Kundera's reading, is premised on memory-less-ness, and Prague appears in his fiction as a 'city without memory', one which 'has even forgotten its name' and where nobody 'remembers or recalls anything' (Kundera 1982, 215). Kafka's genius lies, in Kundera's reading, in producing a fiction of forgetting and forgottenness which extends to a crisis in identity and spectrality. This spectrality emerging out of memory-less-ness in Kafka's fiction bears rich resonance with the absence of identity on the streets of Prague where 'the streets are without names or with names different from those they had yesterday, because a name is continuity with the past and people without a past are people without a name' (ibid., 216). *The Book of Laughter and Forgetting* is a novel about crises in continuity which in turn generate interrupted identities. It is constituted by characters who, like the streets they inhabit, are muted and mutated by the structures and silences of remembering and un-remembering.

The changing street names in Prague correspond to changing political as well as existential identities in Kundera's novel, where memory-less-ness is also equated with silence, slowness, and surveillance, symbolized by the statues of thousands of Jesuit saints built after the failed Czech Reformation in 1621, 'gazing at you from all sides and threatening you, spying on you, hypnotizing you' (ibid., 216). Memory as spectrality appears in *The Book of Laughter and Forgetting* in the form of abandoned monuments and torn-down buildings in Prague which stand as markers of historical change, from the Czech Reformation to the communist era. The current political spring in Kundera's novel sees statues of Lenin 'springing up in Bohemia by the thousands, springing up like weeds among ruins, like melancholy flowers of forgetting' (ibid., 217). The melancholia of forgetting in *The Book of Laughter and Forgetting* is associated with an absence of agency that is political as well as existential in experience and scope.

This is instantiated in the figure of Tamina who appears as an emergent symptom of silence and censorship while also foregrounding the fictional medium in Kundera's novel. Thus, the narrative voice constructing the characters in the novel informs: 'The silence of my father, from whom all words slipped away, the silence of the hundred forty-five historians, who have been forbidden to remember, that multiple silence resounding through Bohemia, forms the background of the picture I am painting of Tamina' (ibid., 221). This brings to attention the politics of representation apropos of remembering in a state of censorship, whereby the production of fiction foregrounds memory as well as what is un-remembered, through an interplay of information and imagination. In doing so, *The Book of Laughter and Forgetting* dramatizes the 'inherent fictionalizing of reality and the inherent reality of fiction' (Berlatsky 2003, 119).

The remembrance of political events in Kundera's novel is also simultaneously a process of forgetting, dramatizing the ontology as well as the movement of memory as a shifting and slippery narrative which produces its own absences. Thus, the narrative voice informs, '[t]he assassination of Salvador Allende quickly covered over the memory of the Russian invasion of Bohemia, the bloody massacre in Bangladesh caused Allende to be forgotten, the din of war in the Sinai Desert drowned out the groans of Bangladesh, the massacres in Cambodia caused the Sinai to be forgotten' (Kundera 1982, 9–10). The concatenation of moments of political violence makes memory into a shifting sequential experience at a collective level that paradoxically produces amnesia, 'until everyone has completely forgotten everything' (ibid., 10). Kundera's novel thus dramatizes how memory in the public sphere operates through an entanglement of production and consumption where every event appears as an erasure of the one preceding it. This problematizes the ontology of the event itself in *The Book of Laughter and Forgetting*, where '[h]istorical events mostly imitate one another without any talent' (ibid., 18) and where certain anniversaries pass in silence and certain names 'are carefully erased from the country's memory, like mistakes in a schoolchild's homework' (ibid., 19). The erasure and effacement of certain names from public memory underline the textuality and the referentiality of the remembering process itself which, by extension, highlight how memory as reconstruction is mimetic as well as mutative in quality. Kundera's novel foregrounds this fluid mimesis and mutability in memory through the medium of fiction, combining event and eventuality in the same spatiotemporal frames.

A fictional work on philosophy and forgetting which also offers a complex commentary on the major political changes in his country of birth, Kundera's *The Book of Laughter and Forgetting* is set in Czechoslovakia but was finished in 1978 after the writer moved to France. A novel about liminality, loss, and laughter, about borders between remembering and forgetting, *The Book of Laughter and Forgetting* is a powerful example of fiction's ability to offer a fluid framework to remember complex historical events and lost possibilities. This is instantiated in the section titled 'Borders':

> It takes so little, so infinitely little, for a person to cross the border beyond which everything loses meaning: love, conviction, faith, history. Human life – and herein lies its secret – takes place in the immediate proximity of that border, even in direct contact with it; it is not miles away, but the fraction of an inch. (ibid., 206–7)

What becomes immediately evident in Kundera's writing above as well as elsewhere in the novel is the experience of movements across matter, metaphors, and memories, whereby the moving subject recognizes reality as a play between presence and absence. In structural as well as functional ways, this is quite similar to Palmer's idea of shading which foregrounds the location between event and imagination, between fact and fiction. Describing human life as an activity that inhabits the border between meaning and its loss, *The Book of Laughter* also articulates the proximity of desire and death in totalitarian systems of control. More importantly, laughter is used bidirectionally in Kundera's novel, as Mark Weeks argues, to 'forget the horrors of Soviet domination, but it is also projected as a joyful herald of the future' (Weeks 2005, 139). The experience of laughter in Kundera's novel thus also entails the production of forgetting as a subversively aspirational category, one which sometimes situates itself against forms of totalitarian control and identity preservation.

If metaphor may be defined as a compression of several semantic systems, laughter also emerges in Kundera's work as a compression of several orders of time 'through the acceleration of joyfully purposeful movements' (ibid., 140). Such movements merge remembering and forgetting in ways which endorse existential experiences that undercut politics of control and coercion, producing and promoting in their wake a laughter of 'willed delusion' (ibid., 142). More importantly, like the medium of fiction itself, Kundera's vision of laughter produces an order of ambivalence that 'precludes some absolute subscription to pessimism, optimism, or endless momentum' (ibid., 147). This non-committal quality of laughter in Kundera's work is precisely what makes it political and ambivalently subversive in scope, whereby non-subscription to any absolute or monolithic mode of reaction makes laughter functionally similar to forgetting. For if forgetting is an interruption to recollection or reconstruction, it also informs such processes cognitively as well as collectively. Likewise, laughter in Kundera is often an interruption in meaning making and dissemination, while also emerging as the only available agentic activity to produce and preserve memories in a world of chaos and totalitarian coercion. The title of Kundera's work evokes as well as equates laughter and forgetting, while also underlining how these two activities may be inscribed in a book of fiction, the medium of fiction offering a performative mix of fact and fabulation. This mix is historicized as well as characterized by a compulsive condition in Kundera's novel, a form of self-serving solipsism which emerges as the most agentic instrument against instruments of inscription and erasure. Connected to writing is also the act of remembering whereby the textuality of inscription and reiteration situates itself against the forces of forgetting induced and necessitated by states of censorship and surveillance. Writing thus emerges as an act of production as well as self-preservation, whereby what is remembered and represented is often situated outside of the dominant discourse and dissemination of knowledge. *The Book of Laughter and Forgetting* displays and dramatizes how knowledge as an ontological category is material, metaphoric, and metonymic in quality – encoded, effaced, and consumed by complex forms of forgetting and remembering.

The play between the politics of forgetting and the forgetting of politics is immediately embodied in part 6 of Kundera's novel in the figure of Gustav Husak, appointed by Russia in 1969 as the seventeenth president of Czechoslovakia, one who is commonly called the 'president of forgetting'. Addressing a group of children in a section in *The Book of Laughter and Forgetting*, Husak calls them the future of the country, while also advising them to never look back (Kundera 1982, 173–74). As Ellen Pifer argues, the *infantocracy* symbolized by a state forbidden to remember its past is foregrounded in the addressed children not experienced enough to form a strong and stable memory (Pifer 1992, 87). Therefore, bestowing a future-looking status on the chosen children, appropriately articulated by a political figure famed for his erasure of the past, is in alignment with the politically induced forms of forgetting in Kundera's book. With no 'burden of memory', childhood emerges in *The Book of Laughter and Forgetting* as the chosen 'image of the future' (Kundera 1982, 186–87), exhibiting how effacement and erasure of undesirable information and history are embodied as well as politicized. At a broader discursive level, it is also emblematic of a strategic vision of a future which is mindless in its production and consumption of collective amnesia whereby the 'contemporary culture risks losing not only its collective memory but the very source of individual identity' (Pifer 1992, 87). Memory and its loss affect individual identity at a cultural as well as a corporeal level in Kundera's novel, manifested in the metaphor of *shrinking*. Thus, as the character Tamina realizes with increasing frequency in *The Book of Laughter and Forgetting*, 'the sum total of her being is no more than what she sees in the distance, behind her. And as her past begins to shrink, disappear, fall apart, Tamina begins shrinking and blurring' (Kundera 1982, 86). Shrinking emerges as an epistemic as well as a corporeal condition in Kundera's novel, an interruption followed by disorientation and reorientation which are spatiotemporal in quality, affecting the subject's situatedness as well as embodied engagement in their social and cognitive schema. Blurring appears as a similar cognitive and corporeal crisis in *The Book of Laughter and Forgetting*, affecting the subject's recognition of reality and often manifesting in condensed and confused acts of remembrance. It also emerges as a natural response to state-induced forms of forgetting, whereby the remembering subjects transpose and transport themselves by deliberately mixing and merging several and different orders of space and time.

In part 2 of *The Book of Laughter and Forgetting*, Karel's ageing Mother moves to and inhabits an imagined past as 'tanks of a huge neighboring country came and occupied their country', producing a numbed fear which was 'so great, so terrible, that for a long time no one could think about anything else' (Kundera 1982, 40). Against the current reality of political terror and territorialization, the human subjects appear to have 'moved on to the different world' of a second and reimagined childhood, emerging as a 'different order of creature: smaller, lighter, more easily blown away' (ibid., 42). The textuality of memory and remembering is foregrounded as well as informed by absences in *The Book of Laughter and Forgetting*, manifested performatively in Mama's recitation of a patriotic poem whose last stanza she had forgotten and her insertion of lines 'about a Christmas tree and the star of Bethlehem' (ibid., 63) which nobody notices. The original experience of the forgotten stanza appears to Mama when she was in school, and this story of forgetting is retold and in turn forgotten several times in Kundera's novel. Shrinking and shrunkenness appear in Kundera's novel as forms of *corporeal compression* that also compress memory and modes of remembering, incorporating fantasies of pasts which are integrated imaginatively. Later in *The Book of Laughter and Forgetting*, Karel looks at Mama and feels that 'all her life has been a slow process of shrinkage' (ibid., 72), which is a move towards dimensionless-ness with old age as well as an 'optical illusion' (ibid., 72) due to the distance between the figures. The sense of shrunkenness as compression of temporal frames also transforms into an experience of imaginative liberation in Kundera's novel as the character Karel recalls an erotic figure from his childhood memory and realizes that 'beauty is an abolition of chronology and a rebellion against time' (ibid., 73). Beauty as an emotional experiential category is often a subversive instrument in *The Book of Laughter and Forgetting*, producing in its wake a formal fictional method which 'flagrantly juxtaposes historical reportage and documentary with the symbolic landscape of fantasy and fable' (Pifer 1992, 92).

The Book of Laughter and Forgetting begins with a description of a performatively mutable mode of memory that also highlights the textuality and entanglement of remembering and forgetting at broader political levels. It depicts a scene from the Old Town Square in Prague in February 1948 when the communist leader Klement Gottwald steps out of a Baroque palace to address a crowd of hundreds of thousands gathered to greet him. Bareheaded in falling snow, Gottwald is given a fur hat by his comrade Clementis as the former spoke to the massive crowd at a heavily photographed moment 'when the history of Communist Bohemia began' (Kundera 1982, 3). Kundera's narrator emphasizes how the fetishization of this moment takes place through propaganda photography which shows the spectacle of Gottwald addressing the crowd. Four years later, Clementis is executed on charges of sedition, and the same propaganda section seeks to efface all traces of his historical presence from public memory and photography. Consequently, Gottwald now appears alone in the same photograph addressing the crowd while 'Nothing remains of Clementis but the fur hat on Gottwald's head' (ibid., 4). The drama depicts the mutable as well as the metonymic quality of memory in complex political settings whereby identities appear as well as disappear in selective fragments in collective imagination. It also displays the entanglement of encoding and effacement that informs complex orders of remembering in private intimate spaces as well as in public discourses, highlighted by Eric Berlatsky's examination of the novel which shows how memory 'is inextricable from textuality and can itself be a mode of political oppression' (Berlatsky 2003, 102). Kundera's novel highlights how the encoding of memory is also an effacement, sometimes simultaneously, and how both operate through forms of physical as well as epistemic violence. Thus, later in the novel, Milan Hübl, a dissident historian displaced by the President of Forgetting Husak exclaims: 'You begin to liquidate a people . . . by taking away its memory. You destroy its books, its culture, its history. . . . Then the people slowly begins to forget what it is and what it was. The world at large forgets it faster' (Kundera 1982, 218). Forgetting thus appears in Kundera's work as an act of liquidation and destruction which is also one of manipulative production, enmeshed with the politics of privilege informing the construction and consumption of memory, history, and knowledge, through censorship, silence, and slow time. Slowness appears in *The Book of Laughter and Forgetting* sometimes as a strategy of remembrance, in resonance with Kundera's description of the same in the novel *Slowness*: 'There is a secret bond between slowness and memory, between speed and forgetting' (Kundera 1996, 34). Such slowness situates itself against the force of forgetting which 'hinges on the logic of speed and watered-down but widely marketable versions of history' (Kovacevic 2006, 635).

Against such politics and production of forgetting, the figure of Mirek in *The Book of Laughter and Forgetting* situates the slowed-down personal memory against forgetting as a 'struggle of man against power' (Kundera 1982, 4) and keeps all his correspondences – from personal to intimate ones – as an instrument to internalize information and preferred identity formation. This corresponds to a different description of memory and history respectively, with the latter emerging as 'the reconstruction, always problematic and incomplete, of what is no longer', while memory is 'a perpetually actual phenomenon, a bond tying us to the eternal present' (Nora 1989, 8). The organicity of memory and the discursivity of history are frequently contrasted in Kundera's novel, which also depicts how both categories (memory and history) may be mutated and manipulated by the brain and the powers that be. More significantly, *The Book of Laughter and Forgetting* offers a tragicomic tale of human freedom and its absence in the face of political totalitarianism and information control, whereby personal memory with all its unreliability becomes the only available instrument to embed and enact agency. Depicting a state of coercion and consent manipulation, Czechoslovakia in Kundera's novel exemplifies Roland Barthes's notion that '[h]istorical discourse does not follow the real; rather, it only signifies it, endlessly reiterating that it happened' (Barthes 1967, 73–74) without empirically engaging with any need to really validate it. In the section titled 'Lost Letters', Mirek's memory emerges not only as a cognitive function but as a vital existential experience which is also selective, textual, and constructed in quality. Thus his 'connection to his life was that of a sculptor to his statue or a novelist to his novel' (Kundera 1982, 15), highlighting issues of authorship and authority associated with memory, especially when state-induced forms of forgetting operationalize and shape similar states of censorship.

Photographs, notebooks, and journals play key roles in Kundera's novel as artefacts and material markers for abstract emotions and recollections. However, instead of the auratic quality of photography as a mode of preservation, *The Book of Laughter and Forgetting* displays and dramatizes the mutability and materiality in such processes of preservation, whereby photographs can encode as well as efface, as evinced in the very opening of the novel where Clementis's image is subsequently excluded and deleted from public records. This makes photography an effective instrument in reconstruction and re-creation whereby 'the line between memory and photography blurs' (Rugg 1997, 23), and by extension, remembered subjectivity emerges as a 'prosthetic process, with external (and manipulatable) items like photographs and journals being indispensable in the construction of the self' (Berlatsky 2003, 117). Kundera emphasizes the textuality of memory and the incompleteness of its inscription through the metafictional characterization of Tamina who managed to reconstruct memories in her head but failed to arrange those in the right sequence on the notebook page as the 'chronological order was irremediably lost' (Kundera 1982, 117). Tamina's presence as a hyper-fictionalized figure (she is introduced and described as a purely fictional character by Kundera) lends special currency to the textuality and materiality of the remembering process. Such textuality and materiality emerge as a spatiotemporal framework in Kundera's novel, an experiential location situated against the forces of forgetting. Thus Tamina 'wants to have her notebooks so that the flimsy framework of events, as she has constructed them in her school notebook, will be provided with walls and become a house she can live in' (Kundera 1982, 119). The ontology and experience of the self in *The Book of Laughter and Forgetting* is thus a play of matter, metaphor, and memory, whereby presence is performative as well as being informed by absence, whereby remembering is also a function of forgetting.

The centrality of playful imagination in the novel is most immediately instantiated by the rejection of all grand signifiers of referentiality in political as well as in intimate spaces. Instead, the novel offers a process of rewritings and reinscriptions through which the self is produced and reproduced. Connected to this is the issue of identity which too emerges as a playful prosthetic process of imaginative integration whereby all claims to objective history and memory-knowledge are dramatized and deconstructed. Remembered identities operate as textual, metonymic, and affective processes in Kundera's novel, as evinced in Mama's deliberate refusal to disbelieve the anachronism associated with her version of reciting a patriotic poem in school and her preference to hold on to her own version of the event as the *official truth*, as that situates her sense of self through preferred modes of memory and reinscription. Equally, Karel's knowledge of Mama's flawed retelling does not preclude but rather produces affective possibilities as 'he is inspired to a rebellion against time' and 'symbolically keeps the past, however flawed, alive in the present' (Kovacevic 2006, 647). Flawed and manipulative memory appears as a deliberate and recursive trope in Kundera's Czechoslovakia fictionalized in *The Book of Laughter and Forgetting*, operating against the powers of amnesia and experienced often as the complex emotion of *litost*, 'a state of torment created by the sudden sight of one's own misery' (Kundera 1982, 167). Such despair often penetrates human subjects and produces acts of remembering, as in the fictional figure of Tamina who finds herself in such sadness that 'she was thrilled suddenly, surprisingly, to find in it a lost fragment of her past' (ibid., 229). The ambivalent appearance of loss and laughter, of despair and discovery in memory, in Kundera's novel makes it a complex work about borders and border crossing. *The Book of Laughter and Forgetting* foregrounds the medium of fiction and fictional figures in its depiction of the liminal location between remembering and un-remembering, between matter and metaphor, in its description of the border which 'is not a product of repetition' but rather 'is covered with dust, and repetition is like a hand whisking away dust' (ibid., 298). In doing so, it brings into play tragedy and comedy, fact and fabulation, encoding and erasure, also highlighting how these entanglements inform identities and identity formations in intimate as well as politically charged locations.

Kundera's novel shows how similar strategies of remembering and forgetting operate across broader political and personal orders. Thus, just like the Communist Party in Czechoslovakia effaces, rewrites, and produces absence apropos of the fallen comrade Clementis, Mirek attempts to efface all traces of his former lover Zedna 'from the photograph of his life not because he had not loved her but because he had' and, in the process, 'rewrote history just like the Communist Party, like all political parties, like all peoples, like mankind' (ibid., 30–31). This underlines how institutional and intimate forms of forgetting and remembering both rely on selective production and preservation apropos of identity formation and re-formation. As in the powerful political forces informing identity production and preservation, memory in the intimate emotional space is never innocent but also operates through strategic reification that corresponds to preferred emotions and orders of imagination. This is performatively evinced in Mama's retellings and reinscriptions of her youthful patriotism and Karel's erotic objectification of Mama's friend Nora. Both rely on and construct their remembered nationalist and erotic identities through selective emplotment and narrative functions that draw more on manipulative imagination than on empirical information. In keeping with the material and metonymic markers of memory production in Kundera's novel, the section 'Lost Letters II' depicts the character of Tamina who attempts to reconstruct her identity as well as remembrance of her dead husband Pavel through notebooks and love letters. The inscriptive quality of memory and remembering is highlighted here in Tamina's mental drawings of her dead husband from his old passport photo and projecting those images onto every man she sees subsequently. However, the repetitions and reinscriptions in Kundera's novel do not necessarily lead to consolidation of memory but rather sometimes contribute to its slippage, as in the case of the deliberately fictionalized character Tamina struggling to reconstruct her dead husband in her head as the 'colors her memory supplied were unreal, and with such colors there was no way to simulate human skin' (ibid., 116). This underlines the experience of memory as forgetting which runs across Kundera's novel, as Tamina's 'efforts only showed that her husband's image was irrevocably slipping away' (ibid., 117), the loss of memory subsequently depleting her sense of selfhood and identity. Her eventual retreat from the real world and merging with the dreamlike world of children further dramatize the depletion of embodiment and agency associated with the loss of memory in *The Book of Laughter and Forgetting*.

As Maria Nemcova Banerjee argues in her study of the *terminal paradoxes* in Kundera's novels, *The Book of Laughter and Forgetting* describes how while 'the Prague of lived experience disappears in the recessional of memory, distance creates an inner intensity that abolishes the borderline between the fantastic and the real, muddles time' (Banerjee 1990, 66). Time appears as a mimetic activity in Kundera's novel, which also showcases how memory as negotiation with temporality produces its paradoxes and absences. If one examines *The Book of Laughter and Forgetting* as a work of fiction that unleashes 'the emotional power of memory in the *anachronistic imagination*' (Banerjee 1990, 2), such reading also reveals how Kundera's fiction engages with the possibilities and the precarity of remembering. Like Manto's short stories on the violence of Partition, Kundera's *The Book of Laughter and Forgetting* situates memory and the activity of remembering as the only available instruments to enact agency at a time where human life, its value, and its dignity are increasingly depleted. Both Manto and Kundera rely on and exhibit the unique medium of fiction as a fluid framework to focalize human stories of love and loss in times of unbearable suffering. Thus focalization, narrative condensation, metaphors, and inner monologues become key qualities through which remembering minds are depicted as producing memory as well as its slippages and absences, corresponding to complex entanglements of embodiment, intentionality, and intersubjective agency. Such stories of reality and imaginative possibility, of memory, fantasy, and liminal identities played out against violent political backdrops emerge with renewed relevance in the world we inhabit and internalize today.

REFERENCES

Ahmad, Aijaz. 1992. *In Theory: Classes, Nations, Literatures*. London: Verso.

Amin, Shahid. 1995. *Event, Metaphor, Memory: Chauri Chaura, 1922–1992*. Delhi: Oxford University Press.

Anderson, Benedict. 1983. *Imagined Communities: Reflections on the Origin and Spread of Nationalism*. London: Verso.

Arendt, Hannah. 1973. *The Origins of Totalitarianism*. San Diego: Harvest Books.

Assmann, Aleida, and Linda Shortt, eds. 2012. *Memory and Political Change*. London: Palgrave Macmillan.

Augé, Marc. 1995. *Non-Places: Introduction to an Anthropology of Supermodernity*. Translated by John Howe. London: Verso.

———. 2004. *Oblivion*. Translated by Marjolijn de Jager. Minneapolis: University of Minnesota.
Banerjee, Maria Nemcova. 1990. *The Novels of Milan Kundera*. New York: Grove Weidenfeld.
Barthes, Roland. 1967. 'Le discours de l'histoire'. *Social Science Information* 6(4): 65–75.
———. 1977. *Roland Barthes by Roland Barthes*. London: Vintage.
Berlatsky, Eric. 2003. 'Memory as Forgetting: The Problem of the Postmodern in Kundera's "The Book of Laughter and Forgetting" and Spiegelman's "Maus"'. *Cultural Critique* 55:101–51.
Bhalla, Alok. 2001. 'The Politics of Translation: Manto's Partition Stories and Khalid Hasan's English Version'. *Social Scientist* 29(7/8): 19–38.
Bradbury, Peter. 1992. 'Sexuality and Male Violence'. In *Men, Sex and Relationships: Writings from Achilles Heel*, edited by Victor J. Seidler, 156–71. London: Routledge.
Burke, Michael, and Emily T. Troscianko, eds. 2017. *Cognitive Literary Science: Dialogues between Literature and Cognition*. London: Oxford University Press.
Calvino, Italo. 1986. *The Uses of Literature: Essays*. Translated by Patrick Creagh. San Diego: Harcourt Brace Jovanovich.
Cassirer, Ernst. 1944. *An Essay on Man*. New Haven, CT: Yale University Press.
Clark, Andy. 1998. 'Where Brain, Body, and World Collide'. *Daedalus: Journal of the American Academy of Arts and Sciences* 127(2): 257–80.
Daiya, Kavita. 2008. *Violent Belongings: Partition, Gender, and National Culture in Postcolonial India*. London: Temple University Press.
Damasio, Antonio R. 2000. *The Feeling of What Happens: Body, Emotion and the Making of Consciousness*. New York: Vintage.
Daniel, Valentine. 1996. *Charred Lullabies: Chapters in an Anthropography of Violence*. Princeton, NJ: Princeton University Press.
Das, Veena. 1996. 'Language and Body: Transactions in the Construction of Pain'. *Daedalus: Journal of the American Academy of Arts and Sciences* 125(1): 67–91.
Draaisma, Douwe. 2001. *Metaphors of Memory: A History of Ideas about the Mind*. Cambridge: Cambridge University Press.
Eichenbaum, Howard. 2012. *The Cognitive Neuroscience of Memory: An Introduction*. New York: Oxford University Press.
Gazzaniga, Michael S. 2005. *The Mind's Past*. Berkeley: University of California Press.
Gopal, Priyamvada. 2002. 'Bodies Inflicting Pain: Masculinity, Morality and Cultural Identity in Manto's "Cold Meat"'. In *The Partitions of Memory: The Afterlife of the Division of India*, edited by Suvir Kaul. New Delhi: Permanent Black.
Herman, David. 2017. *Storytelling and the Sciences of Mind*. Cambridge, MA: MIT Press.
Hogan, Patrick Colm. 2017. 'Simulation and the Structure of Emotional Memory'. In *Cognitive Literary Science: Dialogues between Literature and Cognition*, edited by Michael Burke and Emily T. Troscianko, 113–34. London: Oxford University Press.
Jalal, Ayesha. 2013. *The Pity of Partition: Manto's Life, Times, and Work across the India-Pakistan Divide*. New York: Princeton University Press.

Kandel, Eric R., and Larry R. Squire. 2009. *Memory: From Mind to Molecules*. Greenwood Village, CO: Roberts.
Kaur, Navdip. 2011. 'Violence and Migration: A Study of Killing in the Trains during the Partition of Punjab in 1947'. *Proceedings of the Indian History Congress* 72(1): 947–54.
Kermode, Frank. 1967. *The Sense of an Ending*. Oxford: Oxford University Press.
Kovacevic, Natasa. 2006. 'History on Speed: Media and the Politics of Forgetting in Milan Kundera's Slowness'. *Modern Fiction Studies* 52(3): 634–55.
Kundera, Milan. 1982. *The Book of Laughter and Forgetting*. London: Faber & Faber.
———. 1996. *Slowness*. London: Faber & Faber.
———. 2015. *Testaments Betrayed: An Essay in Nine Parts*. Translated by Linda Asher. New York: HarperCollins.
LeDoux, Joseph. 2014. *Synaptic Self: How Our Brains Become Who We Are*. New York: Penguin.
———. 2016. *Anxious: Using the Brain to Understand and Treat Fear and Anxiety*. New York: Penguin.
Lodge, David. 2002. *Consciousness and the Novel: Connected Essays*. London: Secker & Warburg.
Malabou, Catherine. 2012. *The New Wounded: From Neurosis to Brain Damage*. Translated by Steven Miller. New York: Fordham University Press.
Manto, Saadat Hasan. 2008. *Bitter Fruit: The Very Best of Saadat Hasan Manto*. Edited by Khalid Hasan. New Delhi: Penguin India.
Mellor, Philip, and Chris Schilling, eds. 1997. *Re-forming the Body: Religion, Community and Modernity*. London: Sage.
Menon, Jisha. 2012. *The Performance of Nationalism*. California: Cambridge University Press.
Neumann, Birgit. 2008. 'The Literary Representation of Memory'. In *Cultural Memory Studies: An International and Interdisciplinary Handbook*, edited by Astrid Erll and Ansgar Nunning, 333–44. Berlin: Walter de Gruyter.
Nora, Pierre. 1989. 'Between Memory and History: Les lieux de memoire'. *Representations* 26:7–25.
Palmer, Alan. 2004. *The Fictional Mind*. Lincoln: University of Nebraska Press.
Pandey, Gyanendra. 2002. *Remembering Partition: Violence, Nationalism and History in India*. New Delhi: Cambridge University Press.
Parui, Avishek. 2015. 'Memory, Nation and the Crisis of Location in Saadat Hasan Manto's "Toba Tek Singh"'. *Short Fiction in Theory and Practice* 5(1–2): 56–67.
Pifer, Ellen. 1992. '"The Book of Laughter and Forgetting": Kundera's Narration against Narration'. *Journal of Narrative Technique* 22(2): 84–96.
Polvinen, Merja. 2017. 'Cognitive Science and the Double Vision of Fiction'. In *Cognitive Literary Science: Dialogues between Literature and Cognition*, edited by Michael Burke and Emily T. Troscianko, 135–50. London: Oxford University Press.
Ricoeur, Paul. 1984. *Time and Narrative*. Vol. 1. Translated by Kathleen McLaughlin. Chicago: University of Chicago Press.
———. 1986. *Time and Narrative*. Vol. 2. Translated by Kathleen McLaughlin. Chicago: University of Chicago Press.
———. 2004. *Memory, History, Forgetting*. Chicago: University of Chicago Press.

Rothberg, Michael. 2009. *Multidirectional Memory: Remembering the Holocaust in the Age of Decolonization*. New York: Stanford University Press.
Rugg, Linda Haverty. 1997. *Picturing Ourselves: Photography and Autobiography*. Chicago: University of Chicago Press.
Saint, Tarun. 2012. 'The Long Shadow of Manto's Partition Narratives: Fictive Testimony to Historical Trauma'. *Social Scientist* 40(11/12): 53–62.
Sarkar, Sumit. 1983. *Modern India: 1885–1947*. New Delhi: Macmillan.
Schachter, Daniel L. 1997. *Searching for Memory*. New York: Basic Books.
Smith, Sidonie A. 2003. 'Material Selves: Bodies, Memory and Autobiographical Narrating'. In *Narrative and Consciousness: Literature, Psychology, and the Brain*, edited by Gary D. Fireman, Ted E. McVay Jr, and Owen J. Flanagan, 86–111. Oxford: Oxford University Press.
Tamm, Marek, ed. 2019. *Juri Lotman – Culture, Memory and History: Essays in Cultural Semiotics*. Translated by Brian James Baer. London: Palgrave Macmillan.
Tasheer, Aatish. 2010. *Manto: Selected Stories*. Noida: Random House.
Thomas, Alfred. 2015. 'Kafka's Statue: Memory and Forgetting in Postsocialist Prague'. *Revue des études slaves* 86(1/2): 157–69.
Troscianko, Emily T. 2014. *Kafka's Cognitive Realism*. London: Routledge.
Weeks, Mark. 2005. 'Milan Kundera: A Modern History of Humor amid the Comedy of History'. *Journal of Modern Literature* 28(3): 130–48.
Wertsch, James V. 2012. 'Deep Memory and Narrative Templates: Conservative Forces in Collective Memory'. In *Memory and Political Change*, edited by Aleida Assmann and Linda Shortt, 173–85. London: Palgrave Macmillan.
Zohar, Danah. 1989. *The Quantum Self: Consciousness, Physics and the New World View*. London: Bloomsbury.

3

Culture, Consumption, and Technology

In an essay titled 'Literature and Technology', the American formalist critic Cleanth Brooks offers a humanistic approach to the dialogues and possible collaborations between literature as an art form and the machines of technology in modernity. Drawing on Matthew Arnold's notion of poetry as the voice of humanity while also articulating its philosophical and political limits, Brooks takes as a case study Thomas Hardy's poem 'The Conversations of the Twain', which refers to the sinking of the *Titanic*. What arrests Brooks's attention is the fact that Hardy chooses not to mention any date or fact about the accident which was the first defined disaster consumed by global media. Instead, as Brooks examines, '[w]hat evidently caught Hardy's imagination was that the ship and the iceberg had, with precision timing, arrived at the same spot at the same instant, just as if destiny had employed a split-second timetable for the whole affair' (Brooks 1985, 92). Brooks's new critical reading of Hardy's poem about the sinking of *Titanic*, about a natural disaster involving a massive and magnificent machine, is an interesting pointer to the propensity to create and consume stories around events and facts, something Brooks also identifies in the mass culture characterizing 'the situation comedies of the TV shows or the gossip columns in the magazines and newspapers' (ibid., 91). Thus Hardy's poem talks less about the dates and weight of the ship and more about how the shipyard in Belfast and the iceberg in the coast of Greenland get metaphorically as well as experientially connected through this disaster. The choice and bias of representation in poetry – and by extension in literature – of a technological-natural accident which was also a global cultural event is reflective of how matter, metaphor, and memory merge to comment on real events involving humans and machines as well as to recreate the same through the focalized imagination informing fiction.

Literature's relationship with technology – especially in terms of how it acts as a representational medium for human-machine interfaces involved in embodiment and cognitive processes – is often reflective of complex cultural vectors. For if culture may be defined and characterized by the production, reception, and internalization of its contemporary technology, literature's descriptions of human engagements and negotiations with machines produce possibilities of reimagining of as well as offering insights into lived experiences with tools of technology. As Greg Kennedy argues in his ontological study of waste, technology, body, and trash, 'the technology of literature produces metaphysics through the effects it works in and on the human body' (Kennedy 2007, 39), whereby the 'literary technology' (ibid., 40) as a special system of signs 'provides the means to be-in-the-world with diminished physical presence and engagement' (ibid., 40). The formal fluidity and plasticity of fiction as a medium dramatizes as well as sometimes deconstructs human connect to and consumption of technology which can create utopian as well as dystopian possibilities, often blurring borderlines between the two world orders. If culture itself may be defined as a technology – a mutable machine that produces, contains, and consumes material, organic, inorganic, and abstract signifiers and their value systems – literature's representation of the same may reveal insights about how such processes are internalized as well as interrupted.

As emergent as well as connective categories, technologies that augment reality and experientiality redefine and recalibrate corporeality, consciousness, and their associated identities which are phenomenal as well as discursive in quality. Fiction and literary representations of technology-navigation are capable of describing the unique location of the human mind and embodied experience by combining multiple focal points and experiential positions. In describing and dramatizing human embeddedness in machinic networks, literary and fictional narratives foreground some key experiential and conceptual categories such as intersubjectivity, embodiment, and empathy. The stylized and defamiliarizing medium of representation in fiction is uniquely suited to represent the hyperreality and simulated states of cognition, emotion, and experience characterizing human-machine entanglements. As the poet and critic John Hollander argues, the medium of literature itself may be read as a kind of 'primal software' through which technology finds its fullest and most complex representational voice (Hollander 1997, 1248). This takes place, Hollander goes on to state, due to literature's unique ability to articulate 'ad-hoc and apragmatic conceptual schemes and fictional histories' (ibid., 1251) apropos of historical machines and material reality. Technology's potential to produce disruption and literature's ability to generate defamiliarization thus find complex convergences at narrative as well as experiential levels. Especially pertinent in this field of study is literature's ability to animate or *give life* to inorganic forms of matter through focalization and imaginative retellings, and in the process deconstruct common presuppositions about embodiment, empathy, and agency.

In his 1988 essay 'Technologies of the Self', Michel Foucault defines and delineates four different types of technology while also highlighting how these rarely work separately or independently of each other. The first constitutes the technologies of production 'which permit us to produce, transform, or manipulate things' (Foucault 1988, 17). The second type involves the technologies of sign systems which permit us 'to use signs, meanings, symbols, significations' (ibid., 17). The third kind constitutes the technologies of power which are used in the process of 'objectivation of the subject' (ibid., 17). The fourth and final form Foucault defines is the technologies of the self which constitute the means and methods through which subjects attempt to 'transform themselves in order to attain a certain state of happiness, purity, wisdom, perfection, or immortality' (ibid., 18). These self-enhancing technologies are embedded as well as extended in quality, characterized by internalizations which are private and existential as well as by more public performances in shared social spaces. Foucault's examination of the technologies of domination and those of the self extends to a study of governmentality and emerges with renewed relevance in the real-virtual world we inhabit today. More immediately, the blurring of borderlines between technologies of production, power, sign, and self serves as a pointer to the postmodern posthuman orders where the moving and experiencing subject is also simultaneously an object, where fantasy and commodity meet and merge in states of becoming and un-becoming. Literature and literary representations of the various orders of technology are of special significance as a representational medium of these various states. For literature too, like Foucault's classified types of technology, operates as well as dramatizes interconnected orders of production, power, sign, and self in a fluid framework with a rich range of focal points and perspectival positions. The ontology of literature and the literary medium constitutes sign as well as self as interconnected categories informing fictional productions and reconstructions, with matter, metaphor, and memory emerging as entangled entities as well as an interplay of experiences.

Through complex and defamiliarized descriptions of space, self, intimacy, and temporality, literature – especially the kind depicting human engagements with technology – is able to offer original perspectives on how acts of production, inscription, installation, and reiteration correspond to different orders of embodiment which are embedded as well as enactive in quality. In such depictions, consciousness emerges as a marker of the fluid and moving self as well as a consolidated commodity, sometimes simultaneously. With its play of signs which inform the self, while also depicting how the self is capable of recreating and recalibrating such signs through processes of emplotment, literature and fiction about technology underline as well as problematize the matrix of minds, materiality, discourse markers, and affectivity. Such articulations appropriate imaginative remappings of the real orders of experience, ones involving reorientations through recognition, commenting on contemporary engagement with technology as well as showcasing futuristic situations which may appear as simultaneously utopian and dystopian. Literature's ability to draw on as well as to imaginatively recreate known narratives about self and technology makes it a unique medium for representing minds, machines, and memory in their various states of entanglement, excitability, and interactivity. Like Foucault's four types of technology, literature about culture, consumption, and machines provides fresh perspectives on how power, production, sign, and self are constantly encoded and re-encoded through various orders of embodiment and knowledge.

This chapter aims to examine literature as an imaginative exercise of human mind and materials whereby intersubjectivity emerges as an interactive activity through an entanglement of matter, metaphor, and memory, which is the principal subject of enquiry in this book. For if technology may be defined and described as a remapping of materiality, it can also emerge as a pointer to the cognitive disruption and defamiliarization of lived reality, as well as an extension and augmentation of the same, whereby the aim is 'to overlay our experience of the physical world with layers of personalized digital information' (Clark 2003, 52). At an ontological as well as a functional level, literature performs a similar role apropos of materiality and experience, with its blurring of borderlines between subjects and objects, mind, matter, and metaphor. More importantly, like the tools of augmented reality (AR), literary representations too can 'add new layers of meaning and functionality to the daily world itself' (ibid., 53) through a process of defamiliarization and recalibration, with an interplay of figurative, focalized, and literal registers. For a work of fiction is both an object as well as a remapping of subjects through a creative combination of information and imagination. In essence, literature may be examined as a creative treatment and representation of minds and materials which inform lived experience as well as social and cultural materiality. If objects carry social as well as semantic significance, material engagement theory (MET) may be interestingly mapped as an interpretive framework onto a study of culture, mind, and technology. Examining technology as an instrument that effectively as well as affectively informs cognition and embodiment, a theory of materials determining culture and cognitive acts offers a fuller understanding of how the mind processes machines and objects of significance.

Drawing on Arjun Appadurai's seminal work on the social and semantic significance of things which argues that 'all things are congealed moments in a longer social trajectory' (Sutton 2008, 41), MET examines cognition and memory as affective as well as material processes of investment and engagement in social networks of extension and exchange. Appadurai's work on objects and subjects is of special significance here as he argues that while theoretically human minds invest semantic significance to things, 'from a *methodological* point of view it is the things-in-motion that illuminate their human and social context' (Appadurai 1986, 5). Objects establish a semiotic relationship in cultural and social structures in this philosophy as they move from being just a commodity or a product to 'essentially a sign in a system of signs and status' (ibid., 45), which in turn is reflective of how 'capitalism represents not simply a techno-economic design, but a complex cultural system with a very special history in the modern West' (ibid., 48–49). Technology as redesigned materiality and the reception of the same in the cultural imaginary thus form a major theme in material engagement theory. Literature's location in the cultural matrix as a special representative medium capable of describing the embedded as well as the enactive orders of consciousness and the *situated subject* amid materiality is of unique significance in this study. Appadurai's thesis on things and their re-formation of the subject carries special resonance in a hyper-technological imaginary where interactivity precedes and sometimes supersedes intersubjectivity. This entanglement of subject and object positions generates a cognitive reframing which often informs fiction about technology and its cultural consumption. Literary depictions and representations of technology and the technological imaginary are thus frequently reflective of how the technologized self is not a monolithic seamless entity but one informed and re-formed by an interplay of installations and interruptions. In such an interplay, the human emerges not simply as an organism but also as an 'abstract machine, which captures, transforms and produces interconnections' (Braidotti 2002, 226). This is explored and described by Arthur Kroker in an essay titled 'Panic Value' in *Life after Postmodernism*, which examines the move from the Cartesian subject to a 'fractal subjectivity' characterized by 'parallel processing as the epistemological form of postmodern consciousness', which is also associated with the production of 'toxic bodies and designer aesthetics as its necessary conditions of operation' (Kroker 1987, 181). The fiction about body and technology thus often dramatizes as well as deconstructs the borders between the real and the virtual, showcasing how the fractal subject operates and experiences through a mix of mind and machines.

If the technology of augmented and mixed reality blurs the borders between the real and the virtual, it also foregrounds the fact that our normal and normative understanding of the self and subjectivity often fails to engage with the inherent mutability which informs neural and cognitive processes. In this context, it is worth remembering that our assumption and awareness of corporeality and seamless embodiment is actually 'an entirely transitory internal construct that can be profoundly altered' and can thus unsettle the belief that the self 'is anchored to a single body that remains stable and permanent' (Ramachandran as cited in Clark 2003, 62). This produces what Andy Clark defines as the *negotiable body* whereby the cognitive schema of the subject emerges both opportunistic and occlusive, with plastic brains and hybrid minds (Clark 2003, 59). What informs this theory is the notion of the mutable and manipulatable brain, whereby the image of the body emerges as 'a mental construct, open to continual renewal and reconfiguration' (ibid., 61) as the brain relies on '*perceived correlations*' (ibid., 61). MET builds on the theory that the human brain is 'both an artefact of culture and a cultural artefact' (Mithens and Parsons as cited in Malafouris 2013, 45). The concept of *metaplasticity* – the theory of a plastic mind endlessly enmeshed as well as extended to a plastic culture of codes and material reconfigurations – underlines an interactive engagement that produces intersubjectivity whereby the mind and matter enter into and establish a fluid framework of exchange. Originally a concept from neuroscience which describes activity-dependent neural changes, metaplasticity 'entails a change in the physiological or biochemical state of neurons or synapses that alters their ability to generate synaptic plasticity' (Wickliffe 2008, 387). This theory of plasticity producing plasticity has been drawn on in MET to describe the mind-matter entanglements in cultural and materialist frameworks, whereby cognition appears as an enactive method in which 'the brain, far from being a hard-wired modular organ, emerges as a dynamic co-evolutionary process of deep enculturation and material engagement' (Malafouris 2013, 45). Metaplasticity emerges as a neural as well as an extended cognitive category in MET whereby the plasticity of neural connections as well as synaptic assemblages determines cognition just like the plasticity of materials and minds involved in cultural coding and the production of values and meanings.

The affective economy between mind and matter in material engagement theory is established by the principle that '*cognition has no location*' and that cognition does not exist within a particular property but operates between properties, agents, and entities (ibid., 85). This fluid framework of mind and matter makes memory, storytelling, and sense making an interactive intersubjective phenomenon where the organic and the inorganic orders are asymmetrically entangled and enmeshed. More importantly, it underlines the distributive quality of technology and cognition alike, where the focus shifts from the body of the subject to the intercorporeal processes determining discourse networks and affective interchange and interactivity. This makes literature and the frame of fiction a unique form of retelling and representation whereby storytelling underlines the enactive mode of cognition informing fictional characters' embodiment through emplotment. This takes place largely due to the fictional production of meaning as 'the temporally emergent property of material engagement, the ongoing blending between the mental and the physical' (ibid., 117). This interplay of mindfulness, meaningfulness, and materiality through focalized narratives lends the literary form of representation a unique perspectival position to celebrate technology as well as to offer cautionary tales. More complexly, literature is also capable of assuming an ambivalent position which can accommodate and articulate both forms of responses whereby the matter and the metaphor of technology and technological materiality can establish complex cognitive associations and disruptions in *fictional minds*. What gets foregrounded in such representations is how objects and things can establish human associations as well as dramatize the *thingness* of things which depart from human control and establish agentic and ontological orders of their own. Fictional retellings and re-encodings with the thingness of things through an interplay of matter and metaphor help generate newer perspectives into how agency, empathy, and intersubjectivity operate across human as well as material networks.

MET's engagement with current cognitive theories on embodiment further accentuates a non-anthropocentric model of cognition where interactivity between mind and matter generates an intersubjective economy of metaphor and memory. For if memory as a cognitive activity draws on an engagement with materiality through the mind, it also produces a focalized and metonymic representation of matter in an embedded as well as an enactive process. This is examined by the cognitive philosopher Andy Clark who argues in favour of material agency and a move towards a non-anthropocentric approach in which 'the brain is revealed not as (primarily) the engine of reason or quiet deliberation, but as the organ of *environmentally situated control*' (Clark 2008, 10). Coining the term *wideware* to describe cognitive states which are intuitively environmental as well as play a function in an *extended cognitive process*, Clark defines human agency as mediated and generated by 'the ubiquitous devices of language, speech and text' (ibid., 13) whereby our 'cognitive profile is *essentially* the profile of an embodied and situated organism' (ibid., 14). The concept of the *situated brain* is central to Clark's cognitive theory, as is his notion of embodied, embedded, extended, and enactive cognition.

The neural and cognitive profile in Clark's study thus corresponds to the mutable materiality and shape of things around the subject and is a process as well as a product of material engagement. Clark's description of the two types of technology – the transparent and the opaque types – is of special significance here. While transparent technology ensures its own invisibility due to increasing internalization that may operate despite its complexities (Clark uses the example of how the hippocampus works for memory production without the subject's knowledge), opaque technology continues to foreground its own ontological density (Clark's example is that of the home PC which keeps crashing despite the subject's knowledge of its operational processes) through its potential for disruption (Clark 2003, 37–38). Correlating transparent technology with cognitive profiling, Clark describes how, at its highest form, the transparency in this technology becomes 'pseudo-neural' (ibid., 45) in the sense that it appears entirely aligned to the neural makeup of the experiencing subject. What paradoxically creates cognitive complexity for the subject is exactly this alignment with the neural makeup, as it produces difficulties in controlling the technology which can spiral away with an alternative order of embodiment with its interplay of opacity and transparency.

This materialist model of cognition may be extended to a study of memory as well, as evinced in the work of John Sutton who situates the concept of *complementarity* 'at the heart of distributed cognition' in order to underline how 'relations between agents and artefacts may be asymmetric and tangled in different ways and that such relations are often dynamically reconfigured or renegotiated over time' (Sutton 2008, 43). Central to Sutton's argument is the relativist positionality of objects and subjects and the blurred borders between the two categories during processes and moments of memory and cognition which foreground how 'changing media, objects, routines, institutions and practices have long been integral parts of the coordinated, interactive cognitive systems in which our characteristic plasticity is revealed, engaged and transformed' (ibid., 37–38). Such engagements which are neural and cognitive are shaped by the shapes surrounding the subject. Fiction's potential to *change the subject* and *orient the object* is of special significance here. For if subjects are formed and re-formed through an enactive process of encoding and engagement with materiality which in turn informs cognition and memory, fiction's ability to remap reality while also being embedded in language makes it a unique medium for *recognition through representation*. In particular, Sutton's notion of complementarity as an active engagement between agents and artefacts finds a complex representation in the field of fiction which dynamically defamiliarizes reality while also proffering possibilities involving imaginative re-creations. The *cognitive profiling* and plasticity performed by fiction operate through a distributive process whereby multiple minds and modes of cognition can be simultaneously accommodated and articulated. The fictional productions and representations of mindfulness and materiality often involve a renegotiation with matter and technology in ways which blur the borders between subjects and objects, making agency an intercorporeal interactive process of appropriation and action.

In close correspondence to material engagement theory, actor-network theory (ANT) examines the human-nonhuman interfaces that inform and influence the production and consumption of materials and their meanings. It proposes a semiotic structure of material correspondence which symmetrically incorporates human as well as nonhuman agents (Law as cited in Malafouris 2013, 123). ACT's theory of relationality offers a fluid framework for identity 'in order to focus on the multiplicity of mutually constitutive and positioning "actants" which together serve to hybridise agency' (Malafouris and Knappett 2008, 81). Bruno Latour's *Reassembling the Social: An Introduction to Actor-Network Theory* defines the *social* as a 'movement, a displacement, a transformation, a translation, an enrollment' (Latour 2005, 64–65) and the project of ANT as 'simply to extend the list and modify the shapes and figures of those assembled as participants and to design a way to make them act as a durable whole' (ibid., 72) in social structures of materialization. In such a theory, 'agency comes to be distributed across a network, inhering in the associations and relationships between entities, rather than in the entities themselves' (Knappett cited in Malafouris 2008, 127). Latour's metaphor of *reshuffling* is particularly pertinent in this work as the social is defined in ANT as 'a type of momentary association which is characterized by the way it gathers together into new shapes' (Latour 2005, 65). This association operating across objects and subjects, in Latour's study, becomes social at the 'brief moment when they are reshuffled together', as in the multiple reconfigurations and repackagings in a supermarket, the metaphor Latour uses (ibid., 65). Inherent in both MET and ACT is a call to move away from an anthropocentric understanding of the world and its material engagements and instead embrace a more inclusive plastic condition where actants and actions mix and merge in organic as well as in inorganic forms. This appears to anticipate and appropriate a more posthumanist perspective on materiality and its representation, which defamiliarizes commonly consumed reality and its presuppositions, producing in its wake a convergence with the fiction and philosophy of radical re-evaluations of subjectivity. In such a perspective, culture, cognition, and embodiment become activities whose ontological validation does not rest on the human agent alone but is distributed across a map of materials which inform as well as re-form the subject.

The fluidity of the re-radicalized subject informed as well as re-formed by technology is explored in the works of Rosi Braidotti, particularly in her examinations of metamorphoses and re-corporealization in the posthuman technological imaginary and its creation of *nomadic subjectivity*. This bears strong and complex resonance with some of the key tenets of material engagement theory, as examined earlier in this chapter. Particularly pertinent here is Braidotti's thesis on the entanglement of technology and the body and how cyberspace problematizes orders of embodiment in ways which are simultaneously subversive and hegemonic. This appears abundantly in Braidotti's *Metamorphoses: Towards a Materialist Theory of Becoming* (2002) where she examines how the 'teratological imaginary expresses the social, cultural, and symbolic mutations that are taking place around the phenomenon of techno-culture' whereby, following the electronic revolution, a 'disembodied gaze constitutes a collision of virtual spaces with which we co-exist in increasing degrees of intimacy' (Braidotti 2002, 181). Intimacy as an affective condition is significant in Braidotti's study, emerging less as an intersubjective and more as an interactive quality where mind and matter mix asymmetrically, generating and re-generating societal and experiential identities. This ontology and experience of intimacy through interactivity find complex and fuller forms of representation, in Braidotti's study, in special kinds of fiction, which move 'beyond the irreconcilable classical conflict between utopia and dystopia, moving instead towards heterotopia, the coexistence of mutually undermining meaning systems which point to the dissolution of the unitary notion of the subject' (ibid., 183).

Evident in Braidotti's examination here, and also elsewhere in similar philosophical engagements on fiction and technology, is the mobility of the subject moving in space and time, one which is always mutable and mutating. Fiction's ability to describe and further defamiliarize this mobility blurs the borderlines between the utopian and dystopian conditions created by technology and instead appropriates an order of ambivalence in relation to the subject's situatedness in an experiential engagement with machines. More significantly, and in keeping with the principal philosophical framework of this book, this reveals how the subject-object binary emerges as untenable in a teratological technological imaginary where mind, matter, and metaphors are entangled in a fluid economy of experientiality, interactivity, and affectivity. Fiction about technology and human interactivity thus offers, in Braidotti's study, a 'nomadic approach to contemporary creativity' which may emerge as simultaneously subversive and reflective of futuristic conditions in its 'disaggregations of humanistic subject-positions and values' (ibid., 200–201). What emerges in such representations is a symbiotic interplay where the human, the animal, the artefact, and the machine collude and collide with varying degrees of interconnectedness and intimacy. The nomadic and synthetic subject in Braidotti's study is a moving and mutable assemblage of mind and matter, consciousness and codes, co-inhabiting complex configurations of space and time with similar as well as dissimilar agents. This offers a ludic landscape of mutations and sensations whereby subjectivity emerges as a function of interstitiality and interactivity, producing a shared economy of affect and agency. This affective field of shared subjectivity, which animate as well as inanimate agents co-inhabit, receives representations in literary works where fictional characters, entities, and spaces are assembled through narrative codes and imaginative investments. Literature and literary representations therefore often emerge as entangled modes of empathy and agency through different focal points and existential perspectives. More importantly, in its ability to describe moving and nomadic subjects as well as to vitalize inanimate objects through language and fictional re-creations, literature and literary forms of representation can create enactive modes of cognition and interaction where minds, matter, and metaphors meet in varying degrees of intensity and interactivity.

Comparable with Andy Clark's idea of neural profiling and manipulative corporeality examined earlier, Brian Massumi's work on affect, embodiment, and movement offers original insight into how technology, affectivity, and body can merge in ways which are asymmetric as well as unquantifiable. In *Parables for the Virtual* (2002), Massumi examines how the metacognitive quality informing embodiment (the way in which the body generates and experiences awareness of its own corporeality) rests on two fundamental features: *movement* and *feeling*. Defining the virtual order of embodiment as an entanglement of the real but abstract intercorporeality (Massumi 2002, 21), Massumi locates affect as 'central to an understanding of our information- and image-based late capitalist culture, in which so-called master narratives are perceived to have foundered' (ibid., 27). The movement of affect inasmuch as it informs embodiment and cognition exists, in Massumi's study, as *'virtual synesthetic perspectives* anchored in (functionally limited by) the actually existing, particular things that embody them' (ibid., 35). The autonomy of affect in Massumi's theory thus transcends corporeality as well as materiality, and the intersubjectivity and interactivity of subjects and objects are affectively determined by the departure and dislocation from any fixated frame, in resonance with Clark's notion that *cognition has no location*. Both Massumi's philosophy of affective embodiment (characterized by movement and feeling) and Clark's theory of embedded and enactive cognition find unique forms of representation in literary depictions of the mind's entanglement with materiality.

As a moving medium which is both embedded in language as well as uniquely capable of extending the same through re-encodings and defamiliarization, literature emerges as a special function of cultural representation, especially in terms of navigation with and consumption of technology. As Alan Clinton argues in *Intuitions in Literature, Technology, and Politics*, digital technology and its convergences with decentred and global structures of power can perhaps best be examined by literature's 'ability to make unexpected connections' in ways which 'navigate the hidden structures animating the ever-expanding archive of the spectacle' (Clinton 2012, 125). Literature's potential to defamiliarize and revitalize through a shared medium of language is especially pertinent here, connecting the animated spectacle and the privately feeling self through a charged economy of matter, metaphor, and memory. What makes literary representations even more significant in a study of technology, its consumption, and identity production is its embeddedness in everydayness and in language while also being able to stylize the same through creative reconfigurations of phenomenality and materiality. This makes it possible to view the literary text itself as an act of animated and augmented reality, one which situates human subjects and inanimate objects across complex affective and discursive fields.

Examining the convergence of literature and technology in terms of how both can produce radical revaluations of subjectivity and lived experience, this chapter offers a textual as well as a philosophical study of culture, consumption, and technology through selected literary texts. The two primary texts chosen for this study, Oscar Wilde's *The Picture of Dorian Gray* and Will Self's *Dorian*, offer a combination of utopian and dystopian possibilities in fiction in their depiction of human immersion in what may be considered augmented technology, which operates as art in Wilde's cultural milieu and as electronic interconnectedness in Self's. In doing so, these texts provide a complex commentary on and reflection of the ontology of technology as a cultural instrument that affects embodiment and intersubjective experience. At a more fundamental level, this representation of technology, textuality, and body, as reflected in the selected literary texts, foregrounds the interplay of matter, metaphor, and memory which constitutes culture as an activity involving abstraction and materiality. If Wilde's fin de siècle fiction about decadence, masculinity, and monstrosity examines the consumption of the human self in an extended and perversely permanent art frame, Self's intertextual retelling of Wilde's novel in a postmodern cynical setting celebrates shallow simulation and endless dissemination. Crucial to both works of fiction is the emotional and existential ambivalence to technology emerging as an act of consumption which appears as liberation as well as imprisonment. Despite the ostensible moral message at the end of Wilde's novel which may be read as a neo-Faustian tale, *The Picture of Dorian Gray* is a story of possibility and panic, mediated through the uncanny orders of art and technology.

Self's more postmodernist take of this tale situates hollow hedonism and ennui as the emergent sentiments out of technological violence and velocity which experientially appear as an urban activity and markers of metropolitan identities, where fluid forms of interactivity and intersubjectivity emerge electronically as well as existentially connected through video installations and television screens. In doing so, *Dorian* undercuts, as Katherine Hayles argues, 'the presuppositions underlying the social formations of late capitalism' and in the process opens 'new fields of play where the dynamics have not yet rigidified and new kinds of moves are possible' (Hayles as cited in Flanagan 2014, 156). This happens through plays of matter and metaphor which produce, de-produce, and reproduce semantic mappings across minds and machines. Both Wilde's original novel and Self's retelling of the same situate the story and the act of story-telling itself as technology, operating with an affective web of minds and machines that connect as well as disrupt.

Oscar Wilde's *The Picture of Dorian Gray* (1890) is a fictional representation of the fears and fantasies characterizing the fin de siècle cultural imaginary where imperialist expansion and xenophobia, political territorialization and sexual panic, co-existed simultaneously. As Pamela Thurschwell argues in her study of fin de siècle fiction and technology, 'fantasies about language, communication, and suggestions are being worked out in economic models' even as turn-of-the-century literary and scientific texts engage with the panic of disabled communication (Thurschwell 2001, 12). Like Bram Stoker's *Dracula* (1897), which articulates an economic and sexual panic by merging the two together, Wilde's *The Picture of Dorian Gray* dramatizes the human body enmeshed by cultural artefacts and machines which include a grotesquely ageing portrait as well as the language games of wit. If the male body becomes an ageless machine in Wilde's novel, what also gets exhibited is the propensity of that human-machine towards violence and transgression which are directed against established social and sexual mores. It is reflective of a culture where 'the body was the machine in which the self lived; the site of an animal nature which required conscious regulation' (Armstrong 1998, 2). At a time when the difference between the organism and the machine was increasingly unclear and untenable, Wilde's *The Picture of Dorian Gray* also represented a political panic about 'anarchism, crime, population decline and sexual deviance' (Bernheimer 2002, 156). The cultural milieu in the novel reflects constant commodification whereby the mind and the marketplace meet, while the permanently beautiful and youthful Dorian himself becomes a perversely unchanging machine which reveals, as Parui describes in an introduction to the novel, the 'curious entanglements of art, ageing, and consumption' (Parui 2015a, xii). Wilde's own status and performative sexuality as a celebrity writer and the supposed sightings of him after his reported death (Sherard 1917) further reflect the mutability and reversible relationship between the living and the dead body in the fin de siècle cultural imaginary, converting life and death into performative acts, 'as if the difference between alive and dead were purely a matter of taste' (Armstrong 1998, 162). The moving male dandy in Wilde's novel is thus an organism as well as a techno-cultural attaché, equipped with the sartorial and linguistic apparatus to impress, seduce, and intimidate. The performative quality of the male body in *The Picture of Dorian Gray* blurs the boundaries between the animate and the inanimate, 'offering a complex commentary on the *fin de siècle* fetish for ostentation and reification' (Parui 2015a, xii).

In a psychological understanding of reality and materiality which was beginning to be systematized in fin de siècle scientific and cultural discourses in the works of W. K. Clifford, James Sully, and William James, all matter, organic as well as inorganic, begins to assume fluid relationships with mind and things, making the connections between the mental and the material orders complex and contingent in quality. In his 1879 essay 'Are We Automata?', William James examines what he describes as 'the efficacy of Consciousness' (James 1879, 3) whereby the mind is seen as a chemical process in which data is 'sifted' to generate a 'distillate' (ibid., 13), making the mind a product of as well as a creative negotiation with the material world. In this theory of consciousness, the mind can recreate materiality through its innate proclivities and ability to prioritize, thus making the human subject situated as well as agentic in their navigation with their external environment. James's most famous examination of consciousness as a stream occurs in the 1884 essay 'On Some Omissions of Introspective Psychology' where an atomistic understanding of the mind is replaced by a fluid movement across materials in which the mind 'is steeped and dyed in the free water that flows round it' (James 1884, 16). Evident in James's theorizations, and also elsewhere in early twentieth-century discourses on psychology, is a move away from an atomistic understanding of physicality and consciousness which sees the mind and matter as different entities and instead a move towards a more fluid model of the mind whereby materiality and phenomenality emerge as connected categories, where mindfulness is always already materially determined. Wilde's novel dramatizes similar models where the mind and matter merge, producing 'phantoms more terrible than reality itself' (Wilde [1891] 2003, 126), while acknowledging the inability to determine 'where the fleshly impulse ceased, or the psychical impulse began' (ibid., 57), arguing instead that 'life is a question of nerves, and fibres, and slowly built-up cells in which thought hides itself and passion has its dreams' (ibid., 206). In describing a state of aesthetic absorption in a decadent consumerist culture of commodification and contamination – Dorian's addiction to opium makes him like an 'automaton' (ibid., 181) – Wilde's novel reflects the fantasies as well as the anxieties 'in late-Victorian culture, about mind, matter, and their connections' (David 2013, 558). It does so by showcasing the transformed body which moves from the aesthetic to the monstrous order with an interplay of plasticity and permanence. More importantly, such movements and interplays showcase how the self is always already mutated by materiality as well as by the experiences that emerge out of it. In doing so, Wilde's novel corresponds to as well as reflects some of the most central debates and discourses on science, mind, and materiality in fin de siècle cultural imaginary.

Wilde's fictional representation of a portrait which grows old instead of a man, and how the latter is consumed by the disease of agelessness and moral degeneration, inhabits the complex cultural moment where technological transformations and the sciences of the mind begin to be systematized in Western Europe. The neurological research of David Ferrier and John Hughlings Jackson in Wilde's England and the related research on language and cognition in France and Germany by Paul Broca, Gustav Fritsch, and Eduard Hitzig are particularly reflective of this. Anne Stile's work on popular fiction and brain science in the late nineteenth century examines how some key psychologists at that time appropriated a cerebral-localizationist model whereby certain parts of the brain were considered to control certain specific emotions and behavioural patterns, which in turn undercut 'the popular belief in a unified soul or mind governing human action, thus narrowing possibilities of human agency' (Stiles 2011, 10). The notion of the *vanishing subject* of the fin de siècle, as Judith Ryan studies, 'rejected the dualism of the subject and the object' (Ryan 1991, 2) and was instead informed by contemporary interventions in psychology and technology which foregrounded the self as less stable and permanent and more fractured, fissured, and performative, fragmenting 'the body into competing systems with their respective tolerations, limits, and interfaces' (Armstrong 1998, 187). This had bearings in contemporary craft and literary productions as well, which become 'progressively more fragmentary, the art no longer being present in its shaping, but rather in the attempt to physically embody the metaphors which it has projected' (ibid., 172). The body of writing and the writing of the body in fin de siècle were thus both informed and accentuated by performative and prosthetic qualities, foregrounding how corporeality and cognition emerge as always already interstitial and incomplete processes. This receives a dramatic treatment in Wilde's fiction where the organic body becomes the site of a projected fantasy of agelessness and where the techno-artefact quality of the portrait absorbs and responds to markers of human ageing and degeneration.

Technology in *The Picture of Dorian Gray* emerges as a pointer to the commodity fetish characterizing the high-capitalist culture where the mind and the market meet asymmetrically. This is corroborated in Wilde's novel itself which describes the 'mind of a thoroughly well-informed man' as a 'dreadful thing', like 'a bric-a-brac shop, all monsters and dust, with everything priced above its proper value' (Wilde [1891] 2003, 12). The mind of man is thus described with material and metonymic markers, where the mythic and the synthetic states mix seamlessly. The proximity and reversible relationship between monsters and dust, between commodity, sublimity, and monstrosity in Wilde's novel, are represented, as Jonathan Dollimore argues, 'obliquely through irony, ambiguity, mimicry, and impersonation' (Dollimore 1991, 310). *The Picture of Dorian Gray* pushes the ontological merger between the organic and inorganic orders even further with what Regenia Gagnier describes as an 'ornate description of material conditions and an obsession with physical beauty' (Gagnier 1986, 56–57), reflective of a culture of capitalism which is consumerist as well as quasi-cannibalistic in its visual-voyeuristic quality. Thus the body of art and the body of the human subject are transposed onto each other in Wilde's novel while also carrying the new orders of masculine desire and intimacy emerging at the turn of the century (Sedgwick 1993, 55–56). The nature and quality of gaze in Wilde's novel corresponds to the emergence of the new optical and visual technologies, with the first commercial camera, the Kodak, having appeared on the market in 1888, two years before the publication of *Dorian Gray*. Wilde's wife Constance purchased a Kodak in 1892, and Wilde himself 'famously used photographic portraiture as a means of self-expression and self-promotion' (Dobson 2020, 146). In such a culture of consumption and technologized voyeurism, the ageless body of Dorian emerges as a reified machine, one that displays the 'concrete embeddedness of Aestheticism in late-Victorian market economy' (Gagnier 1986, 11). More importantly, such embeddedness of the body in the marketplace reflected how the culture of commodification that was quickly consolidating during Wilde's novel showed the soul of man as infused and manipulated by machines, while the animated organ was revitalized by material markers and affective artefacts.

The French Symbolist poet Stéphane Mallarmé wrote to Wilde on reading the novel, describing how the 'disturbing, full-length portrait of a Dorian Gray' haunts his senses 'as writing, having become the book itself' (Hart-Davis 1962, 218). What is evident in Mallarmé's reading of Wilde's novel is how the body of Dorian and the body of writing (embodied by the book itself) merge in the decadent fin de siècle marketplace as well as in the cultural and aesthetic imaginary, underlining how the act of writing itself emerges as a techno-spectral activity. The book as machine and technology gets foregrounded in Mallarmé's reception of the spectrality in *The Picture of Dorian Gray*, ironically corroborated by the undead status of Wilde's novel itself which continues to charm and haunt readerly imagination. The ontology of the artifice in *The Picture of Dorian Gray* inhabits the sociocultural as well as the corporeal orders where Lord Henry confesses that '[b]eing natural is simply a pose, and the most irritating pose I know' (Wilde [1891] 2003, 6), thereby highlighting how embodiment is essentially a performative process always already enmeshed with the self's enactive engagements with the surrounding synthetic materiality. But Mallarmé's description of the revenant-like quality of Wilde's novel and the book itself is further reflective of a broader culture of writing, textuality, and corporeality in the late nineteenth century as examined by Friedrich Kittler's *Discourse Networks* (1985), one of the earliest and most significant works on technology, information, and discursivity. Examining the emergence of technologies of writing such as the typewriter, Kittler argues that the act of writing itself at the turn of the century was 'no longer based on an individual capable of imbuing it with coherence through connecting curves and the pressure of the pen' but rather materialized into an 'apparatus that cuts up individuals into test materials' (Kittler 1990, 223). Instead of being a purely creative activity that is reflective of the writer's imagination and individuality, writing at the turn of the century was perceived as an act of automatic production through machines, resulting in bodies of books which 'disconnected the production of language from time, distance, and the individual body' (Armstrong 1998, 193).

Technology thus quite directly informs and intervenes in writing, cognition, and corporeality in the fin de siècle cultural imaginary, making Wilde's novel about the body turning into an ageless machine an artefact in itself, capable of haunting with its materiality and spectrality. As Pamela Thurschwell argues in her study of Wilde's body and body of works, the scandal caused due to the writer's supposed deviant sexuality was conveniently connected to his fiction during the 1895 trials for indecency, whereby the novel *The Picture of Dorian Gray* and its writer's homosexuality appeared 'as substitutable for one another; both were dangerously seductive and contaminating' (Thurschwell 2001, 43). The body as a new form of affect and technology appears at the beginning of Wilde's novel when the painter Basil Hallward confesses to the witty dandy Lord Henry Wotton that Dorian defines for him 'an entirely new manner in art, an entirely new mode of style', such that he now sees 'things differently' and 'can now recreate life in a way that was hidden' from him earlier (Wilde [1891] 2003, 10). The body and the personality as triggers for new visual modes and markers for reconstruction inhabit the techno-corporeal interface operating as art in Wilde's novel, while also revealing how such *aesthetic addiction* is connected to the consumerist commodity fetish in the fin de siècle marketplace. As Wilde's novel makes abundantly clear, the desire to recreate life becomes more than a metaphor in the course of the plot, as the picture of Dorian Gray quite literally becomes the animated order of life with its ageing and grotesque degeneration. This foregrounds the interplay of matter and metaphor in the novel's fictional frame while offering a complex commentary and critique of the fin de siècle fetish for beauty as commodity. More importantly, the animation of matter (the ageing portrait) in Wilde's novel and the frozen frame of the organic mutable body (the ageless Dorian) blur the borders between the subject and the object and instead generate a fluid frame of affect which mixes materials, minds, and actants in a complex cognitive economy. In its depiction of art, body, morality, and materiality, *The Picture of Dorian Gray* may be read as a story about the *synthetic subject*, one always already entangled with affective and artificial markers and inhabiting the interface between the real and the virtual orders. In many ways, it may be considered one of the earliest novels about the production of virtual reality through an aesthetic experiment that may also be described as transformative technology.

Art operates like an 'immoral science' (Wilde [1891] 2003, 17) in Wilde's novel, appearing as an affective instrument that can convert the organically ageing body into an ageless artefact, one that corresponds to the sentiment expressed in the novel that 'all influence is immoral' and the 'aim of life is self-development' (ibid., 17). The ontology and experience of influence in the fin de siècle cultural imaginary move from fantasy to fear, with influence frequently equated with the evil of hypnosis. As Pamela Thurschwell argues in her work on literature and technology in the late nineteenth century, 'the life-sucking, vampiric aesthete encapsulated a constellation of fears and desires in the 1890s about the potentially hypnotic effects of newly visible sexual acts and identities' as these anxieties 'asserted themselves in relation to versions of the body, mind and soul as potentially alienable and marketable, capable of being bought, sold or stolen' (Thurschwell 2001, 39–40). If the self-enhancing art in *The Picture of Dorian Gray* corresponds to Foucault's notion of the technologies of the self as discussed earlier, what makes Wilde's novel even more complex is its depiction of how the very ontology of such selfhood and subjectivity is a function of artificially invested animation whereby the subject of Dorian 'is simultaneously artist, scientist and experiment, instigator and victim of his desire for self-substitution' (Raitt 2017, 170). In blurring the borders between the subject and the object of aesthetic experiments, *The Picture of Dorian Gray* foregrounds contemporary anxieties around technology and the body and the related concerns about commodification and the menace of the invasive marketplace which displayed desire as well as dangerous difference. Connected to the commodification of the market was the new order of visual culture at the turn of the twentieth century, exemplified by the emergence of technologies such as X-rays and the camera, which generated new forms of machinic materiality that were ironically also associated with spectrality. This changed the nature and scope of visual and experiential possibilities and connected to the 'corresponding fascination of the limitlessness of the inapprehensible world' whereby seeing became deeper and 'opened up intimations of more, elusive, and inapprehensible phenomena' (Warner 2006, 224).

The fin de siècle self-fashioning in *The Picture of Dorian Gray* corresponds to Wilde's very own 'anti-essentialist, transgressive aesthetics' (Dollimore 1991, 6), but what invests further layers to it is how the body and the experientially *situated self* can be intervened and manipulated by artifice and influence. Technology as a transformative art form operates through abstract as well as materially marked signifiers in Wilde's novel, as evinced in the reifying aesthetic gaze of Lord Henry on Dorian's beautiful body: 'Grace was his, and the white purity of boyhood, and beauty such as old Greek marbles kept for us. There was nothing that one could not do with him. He could be made a Titan or a toy' (Wilde [1891] 2003, 35–36). The interplay of possibilities between Titan and toy exemplify the entanglement of matter and metaphor in Wilde's novel, where the organic body becomes playfully plastic in its interchangeability with mythical masculinity and synthetic commodity. If the body of Dorian appears godlike and plastic alternatively, it also reveals how the self can be materialized and manipulated by the aesthetic as well as by synthetic investments and then made to appear as an object in the marketplace. The market as an instrument and a sentiment is central to Wilde's novel, invading the intimate space of the home as well as the inner space of the body and brain. In its depiction of commodities and aesthetic artefacts, *The Picture of Dorian Gray* shows how the synthetic state can produce the sublime, which is also monstrous and immoral. It also depicts art as a non-innocent activity and aesthetic culture as a form of corruption and corporeal intervention. If the flawless body of Dorian emerges as a fantastic and monstrous machine and the plastic portrait as an ageing organism, those also become signifiers of a culture where consumption and contamination were simultaneous activities. At an affective level, the novel emerges as a fictional representation and reflection of an economy of commodification where fantasy, phobia, and fetish are inextricably interlinked and where the transcendental quality and aura of art can also produce menacing mimesis which can re-ontologize and re-corporealize reality. Wilde's novel does all this with its complex and dark depictions of influence, impressionability, and interchangeability, which question common notions about embodiment, body, and existential agency.

The Picture of Dorian Gray extends the ontology of influence to abstract and aesthetic desires while further problematizing the politics of fantasy and fetish, reflecting a culture of commodification and contamination whereby influence 'comes to stand for a nexus of 1890s fears about the porous constitution of the self and its desires' (Thurschwell 2001, 38). Thus Lord Henry seeks to dominate Dorian and 'make that wonderful spirit his own' (Wilde [1891] 2003, 36), revealing the mix of erotic and metaphysical registers in Wilde's novel, while also reflecting how self-fashioning as a porous and performative process operates through markers which are alternately spiritual and synthetic in quality. The porosity of life and art in the fin de siècle imaginary becomes spectacularly clear during Wilde's trials where his word plays and epigrams are seen to be as insidiously influential as his homosexuality, reflecting a phobic culture where '[l]ife leaks into art and art leaks into life' (Thurschwell 2001, 57). In depicting and dramatizing a plastic portrait which grows old instead of its human subject, *The Picture of Dorian Gray* showcases a decadent consumerist order where commodification and contamination operate simultaneously, producing in its wake artefacts which begin to age, degenerate, and waste. This is exemplified graphically in the novel in the scientific disappearance of the painter Basil Hallward's murdered body through vapourizing chemicals, dramatizing how the body of the artist can be consumed and turned to complete waste by the machines of the scientist. The ontology of art and the ontology of waste thus emerge entangled and eventually indistinguishable in Wilde's novel, foregrounding a cultural and a representational frame which corresponds to the contemporary fin de siècle panic about degeneration, criminality, and waste. This was exemplified in the works of the cultural critics Max Nordau and César Lombroso, whose theories, as Parui states in his introduction to Wilde's novel, 'were rapidly translated and circulated in England as well as appearing in contemporary popular literature like Bram Stoker's *Dracula* (1897), which combined vampiric terror with xenophobic panic' (Parui 2015a, vii). Ironically fueled by the engines of imperialism, the fear of degeneration prevalent during this time reified into racism drawing on the erstwhile anxiety about the Gothic (Parui 2015b).

While influence as inflow connects and transforms subjects in *The Picture of Dorian Gray*, it also inhabits the interface between the human and inorganic matter in its flow between and across affective frames. Thus Dorian muses on the question, 'If thought could exercise its influence upon a living organism, might not thought exercise an influence upon dead and organic things?' (Wilde [1891] 2003, 106), foregrounding the fluid interplay of consciousness, materiality, and spectrality in Wilde's novel. More importantly, and closely connected to the context and scope of this book, such an interplay also displays the interchangeability of matter and metaphor in consciousness as well as in the cultural imaginary, with Wilde's novel emerging as an excellent example of how the fictional frame of literature becomes the perfect medium to represent the same. The ontology of experiment in *The Picture of Dorian Gray* connects the realms of art and science, with both Lord Henry and Dorian emerging as immoral artists fantasizing transgressive transformations which turn real. More importantly, such experiments merge the self and the other, the experimenting subject and the experimented upon object, in ways which make mind, matter, consciousness, and commodity entangled entities. Thus Dorian confesses in Wilde's novel, '[W]hen we thought we were experimenting on others we were really experimenting on ourselves' (ibid., 59). Similarly, after the tragic death of his former lover Sybil Vane, Dorian looks at the changed and more degenerated portrait of himself and experiences that 'his own soul was looking out at him from the canvas and calling him to judgement' (ibid., 119), dramatizing how the ontology of gaze in Wilde's novel assumes necrophilic dimensions while also being embedded in and emerging out of material orders and plastic structures. The interface of mind, technology, and materiality in *The Picture of Dorian Gray* thus connects the spectral and the synthetic frames, also foregrounding the interchangeability and reversible relationship between permanence and decadence. While the plastic portrait begins to simulate the growing moral degeneration of Dorian Gray, his unchanging physical body operates like an ageless machine which paradoxically becomes the signifier of waste despite its flawless frame. Wilde's novel foregrounds the moral and existential dilemma which is also mediated by materiality and the corporeal condition as Dorian wonders 'which were the most terrible, the signs of sin or the signs of age' (ibid., 128).

The end of Dorian Gray exemplifies the panic in the fin de siècle cultural imaginary where waste, like fatigue, 'signals the point at which the body and the machine cannot readily be reconciled' (Armstrong 1998, 65). The real as well as symbolic suicide of the protagonist at the end of Wilde's novel dramatizes the destruction 'by what can neither assimilate nor escape, the very by-products of his hateful and wasteful life' (Raitt 2017, 175). The quasi-cannibalistic quality of the novel's ending whereupon the human is consumed by the image-object also restores the biological and scientific order with the corpse of the human and ugly Dorian lying 'withered, wrinkled, and loathsome of visage' (Wilde [1891] 2003, 183), recognizable only by his rings. If the novel signals a return to the normal order with an associated moral message at the end, what also gets foregrounded yet again is how the borders between life and death, between restoration and permanence, are precariously plastic in a fast-changing decadently consumerist world. The grotesque corpse of Dorian at the end of the novel becomes the paradoxical pointer to his human redemption which is only available posthumously, whereas the shift of the portrait back to its beautiful image becomes the machinic move towards a purely passive artefact which is not animated anymore. The disappearance of the animated virtual object and the end of Dorian's biological life thus inhabit the same temporal point in Wilde's story, which foregrounds the novel's reflection of the fin de siècle anxieties about the material processes of the physical world. Particularly pervasive in Wilde's novel is the experience of panic where evolution and degeneration are sometimes simultaneous processes, whereby 'the very distinction between organic and inorganic may be blurred' with the 'vertiginous sense that human evolutionary kinship extends beyond even the simplest organisms to matter itself' (David 2013, 547).

If Wilde's *The Picture of Dorian Gray* dramatizes the interchangeability of body and artefact as a precarious possibility that is couched in moral fears of degeneration, Will Self's novel *Dorian: An Imitation* (2001) presents a sequel set in a world where the human is always already a machine, connected to other machines in various states of consumption and interactivity. The moral message in Wilde's original novel and the anxieties about the authentic organic self being consumed by the plastic aesthetic order are replaced by a celebration of disembodied exchange and shallow simulation in Self's novel. *Dorian* presents a world of interconnectedness which is also one of distributive cognition, moving away from fears of contamination and appropriating a world order where entangled entities produce and reproduce kinetic identities, sexually as well as technologically. Set in the London of 1981–1997, with homosexuality and drug use as the major markers of urban masculine identities, Self's story started off as a screenplay which eventually became a novel (Hayes 2007, 149). Appropriately subtitled 'An Imitation', *Dorian* depicts a world of television sets and televised images where the human is always already a floating image which can be endlessly produced and consumed. Extending the mimetic frame from Wilde's novel, Self represents Basil Hallward as a conceptual artist in the postmodern tradition of Andy Warhol who, instead of painting Dorian, captures his youth and beauty in a video installation called *Cathode Narcissus* which runs on nine monitors, where 'the sensations imparted as all nine monitors came to life was of the most intense, carnivorous, predatory voyeurism' (Self 2001, 12). The aesthetic narcissism in Wilde's novel thus manifests itself in an electronic transmission in *Dorian* which constantly connects the protagonist to his own simulacra, producing a visual culture where the subject's 'cathodic ego and *alter egos* are superficial, mobile and curvilinear' (Yebra 2011, 26). What emerges in Self's novel is a projection and experience of embodiment as a partial as well as an excessive process whereby the difference between the mirrored media image and the corporeal understanding of the same is blurred. In the process, *Dorian: An Imitation* extends the Lacanian understanding of identification as 'always already an ongoing struggle, one that occurs not only between bodies, but as a virtual body in itself' (Neveldine 1998, 140). Such experiences of virtuality and corporeality are situated in Self's novel amid the politics of capitalist and consumerist fantasies, informing individual desires as well as government policies.

The HIV- and AIDS-infested London gay world in Self's novel presents not so much the fear of sexual disease and degeneration but an order of contagion ironically informed by alienation, characterized by 'a Government at once regressive and progressive, a monarchy mired in its own succession crisis, an economic recession both sharp and bitter' (Self 2001, 3). In the world of hedonistic sexuality and drug abuse, the natural and seasonal differences begin to blur inside the endlessly artificial ambience of intimate domestic spaces. Thus, 'Once you were inside the Chelsea home of Henry and Victoria Wotton it was impossible to tell whether it was day or night-time. Not only was there this crucial ambiguity, but the seasons and even the years became indeterminate' (ibid., 3). This corresponds to the machines of manipulation and consumption in Self's novel, which point to Lyotard's notion of the postmodern sublime which occurs 'at the price of suspending the active powers of the mind' (Lyotard 1991, 124). In such a theory, mindfulness is replaced by cognitive absorption which extends into a state of suspension, whereby the experiencing subject also becomes a passive object stylized into sublimity and hyperreality, producing in its wake what Jose M. Yebra defines as a 'neo-baroque vertigo' that is not tied to any transcendence but to a 'web of never-ending references' (Yebra 2011, 30). This is comparable with Baudrillard's notion of 'baroque over-signification' (Baudrillard 1979, 28), which is about the politics of the production of excess and which borders on the pornographic. In an ironic twist which appears as a funny passage in Self's novel, Dorian explains Baudrillard's philosophies of the virtual and the loss of the real to Hester Wharton during a dinner by arguing that the Gulf War did not happen, ending with the assertion that it is "simply expression ... that gives reality to things"' (Self 2001, 144), highlighting the fluid all-absorbing mimetic medium of the literary novel in a postmodern world of intertexts and interruptions. *Dorian: An Imitation* produces an excellent example in fiction of the ways in which 'contemporary technologies may offer new ways of articulating virtual images and of thinking through the traditional binary opposition of mind and matter, conceptual and corporeal' (McMullan 2000, 166). This connects closely to the principal enquiry of this book, which seeks to examine how fiction and the literary medium may be seen as offering interfaces across mind, materiality, and corporeality through an imaginative interplay where cultural codes and emotional experiences merge, producing in its wake real as well as imaginative descriptions of embodiment, existential movements, and cultural identities.

Divided into three sections appropriately titled 'Recordings', 'Transmission', and 'Network', each of which ends with a death, Will Self's *Dorian* dramatizes the close and problematic proximity of production and destruction, re-creation and annihilation, in a 1980s London characterized by complex subcultures of gay circles, drug addicts, and AIDS victims. A subversion of natural orders and bodies, and a cynical celebration of dangerous lifestyles and sexuality, Self's *Dorian* emerges as an extreme extension of the decadent consumerism in Wilde's fin de siècle setting. If the portrait of Dorian Gray in Wilde's novel carried associations of fear and spectrality, the electronic installation of 'reflective surfaces' (Self 2001, 15) in Self's novel is indicative of a narcissistic and self-indulgent consumerist culture where '[e]veryone who isn't a pseudo-intellectual loves television – it's so much *realer* than reality' (Self 2001, 66). The interplay of art and life through aesthetic instruments – which offers the complex and morally ambivalent frame in Wilde's novel – is thus extended to an obscene and passive consumption of simulation and the simulacra in Self's novel, which depicts in its machines, drug addiction, and sexual diseases the 'interlocking relationships between place, identity and cognition' (Hayes 2007, 7). This entanglement of machines, spaces, and the mind is dramatized in *Dorian* in the protagonist's movements around Chelsea where 'he could hear nothing save the scream of his shredded psyche through the taut steel rigging of consciousness' as the rise of brain waves takes place simultaneously with 'the strange weather in the streets deteriorating', as the 'frightening vortices of low-pressure cyclones formed over Redcliffe Gardens and Edith Grove' (Self 2001, 169–70). The mental movements are thus described in machinic metaphors here, connecting also to the worsening weather which is less natural and more estranged in quality in its stretch across spatial and existential conditions.

As Magdalena Maczynska argues, Self's writing belongs to a culture of 1990s city fiction where the 'escalation of street violence, desiccation of urban nature, and abnormal weather and human behaviour patterns are all indirect consequences of living in a nuclear world' (Maczynska 2010, 81). Technology becomes familiar natural territory in Self's novel, converging hyperreality and corporeality in complex cognitive and collective frames, while natural orders of weather appear alienated and alienating to the human subject, and understandable only through metaphors of machine. In doing so, Self's *Dorian* offers an unsettling account of the manipulated and the manipulatable images and experiences of identities in the postmodern neoliberal city 'through the use of fantastic ontology, defamiliarizing point of view, and comic debunking', depicting the urban spatial experience itself as corresponding to 'soft cities, charged with powerful transformative potential' (Maczynska 2010, 75). The transformative potential of the city and urban experience is additionally reflected in the carnivalesque quality in Self's novel which underlines the cognitive crisis of the human subjects who are also already commodified objects in a quasi-cannibalistic consumerist culture.

The images of the transformative soft city often appear only through the windscreen of speeding cars in Self's novel, depicting how visual consumption becomes a mutable and metonymic process. Far from the fear of new visual modes in Wilde's novel, *Dorian* depicts a cognitive absorption of velocity whereby a riot on the street only appears as a reflection which 'flickered yellow and red on the smooth tan screen' of Dorian's flawless face (Self 2001, 50). The references to contemporary popular culture and cultural icons make Self's novel a complex representation of televised times, where the real and the technologized images arouse private as well as collective empathy, anger, and disgust. This is exemplified most prominently in *Dorian* with references to Princess Diana Spencer who appears 'as blonde, ingenuous and seemingly indestructible as Dorian himself' while also being 'mediated, like Dorian's video-portrait itself, via the deadpan glamour of the TV screen' (Bartlett 2002). The overlap of images of Diana's wedding on the television screen and Dorian's infection with HIV and the eventual destruction of both figures underscore the quasi-cannibalistic quality of 1990s televised Western media where everything, from identity to sexuality, can be consumed and commodified. It depicts a dark consumerist culture which produces and promotes a blur between fact and fiction, making everything 'so ideally *mythic*' (Self 2001, 274). The mythical quality alluded to here in Self's novel is not a function of timeless triumph and heroism but one of hyperreality and endless dissemination through shallow installations and ontological reorientations. This takes place through a process of cognitive profiling mediated through electronic screens and televised gaze whereby the deathless digital image becomes a spectral presence invading public as well as intimate spaces. The endlessly prosthetic and plastic ontology of the body in Self's novel may be seen as an extreme extension as well as a mimicry of what Tim Armstrong defines as 'capitalism's fantasy of the complete body: in the mechanisms of advertising, cosmetics, cosmetic surgery, and cinema; all prosthetic in the sense that they promise the perfection of the body' (Armstrong 1998, 3). The prosthetic body in *Dorian: An Imitation* instead depicts a diseased state, viral in its drugged and media-induced conditions of frenzy and fatigue. Consequently, the performative quality of identity that emerges in Self's novel is a function of textual as well as technological investments which ensure that 'Dorian can be whatever you want him to be – a punk or a parvenu, a dodgy geezer or a doting courtier, a witty fop or a City yuppy' (Self 2001, 108). The range of avatars and identities assumed by the protagonist in the novel points to the hypermimetic quality of the culture depicted, where everyone and everything is always already imitated, indicated by the title of the novel itself.

Henry Wotton's attitude to television as being 'the most intense, carnivorous, predatory voyeurism' (ibid., 12) foregrounds a form of visual addiction which blurs the differences between the viewer and the viewed, the subject and the object. Unsurprisingly, Dorian describes and defines himself as a 'social chameleon' (ibid., 107) whose identity is a function of televised images and media manipulation and consumption. If Wilde's novel retains the organic human quality of painting as an art form even as it transforms into a dangerous and immoral aesthetic experiment, Dorian's electronic avatar Cathode Narcissus celebrates its complete disconnect with any human hand and instead operates overtly as a 'digital virus' (ibid., 271). Self's novel foregrounds the connection and convergence of the technological and medical metaphors, as the digital and electronic virus of Cathode Narcissus inhabits the same spatiotemporal plane as the biological virus of HIV, both operating as instruments of infection and contamination at private as well as collective levels of consumption. Both Diana and Dorian in Self's novel are defined by their digital self-fashioning in the public eye of media, mediated by technologies and televised identity images which make as well as manipulate their personas for private and public consumption. Diana's eventual death on being chased by carnivorous cameras corroborates the definition of murder in Self's novel, which emerges as 'one of the wilder forms of popular entertainment' (ibid., 217) that can in itself become a posthumous visual commodity, endlessly reproduced and consumed collectively, with an absolute disconnect from all forms of ethicality or morality. The immoral art and influence feared in Wilde's *The Picture of Dorian Gray* thus emerges as a celebration in Self's novel where anything can be transformed into an image that is essentially endless and deathless. The posthumous commodification of Diana's televised avatar becomes a pointer to the necrophilic gaze in *Dorian*, where consumption operates alongside death and digitization. It corresponds to a visual culture where 'monitors fizzed into life', generating an endless maze of images that 'forced all who looked upon it to become involuntary voyeurs' (ibid., 42). The production of voyeurism as the normative visual mode is also associated with the absence of agency in Self's novel, whereby the consumer is numbed into a state of absorption which does not correspond to any consistent desire or emotion.

At a fundamental philosophical level, *Dorian: An Imitation* is about the uncanny deathlessness of the image in a digital world, where simulacra operate like spectres that never go away, where human subjects turn into digital objects which never disappear and sometimes become more visible and spectacular after the humans' deaths. The Cathode Narcissus which becomes Dorian's digital avatar in the novel emerges as a pointer to the infection in the visual medium, whereby the viewer as well as the viewed degenerates into a digital abyss which finds its biological counterpart in the dangerous spread of AIDS. The drug abuse in *Dorian* whereby wealthy, decadent, and disillusioned subjects degenerate and contaminate each other through needles and dangerous sex runs parallel to the paparazzi in the novel who hunt celebrities and turn deaths into media spectacles that can be consumed with its infectious information networks and stylized affect. The deathless electronic image in Self's novel is therefore a function of human contagion, contamination, and self-willed destruction, produced out of a cynically and irresponsibly hedonist consumerist world where the media and medical conditions are both determined by their potential to be *viral*. Apart from being an intertextual sequel to Wilde's *The Picture of Dorian Gray*, Self's Dorian pays tribute to as well as mimics several familiar works of literature, including John Donne's poem 'The Flea', which is quoted with its metaphors of mixed blood, ironically during one of Dorian's group drug sessions which sees the 'strange blending of the essence of the five men' (ibid., 67). The allusion to Donne during a drug session emerges less as an intertextual tribute and more as a 'literary hangover' and a 'sacrilegious textfest' that is an unsettling pointer to 'the daily violence of existence, which progressively loses its power to shock' (Gonzalez 2008, 114). The literariness of *Dorian: An Imitation* as an artefact and mimetic act in itself is established by the many metafictional moves it makes as a novel. Thus Henry Wotton in the novel almost writes a brilliant book about the life and times of Henry Wotton, and the character confesses that he would have written a roman à clef had he lost his car keys (Self 2001, 41), ironically losing his car key several times subsequently in the story. Apart from the postmodernist playfulness that Self espouses here, this also foregrounds the novel's ontological status as a constructed cultural artefact as well as a *thing*, an act of fiction which mixes historical reality and materiality with creatively coded imaginative possibilities, ambivalently situated between subversion and celebration, critique and consolidation. Literature thus emerges as a unique and complex form of animated and augmented reality, one which mixes possibilities with events, machines, and identities. This is particularly pertinent to Self's novel which corresponds to a culture 'addicted to imitation and manipulated by ventriloquist narrators whose original premise is the insincerity of the copy and the poetics of consumption' (Gonzalez 2008, 118).

If the metafictional elements in Self's novel are reflective of the metacognitive qualities that fiction can offer as a cultural commentary with its play of matter, metaphor, and memory, a more extreme example of the same appears when Wotton explains his act of giving up Dorian's location in order to cause his death by stating that his decision to kill and finish Dorian is not out of revenge but 'a kind of symmetry we seek, a rounding off of events' (Self 2001, 218), converging the intention to kill Dorian and to arrive at the end of the novel through formal closures. The comparison of literary text and life occurs again at the end of the novel when Wotton prides himself for living his 'life at first hand, rather than filtering it through this paper as part of a literary experiment' (ibid., 220), ironically foregrounding again the fictionality and constructed quality of the events in the novel while also being reflective of how in the post-digital electronic world of images and identities, the biological self is always already a technological experiment. The metafictional quality in Self's novel situates it as a postmodernist artwork which is also a constructed commodity, foregrounding fiction's ability to create and conflate several cognitive registers apropos of cultural materiality. At a larger ontological and representational level, this depicts literature's location as a reflection of cultural conditions through an interplay of realities and possibilities, while being simultaneously a medium embedded within the same matrix of matter, metaphor, and memory that it depicts.

If the metafiction in Self's novel is comparable to metacognition (the awareness of awareness), it also highlights the innate plasticity and self-reflexivity of the postmodern novel, which constantly draws attention to its own artificiality and materiality. This becomes a complex representation of a culture of consumption and absorption which produces and reproduces simulation and stimulation through electronically mediated machines and drug addiction. In doing so, Dorian emerges as a novel 'concerned with the avoidance of predictability, precedent or classification' (Bradford 2007, 52) in its depiction of a culture addicted to stimulation and shock. But Self's novel may also be read as a work that inhabits the interface of textuality and technology, evinced by the copies of Wotton's novel which are gifted to both the biological and the Cathode Narcissus avatar of Dorian in the epilogue, with a mysterious inner voice that affirms that all versions of technologized realities and stories are 'inventions of one sort or the other' (Self 2001, 276). The death of Dorian turns out to be fiction in the epilogue, a part of Henry Wotton's roman à clef as the author himself appears on the verge of death due to AIDS, exposing the entire action as part of the story written by one of the characters, in a classic metafictional move which further underlines the fluid and self-reflexive entanglement of transmission, technology, and textuality in Self's novel.

Both the degenerating portrait of Dorian Gray in Wilde's novel and the video installation Cathode Narcissus in Self's novel may be described as what José Yebra defines as 'metaphors of the abject' (Yebra 2011, 22), which inhabit dark secret rooms and stand for artefacts representing dangerous otherness. More complexly, both the painting and the video installation represent in the two novels the liminal conditions between creation and consumption, 'breaking ontological boundaries and interpellating us through the process of reading' (ibid., 22). If the abject and the subject in Self's novel are both mediated by machines of transmission and consumption, those also reveal how the ontology of the obscene in Dorian is a function of feeling-less-ness, corresponding to Baudrillard's notion in *Cool Memories IV* of needless visibility that does not produce any consistent affect (Baudrillard 2003, 59–60). The hyperreality and the spectacle of the same in *Dorian* are thus the ontological opposite of utility and consistent affectivity, producing instead a state of flatness and passive absorption. This corresponds to the construction of a 'discursive space where constant interference disturbs the inevitability of reproduction' (Gonzalez 2008, 116). At a representational level, *Dorian: An Imitation* exemplifies a merging of the satirical and the fantastic modes which can defamiliarize as well as enact an epistemological elasticity. Self's novel does so by offering a 'hybridized form of urban writing that offers a felicitous surplus of textual economy' that in turn produces 'a new, multimodal and multidimensional experience of the fictional metropolis' (Maczynska 2010, 62).

The textuality of the city is an ontological as well as an experiential condition in Self's novel, a state which emerges subsequent to the loss of any transcendental signifier of meaning and meaningful materiality. This produces a semiotic slipperiness whereby, as Richard Lehan argues, 'a romantic sense of the uncanny becomes exaggerated, and the city takes on the meaning of pure text, to be created by each individual and then read' (Lehan 1998, 287). The mindless production and consumption of simulated images and flattened affects point to the centreless ontological quality of the postmodern world of televised realities depicted in Self's novel. This corresponds closely to Baudrillard's description of the disappearance of reality in a hyper-simulated world which examines how

> [i]mages have entered things. Images are no longer the mirror of reality, they have invested the heart of reality and transformed it into hyperreality where, from screen to screen, the only aim of the image is the image. The image can no longer imagine the real because it is the real; it can no longer transcend reality, transfigure it or dream it, since images are virtual reality. (Baudrillard 2005, 120)

The semiotic instability characterizing the postindustrial Western metropolis is a recursive condition in Self's *Dorian*, where everything is an image to be consumed and recreated, where identity is a function of hypermimetic acts across minds and machines. The imitation quotient in

Self's novel spreads across several textual and technological frames. At the most fundamental level, the novel is an imitation of Oscar Wilde's *The Picture of Dorian Gray*, one which also imitates itself within its own self-reflexive narrative and textual frame, evinced by the metafictional moves in which it emerges as a story written by one of its fictional characters. The plot of *Dorian* reveals how the body is manipulatable and mimetic in quality, with images produced and reproduced electronically and endlessly, flattening all frames of mimesis while also creating a hyper-simulated hyperreal condition of consumption and absorption. This is described in the novel alongside depictions of the drug-abused body which approximates several sexual and medical identities, bringing the technological, textual, and corporeal orders in close and pathological proximities. *Dorian* depicts culture as a contagion and an act of contamination, an infectious viral overdrive which consumes knowledge networks as well as human bodies with a visual overload and a dangerous interplay of simulation and stimulation. If the intertextuality and interconnectivity in Self's novel emerge as reflective of an endless economy of interactivities and hyperrealities, what makes *Dorian: An Imitation* uniquely complex is its depiction of literature's aesthetic and creative possibilities in a world of interrupted cognition and inexhaustible representations.

Both Wilde's *The Picture of Dorian Gray* and Self's *Dorian: An Imitation* offer excellent examples of moving literary frames depicting story worlds where minds, machines, and metaphors mix in asymmetric entanglements. Both dramatize events which show how the human self and its agency are inextricably informed, deformed, and re-formed by materiality through acts of appropriation and consumption. At a fundamental level, Wilde and Self seem to suggest through their novels that the abstraction of affect, fear, and desire are mediated through material markers and machines in a consumerist world where everything and everyone can be commodified. Located at two vital points in the history of human engagement with materials and machines – the fin de siècle with its formative phase of consumerism and commodity fetish and the late twentieth century with its imminent move to a bodiless, digital world of images and signs – *The Picture of Dorian Gray* and *Dorian: An Imitation* both enact a fictional representation of an 'urban visionary fantasy developed and refined in the nineteenth-century British metropolis', one that got subsequently extended in the satirical novels in the 1980s and 1990s which combined a 'nonrepresentational stance of fantasy with the desire to expose and explore the crisis of the contemporary capital' (Maczynska 2010, 62). In doing so, both novels emerge as compelling fictional accounts which appear with increasing relevance in the virtual-real worlds of alienation and affect today.

This chapter has attempted to examine the entanglement of mind, machines, and materiality through literary representations, in correspondence with the central philosophical framework of this book about the role and location of the literary medium in a complex study of culture and cultural formations. By drawing on a range of theoretical frameworks including material engagement theory, actor-network theory, and affect theory, this chapter has explored the concept as well as the experience of cognition and consumption at private existential as well as shared collective levels. Through its readings of the two selected literary texts which are also rich cultural accounts of their times, this chapter has depicted how the mind and the material are not disconnected categories but experiential, affective, and ontological orders which seamlessly and sometimes problematically blend into each other. Additionally, this study has examined how art and transformative technology operate not as outliers to human cognitive systems but as instruments that actively animate and shape such systems through different experiential engagements. In doing so, the chapter underlines the framework alluded to in the subtitle of the book, through a study of the transmission and transformations across matter, metaphor, and memory in terms of how private as well as collective cognitive schema are informed by and in turn inform human situatedness in material and affective networks. It thus throws light on the complex ontology and experience of embodiment, which emerges not just as an embedded state but as an actively extended and enactive one, in relation to a fluid engagement with materials, cultural codes, and objects. The role of literature – with the coded quality of literary language and the interplay of matter and metaphors in fiction – has a perspectival privilege in describing such forms of embodiment in all their corporeal and cognitive complexities. The two literary texts examined here show how culture and cultural subjects consume technology through an affective economy of minds, matter, and memory.

At an ontological and experiential level, literature is capable of offering an ambivalent position in relation to human navigation with technology and technological materiality, especially in relation to questions concerning virtual reality and human embodiment in technologically overdetermined heterotopic conditions. While critics such as Johannes Birringer describe a mood of 'technological-formalist aestheticism that simulates the reproduction of disembodied desire' (McMullan 2000, 165) as one generating ennui and an absence of agency, philosophers such as Kevin Robbins, with a more positive proclivity to posthuman states, argue how cyberspace offers 'possibilities for exploring the complexities of self-identity, including the relation between mental space and bodily other' (Robbins 1995, 140). Both positions underline an ontology of virtuality that emerges in what Anna McMullan defines – in her study of Samuel

Beckett's theatre and technology – as 'the dialectic between embodiment as the located condition of human subjectivity and interaction, and the desire to escape or transform the material limits of the body' (McMullan 2000, 165–66). The literary frame and medium of representation offer a complex and fictional matrix where this dialectic may be accommodated and articulated. In doing so, fictional representations often offer an ambivalent attitude to technology and its consumption, pointing to the possibilities as well as to the precarious conditions characterizing human engagements with machines. As this chapter has attempted to show through its philosophical framings as well as in its close study of selected texts, such fictions on technology demonstrate and dramatize how the human subject is shaped by objects at embodied and existential levels. In their descriptive details and affective forms of representations, such fictional works show the interplay of matter and metaphor as coded processes of transmission and consumption whereby the ontological fluidity of fiction itself emerges as a medium through which human engagements with materiality, corporeality, and the spectrality of memory may be most complexly examined and articulated.

REFERENCES

Appadurai, Arjun. 1986. *The Social Life of Things: Commodities in Cultural Perspective*. Cambridge: Cambridge University Press.
Armstrong, Tim. 1998. *Modernism, Technology, and the Body*. Cambridge: Cambridge University Press.
Bartlett, Neil. 2002. 'Picture of Ill-Health'. *Guardian*, September 12, 2002. https://www.theguardian.com/books/2002/sep/21/shopping.fiction.
Baudrillard, Jean. 1979. *Seduction*. Translated by Brian Singer. London: Macmillan.
———. 2003. *Cool Memories IV: 1995–2000*. Translated by Chris Turner. Paris: Verso.
———. 2005. *The Conspiracy of Art*. Translated by Ames Hodges. New York: Semiotext(e).
Bernheimer, Charles. 2002. *Decadent Subjects: The Idea of Decadence in Art, Literature, Philosophy and the Culture of the Fin de Siècle in Europe*. Baltimore, MD: Johns Hopkins University Press.
Bradford, Richard. 2007. *The Novel Now: Contemporary British Fiction*. Oxford: Blackwell.
Braidotti, Rosi. 2002. *Metamorphoses: Towards a Materialist Theory of Becoming*. Minneapolis: University of Minnesota Press.
Brooks, Cleanth. 1985. 'Literature and Technology'. *Wilson Quarterly* 9(4): 88–99.
Clark, Andy. 2003. *Natural-Born Cyborgs: Minds, Technologies, and the Future of Human Intelligence*. New York: Oxford University Press.
———. 2008. 'Where Brain, Body and Mind Collide'. In *Material Agency: Towards a Non-Anthropocentric Approach*, edited by Carl Knappett and Lambros Malafouris, 1–18. New York: Springer.

Clinton, Alan. 2012. *Intuitions in Literature, Technology, and Politics: Parabilities*. London: Palgrave Macmillan.
David, Michael. 2013. 'Mind and Matter in *The Picture of Dorian Gray*'. *Victorian Literature and Culture* 41(3): 547–60.
Dobson, Eleanor. 2020. 'Oscar Wilde, Photography, and Cultures of Spiritualism'. *English Literature in Transition, 1880–1920* 63(2): 139–61.
Dollimore, Jonathan. 1991. *Sexual Dissidence: August to Wilde, Freud to Foucault*. Oxford: Clarendon/Oxford University Press.
Flanagan, Victoria. 2014. *Technology and Identity in Young Adult Fiction*. New York: Springer.
Foucault, Michel. 1988. *Technologies of the Self: A Seminar with Michel Foucault*. Edited by Huck Gutman et al. Alameda, CA: Tavistock.
Gagnier, Regenia. 1986. *Idylls of the Marketplace: Oscar Wilde and the Victorian Public*. Stanford, CA: Stanford University Press.
Gonzalez, Madelena. 2008. 'The Aesthetics of Post-Realism and the Obscenification of Everyday Life: The Novel in the Age of Technology'. *Journal of Narrative Theory* 38(1): 111–33.
Hart-Davis, Rupert, ed. 1962. *The Letters of Oscar Wilde*. London: R. Hart-Davis.
Hayes, Hunter M. 2007. *Understanding Will Self*. Columbia: University of South Carolina.
Hollander, John. 1997. 'Literature and Technology: Nature's "Lawful Offspring in Man's Art"'. *Social Research* 64(3): 1247–72.
James, William. 1879. 'Are We Automata?' *Mind* 4(13): 1–22.
———. 1884. 'On Some Omissions of Introspective Psychology'. *Mind* 9:1–26.
Kennedy, Greg. 2007. *An Ontology of Trash: The Disposable and Its Problematic Nature*. New York: State University of New York Press.
Kittler, Friedrich. 1985. *Discourse Networks, 1800/1900*. Translated by Michael Metteer, 1990. Stanford, CA: Stanford University Press.
Kroker, Arthur. 1987. 'Panic Value: Bacon, Colville, Baudrillard and the Aesthetics of Deprivation'. In *Life after Postmodernism: Essays on Value and Culture*, edited by John Feteke, 181–93. Montreal: New World Perspective.
Latour, Bruno. 2005. *Reassembling the Social: An Introduction to Actor-Network Theory*. Oxford: Oxford University Press.
Lehan, Richard. 1998. *The City in Literature: An Intellectual and Cultural History*. Berkeley: University of California Press.
Lyotard, Jean-François. 1991. *The Inhuman: Reflections on Time*. Translated by Geoffrey Bennington and Rachel Bowlby. Stanford, CA: Stanford University Press.
Maczynska, Magdalena. 2010. 'This Monstrous City: Urban Visionary Satire in the Fiction of Martin Amis, Will Self, China Mieville, and Maggie Gee'. *Contemporary Literature* 51(1): 58–86.
Malafouris, Lambros. 2013. *How Things Shape the Mind: A Theory of Material Engagement*. Cambridge, MA: MIT Press.
Malafouris, Lambros, and Carl Knappett, eds. 2008. *Material Agency: Towards a Non-Anthropocentric Approach*. New York: Springer.
Massumi, Brian. 2002. *Parables for the Virtual*. Durham, NC: Duke University Press.
McMullan, Anna. 2000. 'Virtual Subjects: Performance, Technology and the Body in Beckett's Late Theatre'. *Journal of Beckett Studies* 10(1/2): 165–72.

Neveldine, Robert Burns. 1998. *Bodies at Risk: Unsafe Limits in Romanticism and Postmodernism*. Albany: State University of New York Press.
Parui, Avishek. 2015a. Introduction to *The Picture of Dorian Gray*, i–xii. Montreal: Universitas Press.
———. 2015b. 'Gothic Horror and Racial Infection in Bram Stoker's Dracula'. In *Gothic and Racism*, edited by Cristina Artenie, 12–28. Montreal: Universitas Press.
Raitt, Suzanne. 2017. 'Immoral Science in *The Picture of Dorian Gray*'. In *Strange Science: Investigating the Limits of Knowledge in the Victorian Age*, edited by Lara Karpenko and Shalyn Claggett, 164–78. Ann Arbor: University of Michigan Press.
Robbins, Kevin. 1995. 'Cyberspace and the World We Live In'. In *Cyberspace, Cyberbodies, Cyberpunk: Cultures of Technological Embodiment*, edited by Mike Featherstone and Roger Burrows, 135–55. London: Sage.
Ryan, Judith. 1991. *The Vanishing Subject: Early Psychology and Literary Modernism*. Chicago: University of Chicago Press.
Sedgwick, Eve Kosofsky. 1993. *Tendencies*. Durham, NC: Duke University Press.
Self, Will. 2001. *Dorian: An Imitation*. New York: Viking.
Sherard, Robert. 1917. *The Real Oscar Wilde*. London: T. Werner Laurie.
Stiles, Anne. 2011. *Popular Fiction and Brain Science in the Late Nineteenth Century*. Cambridge: Cambridge University Press.
Sutton, John. 2008. 'Material Agency, Skills and History: Distributed Cognition and the Archaeology of Memory'. In *Material Agency: Towards a Non-Anthropocentric Approach*, edited by Carl Knappett and Lambros Malafouris, 37–56. New York: Springer.
Thurschwell, Pamela. 2001. *Literature, Technology and Magical Thinking, 1880–1920*. Cambridge: Cambridge University Press.
Warner, Marina. 2006. *Phantasmagoria: Spirit Visions, Metaphors and Media*. Oxford: Oxford University Press.
Wickliffe, Abraham C. 2008. 'Metaplasticity: Tuning Synapses and Networks for Plasticity'. *Nature Reviews Neuroscience* 9:387–99.
Wilde, Oscar. (1891) 2003. *The Picture of Dorian Gray*. New York: Penguin.
Yebra, José M. 2011. 'The "Moving" Lines of Neo-Baroque in Will Self's *Dorian: An Imitation*'. Atlantis 33(1): 17–31.

4

∽

Race, Medicine, Matter, and Metaphor

The final chapter of this book offers an interdisciplinary examination of culture, racial identity, medical politics, and the ontology and experience of waste, looking at literary as well as nonfictional representations of the same which display and dramatize an entanglement of matter, metaphor, and memory for a fuller understanding of those categories. In studying the biopolitical definition and production of life, liveability, and identity, this chapter will offer an examination of the ontology of *lives that matter* and the ones which do not, drawing on the works of Michel Foucault, Giorgio Agamben, and Zygmunt Bauman, among others. Through a close critical reading of the selected texts – Frantz Fanon's *Wretched of the Earth* and *Black Skin, White Masks* and Ian McEwan's neuro-novel *Saturday* – this chapter will provide a finale for this book by examining how cultural identities are formed, deformed, and re-formed through various vectors of medical and racial politics and profiling. Additionally, drawing on the works of Greg Kennedy, the chapter will examine the *ontology of wasted identity* and that of trash as connected categories, while also studying how culture as an act of production and consumption entails an experiential and embodied negotiation with materiality, immateriality, identity, and agency. By using the broad categories of race, medicine, identities, and liveability, this chapter examines – through its selected texts – how culture as a controlled economy and movement of meanings, materials, and bodies also produces its ontological opposites and sites of subversion, often accidentally, through experiences of liminality, epiphany, and interstitiality. This enquiry will thus underline how such subversion may emerge as an act of dissent as well as an *affective insight through accident*, represented by experiential first-person accounts as well as by focalized fictional frames. In doing so, the chapter offers an examination of how medical discourses and political processes often create and consolidate otherness which is manifested as a dehumanizing as well as a deconstructive category through alternate forms of representation, remembering, and storytelling.

Frantz Fanon's revisionist reading and critique of colonial biopolitics and identity formations may be studied as an example of how the medical gaze mapped and reified human bodies and subjects in racially discriminatory settings. This chapter examines Fanon's experiential first-person accounts as a black subject under a white gaze (famously and disturbingly depicted in the 'Mama, see the Negro!' episode in *Black Skin, White Masks*) and his trained psychiatric understanding of colonial violence and mental health (in *The Wretched of the Earth*) as deconstructive engagements with the corporeal and epistemic qualities invested in discrimination. Despite the nonfictional nature of Fanon's accounts, the anecdotal and narrative qualities in his experiences and medical case studies offer a complex combination of matter, metaphor, and memory in an understanding of corporeal and existential unsettling which is also, as Judith Butler argues, a 'recitation of the racist interpellation' in which 'the black body is circumscribed as dangerous prior to any gesture' (Butler 2004, 208). In comparison to Fanon, this chapter studies Ian McEwan's neuro-novel *Saturday* as an experience in *affective unlearning*, whereby the privileged, white, neuroscientific gaze of McEwan's protagonist is deconstructed by an acknowledgement and articulation of epistemic and ontological uncertainty. The medical culture initially espoused by *Saturday's* protagonist Henry Perowne – one which is allied to the neo-Darwinist notion of bioscientific certainty – is juxtaposed with the emotional and political backdrop of a post-9/11 paranoid Western world, accentuating, like Fanon's writings, how medical and political profiles blend to create and consolidate identities and politics of privilege. What makes McEwan's novel even more complex and significant in the context of this book is its *affective understanding of uncertainty* about the human mind, emotions, and culture, foregrounded and focalized by the liminal literary frame of the lyric. The evocative and performative presence of Matthew Arnold's 'Dover Beach' in *Saturday* highlights the central thesis in this book: literature as a special and stylized system of codes reflects, represents, and defamiliarizes culture and lived reality through an interplay of matter, metaphor, and memory.

In his study and recontextualization of the ancient archetype Homo Sacer – the one who can be killed without remorse or fear of penalty and yet not considered worthy enough for sacrifice – and the relationship of that figure with sovereign life, Giorgio Agamben describes how the 'originary figure of life taken into the sovereign ban' (Agamben 1998, 81–82) manifests in the 'memory of the originary exclusion through which the political dimension was first constituted' (ibid., 81–82). The act of exclusion thus emerges, in Agamben's study, as an act of political construction, which is also medically mediated and mutated. In what he defines later as *bare life*, Agamben underlines the 'interlacing of politics and life' (ibid. 81–82) which characterizes the modern biopolitical imaginary that incorporates medicine, political control, and the body, whereby 'the biological life and its needs had become the *politically* decisive fact' (ibid. 81–82). The biopolitical investment in modern Western democracy is so clinically complete, Agamben argues, that the 'absolute capacity of the subjects' body to be killed forms the new political body of the West' (ibid., 138). The ontology of bare life, as defined by Agamben, becomes a site where rights to live and be recognized as a subject and a citizen are determined by an 'ambiguous terrain in which the physician and the sovereign seem to exchange roles' (ibid., 143). Comparable to Agamben's thesis on the biomedicalization of life and the resultant determinations of privileged and non-privileged forms of living is Zygmunt Bauman's work on wasted lives. In his work, Bauman actually draws on Agamben's theory of the Homo Sacer and defines it as 'the principle category of human waste laid out in the course of modern production of orderly (law abiding, rule governed) sovereign realms' (Bauman 2003, 32). Bauman's theory of waste and wasted lives connects to the ontology of knowledge, memory, and forgetting, underlining how these categories operate in liquid and liminal ways characterizing the ambivalence of modernity. In this philosophical framework, in 'the factory of knowledge, the *product* is separated from the *waste*' while also highlighting an ontological condition where 'knowledge is inconceivable without waste, memory without forgetting' (ibid., 18). Describing the production of waste and the notion of wasted humans as by-products of modernization and modernity, Bauman connects the same to the 'inescapable side-effect of *order-building*' and '*economic progress*' (ibid., 15). Defining modernity as a liquid condition of 'compulsive, and addictive designing' (ibid., 30), Bauman underlines how such liquid culture constitutes '*disengagement, discontinuity and forgetting*' (ibid., 117). In such settings, the ontology of waste gets quickly and conveniently connected to the politics informing human identities with an affective economy of matter, metaphors, and memories. Bauman offers a series of examples from fiction, from 'Kafka's monsters and mutants' to the societal and cultural concepts of '[f]lawed beings, from whose absence or obliteration the designed form could only gain, becoming more harmonious, more secure and altogether more at peace with itself' (ibid., 30). Inherent in both Bauman's and Agamben's studies as cited above is an examination and a critique of the biopoliticization of lives and identities and how that connects to key questions about privilege, otherness, and waste.

Greg Kennedy's study of the ontology of trash examines how trash turns to 'the mandatory subject of modern ontology', connoting violence as well as a 'mode of comportment, treating things without care, negatively, and destructively' (Kennedy 2007, xvi). As a mode as well as a signifier of consumerist modernity, trash becomes an act of consumption as well as a production of identity. More importantly, the ontology of trash in contemporary consumerist societies exhibits, as Kennedy argues, how 'the being of commodities is always already trashed' (ibid., xvii), whereby material identities are preceded and defined by their potential to turn to waste. Kennedy's ontological distinction between waste and trash is particularly relevant here. Thus, while waste emerges as a reminder of human finitude and failure to transcend animality, trash 'results from a willful human determination concerning the being of the object' (ibid., 23) whereby the object and ontology of trash is defined as always already disposable, corresponding to a desire which prompts humans to 'create trash to deny waste' (ibid., 23–24). This ontological study of trash demonstrates how violence through uncaring is instrumental in the production and perpetuation of the identity of trash through a process that 'negates the being of beings' (ibid., 123). Such negation and denial of being to bodies may be compared to political processes connected to issues around corporeality, identity, and agency. The ontological violence which informs the production and rejection of trash is reflective of 'the refusal on our part to let beings be' (ibid., 155), which extends to and manifests into violence on and abuse of identities which are politically and medically mediated. Drawing on the studies and philosophical frameworks cited above, this chapter examines how human identities in complex cultural conditions pass through processes of biopolitical, racialized, and discursive determinisms that create and curate notions about desirability and disposability. Frantz Fanon's experiential, cultural, and trained psychiatric accounts of living the *violent otherness* and ontology of blackness under a colonial white gaze and Ian McEwan's neuro-novel about an experiential and affective unlearning of privileged white, male, bioscientific knowledge of mind and matter in the backdrop of a post-9/11 paranoid climate both connect and correspond to questions around the biopolitics of identity, recognizability, embodiment, and agency.

FRANTZ FANON AND THE BIOPOLITICS OF COLONIAL RACIAL IDENTITY

The relevance of Frantz Fanon (1925–1961) in a study of French-Algerian colonial biopolitics – one which *medically* declared that '[t]he Algerian has no cortex' and is dominated, 'like the inferior vertebrates, by the diencephalon' (Fanon [1967] 2001, 243) – is increasingly important in the political world today in the context of racially reified subject formation where certain racially defined and determined lives *matter* less than certain others. Fanon describes colonialism as a culture of violence that operates at visual and visceral levels whereby '[t]he Algerians, the veiled women, the palm-trees and the camels make up the landscape, the *natural* background to the human presence of the French' (ibid., 201). A psychiatrist by training, Fanon studied colonial neurosis in Algeria as a nervous condition born out of a systematic structure of violence, coercion, and repression, inhabiting corporeal as well as existential experiences and unsettling normal knowledge and orders of embodiment, creating what Fanon defines as psychosomatic pathology, 'the general body of organic disorders the development of which is favoured by a conflicting situation' (ibid., 234). Fanon's psychiatric study of neurosis and nervous disorders due to French-Algerian colonial violence defines and delineates the following markers of mental illness: verbal stereotypy characterized by paranoid and anxious repetitions, usually of denial; complete clouding of intellectual and sensory perceptions whereby the 'patient cannot affirm the existence of a given visible object'; a permanent phobia characterizing all private conversations, emerging from 'the acute impression that at any moment a fresh interrogation may take place'; and inhibition which is marked by a neurotic guardedness followed by 'psychical slowing down, interrupted sentences, repetition and faltering' (ibid., 230). As Diana Fuss contends in her assertion of Fanon's position in an understanding of colonial neurosis and trauma, such study of the colonial condition incorporated the medical as well as the political registers and exposed 'the neurotic structure of colonialism itself' (Fuss 1994, 19). Moreover, Fanon was one of the first figures to bring the politics of medicine into the colonial setting as a discursive study of oppression and its subsequent psychopathological subject and abject formations. This took place, as Fanon examines, through processes of corporealization and epidermalization whereby the body of the black subject becomes the *ontology of the abject* through which structures of discrimination, disgust, and difference are produced and perpetuated in a cultural setting where 'apart from the pathology of torture' there is a 'pathology of atmosphere' (ibid., 234) which creates incomprehensibility in doctors trying to treat subjects suffering trauma and other forms of mental illness. As Fanon's study of French-Algerian violence makes amply evident, the biopoliticization of identities in the colonial setting was accentuated by a strategically motivated medical discourse which produced and perpetuated 'a scientific appreciation of the biologically limited possibilities of the native' (ibid., 244).

The violence and neurosis produced out of the process of epidermalization are examined by Fanon by highlighting how 'the emotional sensitivity of the native is kept on the surface of his skin like an open sore which flinches from the caustic agent', causing permanent damage to his psyche and sense of agentic self, which in turn have caused, Fanon sarcastically states, 'certain very wise men to say that the native is a hysterical type' (Fanon [1967] 2001, 44). This creates existential anxieties in the slippery spaces between the black skins and white masks as described by Fanon, a condition that may be compared with Homi Bhabha's analysis of colonial mimicry, the performative acts and language games that constitute the double articulation of difference and dedoublement that 'does not merely "rupture" the discourse, but becomes transformed into an uncertainty which fixes the colonial subject as a "partial" presence' (Bhabha 1994, 123). The identity of the colonized subject thus emerges as fractured and partial, always already insufficient in comparison to the *ideal identity* of the colonizer. The emotional and political states of violence studied by Fanon – creating what he classifies as the 'contingent of cortico-visceral illnesses' (ibid., 235) – manifest themselves in two specific syndromes historically born out of these colonial conditions of coercion and claustrophobia: *pseudomelancholia* and *North African syndrome*. What emerges from Fanon's oeuvre of political and medical work is how the *production of the abject* operates through an interplay of matter, metaphor, and memory and how such discursive designs can be best represented through narrative patterns, albeit in nonfiction. Indeed, the narrative quality of Fanon's critique of colonialism and colonial biopolitics underlines how racially reified identity and identification is an experiential, embodied, and enactive process which receives its fullest representations through anecdotal evidence and forms of storytelling. The ontology of the abject in Fanon's reading is also always an affective process which produces its unique metaphors and metonymic markers, most dramatically exemplified by the body of the black subject which is always already an object, one that is gazed at as incomplete as well as excessive, anarchic, and existing only as an insufficient comparison.

The reified and relativized Algerian black body is denied any ontological or existential completion and instead appears in the white French gaze as a metonymic marker of disgust and difference. In his examination of the spectacular as well as the subliminal processes characterizing the colonial site of corporeal, epistemic, and interstitial violence, Fanon asserts unequivocally, 'The Negro is a comparison. There is the first truth. He is comparison: that is, he is constantly preoccupied with self-evaluation and with the ego-ideal. Whenever he comes into contact with someone else, the question of value, of merit, arises' (Fanon 1986, 211). The constant comparison entails repression, the anxiety to assert as well as accept difference in a discursive field, with the material, metaphoric, and metonymic markers of memories and identities emerging as an entanglement of colonial stereotype and self-fashioning through appropriation. As Jean-Paul Sartre affirms in the preface to Fanon's *The Wretched of the Earth*, the nervous condition characterizing colonialism essentially emerges out of repression, strategic subordination, and violence that operates at visceral as well as epistemic levels. This corresponds to Gramsci's notion that the status of domination necessitates a political condition introduced and maintained by the controller among colonized people *with their* consent (Gramsci 1985, 90). Sartre's study examines the neurosis characterizing the colonial condition which operates through hegemony as well as violence (Sartre [1967] 2001, 25). As Sartre would argue further in his famous preface, 'The native cures himself of colonial neurosis by thrusting out the settler through force of arms. When his rage boils over, he rediscovers his lost innocence and he comes to know himself in that he creates his self' (ibid., 18). In the liminal space between the white skin and the black mask, marked by anxiety as well as performativity; lurks 'the tension of meaning and being . . . demand and desire, which is the psychic counterpart to that "muscular tension" that inhabits the native body' (Bhabha 1986, xxii) in the colonial space which is the site of difference and violence. The violence born out of colonial coercion and oppression is corporeal as well as epistemic in quality, discursively determined as well as experientially suffered. This treatment and culture of control and coercion was historically legitimized, produced, and perpetuated by a medical vocabulary backed by a pseudoscientific discourse which publicly pronounced, as Fanon highlights, how the 'lack of integration of the frontal lobes in the cerebral dynamic is the explanation of the African's laziness, of his crimes, his robberies, his rapes and his lies' (Fanon [1967] 2001, 245).

In his fascinating study of medicine and colonial classification, Fanon further examines the location of medical politics in the discourses of domination that become tools in colonial control. The study examines and deconstructs the ontology of objectivity in Western medicine and reveals how it informs the colonial subject formation through a process of apprehension, anxiety, and mistrust, against which '[t]he black man has no ontological resistance' (Fanon 2000, 258). Asserting the problematic proximity of the military and the medical in the colonial condition, Fanon asserts:

> The colonized perceives the doctor, the engineer, the schoolteacher, the policeman, the rural constable, through the haze of an almost organic confusion. The compulsory visit by the doctor to the *douar* is preceded by the assembling of the population through the agency of the police authorities. The doctor who arrives in this atmosphere of general constraint is never a native doctor but always a doctor belonging to the dominant society and very often to the army. (Fanon 1980, 99)

The 'organic confusion' Fanon describes here is an epiphenomenon of the nervous condition characterizing colonialism where markers of authority are interchangeably shared by doctors, policemen, and schoolteachers. The apparatus of cure and the apparatus of control are thus enmeshed in the colonial condition where diseases are reified as well as racialized and where the doctor appears more as a punitive presence than an empathetic healer. The meeting with the doctor in the colonial condition thus often entailed biomedical objectification whereby colonial sickness and the sick subject were coerced and *corrected*. What gets evident in Fanon's graphic as well as metaphoric descriptions of corporealization and epidermalization of identity in a racially reified and charged setting is how the black 'body is surrounded by an atmosphere of certain uncertainty' (Fanon 2000, 260) whereby the historicity of the subject disappears along with any acknowledgement of agency. This is defined by Judith Butler, in her study of colonialism and corporeality, as the state of the body as the '*deanimated life of that historical condition, without which colonization itself cannot exist*' (Butler 2008, 224, emphasis in original), the deanimation or the production of the deadened non-agentic body being the motive of the machinery and the affective apparatus of colonialism.

In contrast to the anti-Semitic condition theorized by Sartre in *Anti-Semite and Jew*, Fanon foregrounds how the whiteness of the Jew makes their experiential discrimination different from the immediate identification marker of the black subject whose corporealization precedes his performative presence as social identity, whereby the fact of the body's blackness is 'overdetermined from without' (Fanon 2000, 261). Instead of the cultural and ritualistic difference of the Jew, the otherness of the black subject is enacted through the surface, the superficial signifier of the skin which emerges as the deepest and most permanent marker of difference experienced visually as well as viscerally. Fanon's famous episode – where he describes the horror of being identified and epidermalized by the gaze of a white girl who calls out for her mother and says she is frightened of the Negro – emerges as an example of an experiential as well as an ontological assault on presence whereby 'the corporeal schema crumbled, its place taken by a racial epidermal schema' (ibid., 259). Fanon's passage – written in a high literary and affectively charged language – reveals that the black subject in a racially reifying setting is reduced to matter which is always already a metaphor, one which is also a metonymic signifier of identity and its associated possibilities of violence, monstrosity, and savagery. The fear of seeing the dangerous black body is dramatized by the white girl's act of pointing ('Mama, see the Negro!'), which, as Judith Butler argues in her study of the scene, 'is both a pointing and a seeing, a pointing out what there is to see, a pointing which circumscribes a dangerous body, a racist indicative which relays its own danger to the body to which it points' (Butler 2004, 207). It exemplifies as well as experientially demonstrates what Foucault defines as 'biological transcription' (Foucault 2003, 60–61) through which 'dynamic racism' (Foucault 1990, 125) is defined and dramatized.

In order to fully understand Fanon's critique of colonial medicine in the French-Algerian context, it is important to examine the rampant racialization that informed colonial biopolitics from the mid-nineteenth to the mid-twentieth century. The birth of biopolitics, as Foucault informs, was synchronous to that of racism in the late nineteenth century, setting in motion 'the set of mechanisms through which the basic biological features of the human species became the object of a political strategy' (Foucault 2009, 1). Such systematic racialization of medicine in an African colonial context is depicted in the work of John Carothers, the director of Nairobi's Mathari Mental Hospital from 1938 to 1950, who pronounced that '[t]he African makes very little use of his frontal lobes. All the particularities of African psychiatry can be put down to frontal laziness' (as cited in Fanon [1967] 2001, 244). With no formal degree in either psychology or psychiatry, Carothers's first publication was an essay on understanding the general nature of *African insanity* and exposited that the exposure to European culture was the fundamental reason behind the madness of the African whose brain was a cross between that of an innocent child and a lusty animal (Carothers 1940). Describing the normal African as a 'lobotomized European' (cited in Fanon [1967] 2001, 244), and comparing the average African to the European schizophrenic, Carothers classifies the African psychopathology as invested with an attribute that 'sees no sharply defined aspects of reality' (Carothers 1940, 99). In a later but related publication, Carothers theorizes what he saw as the African's innate propensity to lie as a compulsive mental condition that was pathological inasmuch as the liar would cease to believe in the distinctions between truth and fabulation (Carothers 1947, 73). Unsurprisingly, Carothers also examined the African's phases of 'frenzied anxiety' as a more pathological and criminal extension of the European's anxiety disorder and asserted that the African's imbalance naturally extended into irrational homicidal impulses and accounted for murders committed with no ostensible logic for violence (ibid., 71). However, Carothers's most famous as well as notorious contribution to European ethnopsychiatry was his analysis of the African physiognomy and the anatomical markers of sluggishness (Carothers 1951). Examining the *frontal lobe function* of the African and equating it with innate criminality and delinquency, Carothers theorized a medico-anthropological discourse that found many takers during his day, including the World Health Organization which commissioned Carothers to produce a monograph out of his medical experiences in Africa.

During his experience as a diploma student at the Maudsley Hospital of psychiatry in 1948, Carothers had come by the medical practice of frontal leucotomy whereby a section of the patient's brain was deliberately destroyed as part of the medical treatment. The generally perceived effect post-operation was insufficient imagination in the patient and an inclination to be overly cheerful about one's present with little considerations for the complexities the future may hold. Attributing Africans' inferiority to their culture in what was a thinly disguised racist anthropological discourse, Carothers equated the leucotomized European to the average African and went on to assert that '[i]t seems not without significance that at least one of the few Europeans leucotomized in Kenya has, since his operation, consorted much more happily with Africans than with Europeans, in marked distinction from his previous behaviour, and to the great embarrassment of his relations' (Carothers 1951, 38). Carothers's equating leucotomized Europeans with general Africans takes up the obvious racialized discourses operative during his times, and the medically metonymized construct of the leucotomized European offered a convenient metaphor for the *half-developed African*. The theory of the African's *frontal sluggishness* was used to medicalize the black man's inertness, slowness, and violence and prevailed in the cultural vocabulary until much later through the politics of coercion and consent. In his preface to Fanon's *The Wretched of the Earth*, Jean-Paul Sartre alludes to and critiques the constructed quality of the psychiatric classification and signification of 'frontal lobes' and parodies it by demonstrating its perfect applicability to the anarchic violence characterizing the French political condition: 'For we too, during the last few years, must be victims of "frontal sluggishness" since our patriots do quite a bit of assassinating of their fellow-countrymen and if they're not at home, they blow up their houses and their concierge' (Sartre [1967] 2001, 24). As Jock McCulloch asserts in his remarkable study of ethnopsychiatry, Carothers's works were readily accepted and disseminated across a number of published forums, while his near contemporary Fanon, who sought to redeem and redefine the African's location and reification in the increasingly racist medical politics of the times, 'had to content himself with obscure forums such as *Conscience maghrebine* and *Maroc medicale*' (McCulloch 1995, 58). The politics of publication in medical science at that point in time was reflective of a cultural climate that necessitated systematic polarizations through heavily racialized research.

One sees in Fanon's analysis of the colonial nerves a critique of the ethnopsychiatry of his day, the complex yet reductionist composite of ethnography and psychiatry with the assumption of racially determined pathology. This is perhaps most heavily exemplified in Fanon's time in the work of Octave Mannoni, whose *Prospero and Caliban*, an anthropological analysis of the colonial condition of Madagascar through a social Darwinist lens, was published in English in 1950. Mannoni's work rested on a Manichean allegory of machine and magic, the European whiteness with its innate sense of superiority and the colonized community with 'local forces of magic' (Mannoni 1964, 128). Inherent in Mannoni's argument are the concepts of inferiority and dependence, and he draws heavily in his study of hysteria from the theories of Freud's former collaborator Alfred Adler, whose theory of the 'inferiority complex' emerged as the analysis of a unique behavioural pattern that supposedly characterizes the neurotic and constituted 'the outgrowth of the individual's relation to his environment or to his strivings' (Adler 1921, 7). Equating innate inferiority with a propensity to be colonized, Mannoni defined colonialism as a desire to be dependent (Mannoni 1964, 128) and was one of the first psychiatrists to study the colonial condition as a psychosomatic theatre of domination and dependence. The neurotic weakness of the colonized that accounted for the predilection to be protected and dominated was conveniently described using metaphors of emasculation and may be comparable to the criminalization of the Jews in the medical as well as the psychiatric vocabulary of the late nineteenth and early twentieth centuries.

Fanon's critique of the ethnopsychiatry of Mannoni was primarily premised on an attack against the theory of African inferiority that Mannoni sought to systematize through literary (Shakespearean) metaphors, underlining in the process the discursive designs and coded investments that inform metaphor formation and dissemination. In his chapter in *Black Skin, White Masks* (1952) on the alleged dependency complex of the Africans as posited by Mannoni, Fanon alludes to Mannoni's reading of Adler and equates the logic with the racist politics of difference and demarcation:

> While the discoveries of Adler and the no less interesting findings of Kuenkel explain certain kinds of neurotic behaviour, one cannot infer from them laws that would apply to immeasurably complex problems. The feeling of inferiority of the colonized is the correlative to the European's feeling of superiority. Let us have the courage to say it outright: *It is the racist who creates his inferior*. (Fanon 1986, 93)

Inherent in Fanon's analysis is a critique of the reductionism that Western ethnographic gaze into Africa assumes with its racialized discourses. The creation of the inferior as well as dangerous other follows a similar political principal to that of the pleasure principle inherent in the Orientalist discourse that Edward Said studies in his critique of the grand narrative of Western ethnographic classification that needs its *orchestrated alterity* in order to perpetuate its rituals of discourse production, dissemination, and reification. Studying Fanon's famous passage in *Black Skin, White Masks*, 'Look, Mama, a Negro', E. Ann Kaplan examines it as a classic instance whereby the traumatic subject sees himself being seen and reified through a racialized rhetoric of otherness. Kaplan notices how the immediacy of the traumatic moment is internalized in imagination as evident from Fanon's description of the events as a perpetual shock that characterizes the traumatized through 'its recurring present, its not being given a meaning which would assign it a place in a person's history' (Kaplan 1999, 147). The vocabulary of violence and absence in Fanon's description captures the decentring of the subject through an experiential and existential unsettling whereby the subject is 'sealed into that crashing objecthood' (Fanon 2000, 259). In situating an emotional account of racialized negation within a narrative storytelling design, Fanon underlines how the epidermalization and objectification of identity – whereby the black subject simultaneously emerges as the *image of the abject* under a racially reifying gaze – is also associated with epistemic violence through which the identity of the subject is entirely corporealized, fixing the self 'in the sense in which a chemical solution is fixed by a dye' (ibid., 260). The frozenness of the black body as always already determined to be dangerous under the racially reifying white gaze emerges as an example of Judith Butler's characterization of the machinery of colonization as 'the deadening of sense, the establishment of the body in social death' (Butler 2008, 224).

It is important to historicize Fanon's analysis of colonial psychiatry in order to explore the extent to which it emerges as a counter-discourse to colonial ethnographic formations. Such a study will not only throw light on the topicality of Fanon's critique of medical politics but will also help connect to different cultural climates in similar situations of repressive reification. In the Manichaeism characterizing the colonial condition whereby the colonizer and the colonized were classified through a gendered vocabulary, 'the conflict itself was the constitution of madness [and the therapy was] revolutionary praxis' (Gordon 1996, 81). Thus, as Fanon contends unequivocally in *The Wretched of the Earth*, decolonization is always associated with a violence that is phenomenal as well as political, enacted through a violent decentring that is never inconspicuous and that 'transforms spectators crushed with their inessentiality into privileged actors, with the grandiose glare of history's floodlights upon them' (Fanon [1967] 2001, 28). One of the finest examples of this emerges from Fanon's medical and political examination of the North African syndrome.

In his remarkable essay titled 'The North African Syndrome', published as a medical student in 1952, Fanon examines the alleged malingering characteristic of the African as the nervous condition induced by the anxiety of existential dislocation. As Jock McCulloch contends in his historical study of colonial psychiatry, the North African syndrome was a complex condition of mutual misunderstanding, and in the dominant biopolitical gaze, '[i]t was seen to serve the patient's need to escape from work and enjoy the warmth and inactivity of the hospital environment: in short, to become a social parasite' (McCulloch 1995, 124). Fanon's incisive study of the political presuppositions informing the disease asserts thus:

> The medical staff discovers the existence of a North African syndrome. Not experimentally but on the basis of an oral tradition. The North African takes his place in this asymptomatic syndrome and is automatically put down as indisciplined (cf. medical discipline), inconsequential (with reference to a law according to which every symptom implies a lesion), and insincere (he says he is suffering when we know there are no *reasons* for suffering). (Fanon 1967, 9–10)

A critique of the metonymic materiality that governed European medical science (the metonymic correlation between a symptom and its corresponding lesion), Fanon's analysis of the North African syndrome exposes the political-cultural contingencies and the psychic insecurities that constructed and corroborated contemporary colonial conditions. More importantly, in exposing and critiquing the collusion between medical science and the machinery of state control, Fanon reveals how colonial medicine itself may emerge as 'an effect of political action' (Lemke 2011, 31–32).

As Ranjana Khanna contends in her remarkable analysis of psychoanalysis's location in colonial conditions, Fanon's explanations of the North African syndrome eschewed sentimental affiliation as well as biomedical reification. Among Fanon's explanations

> [o]ne was that the North African faked illness in order, for example, to be treated to a warm hospital bed when it was cold. Another was the doctors' failure to interact appropriately with their patients, patronizingly addressing them in the familiar and disrespectful second person singular (*tutoyer*), thus introducing a hierarchical relationship between doctor and patient. And a third was that illnesses were psychosomatic functions of colonial affect, because of expatriation, torture, or cultural confusion. (Khanna 2003, 176)

The charges of simulation appropriated by the North Africans as analysed by Fanon are not dissimilar to the supposed strategies of attention seeking and malingering that were ascribed respectively to the hysterical women of the late nineteenth century and the shell-shocked soldiers of the early twentieth century (Parui 2018, 120–36). Speaking as an insider of the French–North African colonial condition, Fanon argues that the North African on the threshold of French citizenship experiences the same anxiety as that of a medically sick man on the threshold of a hospital or clinic, embodying a pathological condition that is an epiphenomenon of politically produced neurosis:

> Threatened in all his affectivity, threatened in his social activity, threatened in his membership in a community – the North African combines all the conditions that make a sick man. Without a family, without love, without human relations, without communion with the group, the first encounter with himself will occur in a neurotic mode, in a pathological mode; he will find himself emptied, without life, in a bodily struggle with death . . . and what is more pathetic than this man with robust muscles who tells us in his truly broken voice, 'Doctor, I'm going to die'? (Fanon 1967, 13)

The North African syndrome as examined by Fanon dramatized the dislocation that characterized the melancholic and transformed him – according to the racialized colonial psychiatry – from the realm of the suicidal to that of the homicidal. This seemingly unaccountable transition (expounded earlier in the works of Carothers as the African's frontal lobe syndrome) was actually acerbated by the conditions of rootlessness and lack of national identity. The supposed pathology of the North African, whose melancholia, conveniently classified as *pseudomelancholy* by colonial psychiatrists, was a manifestation of not just bodily disorders but also of what Gayatri Chakravorty Spivak classifies in the context of Indian colonial education as 'the epistemic violence of the legal project' (Spivak 1999, 268) that sanctioned the superordination of one system over another. The subversive civility between the black skin and white masks emerges as a nervous/neurotic condition that constitutes and highlights the 'motility of the metaphoric/narcissistic and metonymic/aggressive system of colonial discourse' (Bhabha 1994, 113). As Fanon put it in *Black Skin, White Masks*, '[t]he Negro enslaved by his inferiority, the white man enslaved by his superiority alike behave in accordance with a neurotic orientation' (Fanon 1986, 60), the neurosis emerging as a political as well as an existential condition that is marked by melancholia, anxiety, and fear. It highlights the convergence of the medical and the political conditions of coercion and suffering in Fanon's writing where '[c]olonization affects stomachs and breaths, life and death' (Clare 2013, 65), creating a nervous state where epidermalization and corporealization shape and reshape identities.

The concept of *pseudomelancholia* (a medico-cultural construct that may be examined in line with what Fanon classifies as the 'North African syndrome') was first systematically propounded by Antoine Porot, an honorary professor and practising psychiatrist at the Psychiatric Clinic of the University of Algiers and generally considered the founder of the Algiers School of Psychiatry that sought to clinically prove the innate inferiority of Algerians and their need to be controlled and colonized by a superior race. An entanglement of institutional racism and medicine, pseudomelancholia as expounded by Porot and Carothers (who studied the sub-Saharan counterpart of Porot's Algerian Muslim) was a systematic biomedical analysis of the constitutional difference between the Western and the African experiences of melancholia. Thus, Porot and Carothers would argue, while the Western melancholic was more given to introspective and suicidal tendencies, the pseudomelancholic African was constitutionally inclined to aggression and homicidal tendencies (Carothers 1972; Porot and Bardenat 1960). Inherent in such medical analysis was a neat racialized divide of the minds of men in different cultures of suffering. In consonance with various other contemporary colonial medical analysts, Porot offered a criminological Lombrosian account (offered by Césare Lombroso [1835–1909]) of the innate criminality of the Algerian by equating violent behaviour with the size and structure of the Algerian brain (McCulloch 1995, 106–7; Porot and Sutter 1939). The politics of containment such ethnopsychiatry showcased was premised on a sanctioned science that sought to biomedically legitimize colonial control by reifying and disseminating stereotypes of African inferiority, hypersexuality, and criminality.

The relationship between the colonial circulation of stereotypes and medical analyses of such attributes was thus simplistic, strategic, and racially motivated. In an interesting analysis, Jock McCulloch makes a significant distinction between the ethnopsychiatrists and the colonial anthropologists in terms of their interests and locations in the colonial machinery. Thus, while the anthropologists were usually located at the margins of the colonial state (usually in the interiors or villages) and were more closely involved with the indigenous colonized tribes and populace, the psychiatrists usually occupied more urban centres and 'were better placed than were anthropologists to document and to understand the changes which would lead eventually to the disintegration of colonialism' with a less reified perspective on race, and 'their strategic location did force the ethnopsychiatrists to confront, in an oblique fashion, the major political questions of the day' (McCulloch 1995, 141–42). Fanon's location as a psychiatrist and a cultural critic foregrounds as well as deconstructs the racialized rhetoric of medicine and medical science in the French-Algerian context, while also highlighting the collusion between the medical and the political orders in determining identity production and consumption. In Fanon's reading, the blackness of body and the body of blackness both emerge as experiential and embodied categories that exemplify what Foucault defines as the 'enunciative modality' in biopolitics whereby 'cross-checking of signs, reasoning by analogy, deduction, statistical calculations, experimental verifications and many other forms of statement are to be found in the discourse of nineteenth century doctors'

(Foucault 1972, 55). Drawing further on Foucault, it may also be argued that Fanon's own experience of blackness and being *subjected to the abject* informs his status as a 'specific intellectual' who is embedded 'in a question of real, material, everyday struggles' (Foucault 1980, 127) underlining the quotidian quality of colonial violence and suffering.

The relevance of Fanon in the context of racial politics and production of identities is increasingly relevant and profound. His reading of the racialization of medicine and the medicalization of race highlights the collusive forces that historically informed the engines of imperialism and its subsequent industry of identity production that are re-encoded and replayed even to this day. A work 'hastily completed before Fanon's untimely death in December 1961' (Nethersole 2020, 121), *The Wretched of the Earth* remains a classic text as well as a political manifesto in understanding the visceral and epistemic violence characterizing colonialism and its aftermath. As Sartre states in his famous preface, Fanon may be considered 'the first since Engels to bring the processes of history into the clear light of day' (Sartre [1967] 2001, 13). In a similar vein, Homi Bhabha argues in his 'Foreword: Framing Fanon' that the 'legacy of Fanon leaves us with questions; his virtual, verbal presence among us only provokes more questions' (Bhabha 1963, x). The narrative storytelling quality in Fanon's accounts – first-person as well as studied depictions of violence and suffering – corroborates what Edward Said highlights as the 'formal characteristics of narrative in wider social and philosophical frameworks' as exemplified in the works of Frederic Jameson, Paul Ricoeur, and Tzvetan Todorov, whereby '[n]arrative was transformed from a formal pattern or type to an activity in which politics, tradition, history, and interpretation converged' (Said 1989, 221). Despite not using the fictional framework, Fanon's accounts of colonial violence and its impact on mental health draw heavily on the use of metaphors and focalized storytelling structures, as evinced in his medical case studies and experiential accounts of racial reification. As Stephanie Clare argues, Fanon 'uses organic metaphors and the vocabulary of biology: he writes of muscles and breath, life and death' (Clare 2013, 61), underlining the corporealization and medicalization of identities in colonial violence which are manifested in his use of figurative and focalized language. This is amply evident in Fanon's use of the evocative and affective language of poetry to describe the distress characterizing the North African syndrome where the suffering subject experiences

> A death in the tram
> a death in the doctor's office,
> a death with the prostitutes,
> a death on the job site,
> a death at the movies,

a multiple death in the newspapers,
a death in the fear of all decent folk of going out after midnight.
A death,
Yes A DEATH (Fanon 1967, 13)

Edward Said's remembrance of and acknowledgement of the lasting legacy of Fanon underlines how 'the whole point of Fanon's work is to force the European metropolis to think its history *together with* the history of colonies awakening from the cruel stupor and abused immobility of imperial domination' (Said 1989, 223, emphasis in original). In offering this epistemic revision of European history with a forced acknowledgement of its perpetrated colonial violence, Fanon foregrounds the body of the black subject in historicizing the corporealization and ontologization of the abject in the white imperial imaginary, whereby, as Judith Butler states in her reading of Fanon, 'the body itself becomes historical precisely through an embodiment of social conditions' (Butler 2008, 224). This *abjection of blackness* continues to this day, as Butler would argue elsewhere, through 'a racist organization and disposition of the visible' (Butler 2004, 206), thereby corroborating how the fact of blackness is rematerialized, remetaphorized, and remembered in public discourses from the colonial to the contemporary setting. Fanon's work on race, colonial violence, and the production and reproduction of identities thus showcases how such entanglements operate through the performative, suffering, and inscriptive body which emerges as a vector for mutable matter, metaphor, and memory, which is the primary theme of this book and the central focus of this study.

THE MEDICAL, POLITICAL, AND LITERARY IDENTITIES IN IAN MCEWAN'S *SATURDAY*

The aim of this section is to examine how a literary narrative – Ian McEwan's 2005 novel *Saturday* – can offer complex commentary on the interface of medical knowledge, political events, and literary affect at a time of cultural confusion and uncertainty. Medical knowledge in this study will be read as an epistemic instrument that can quickly collude with other white neoliberal institutions of power, production, and privilege. Against such instrumentality of neuroscience, McEwan's novel situates affect and empathy as more complex experiential categories not mappable by medical machines. This study will show how such affective experiences may be produced by poetry – Matthew Arnold's 'Dover Beach' (1867), which exists as a nested narrative in the fictional frame of *Saturday* – generating awe, amazement, and an eventual admission of ambivalence in the mind of the neurosurgeon protagonist who had hitherto believed in the irrefutable quality of modern medical knowledge. This section examines how the movement from neuroscientific certitude to ambivalence takes place in *Saturday* through witnessing a changing mind in an affective engagement with literature and lyric, which in turn connects to complex questions about the brain, consciousness, affect, and empathy. The section also foregrounds and studies the broader political setting in McEwan's one-day novel – the post-9/11 paranoia in the Western world and the anti–Iraq War protest in London in February 2003 – and examines how it further problematizes cognition and agency at the intersections of experientiality and discursivity.

Commonly classified as an example of the *neuro-novel*, Ian McEwan's *Saturday* (2005) is a narrative that takes as its central theme the ambivalence that the normative medical gaze learns through its existential enquiry about how matter becomes conscious. Set in the Western political climate of post-9/11 attack and pre–Iraq War, *Saturday* is a complex literary text which highlights current debates in neuroscience, psychology, and the study of affect and affective identities. A novel '*about* prejudice, misunderstanding and over-interpretation in an increasingly paranoid London' (Bradley and Tate 2010, 30), *Saturday* depicts the dual potential of a work of fiction to comment profoundly on the political condition of its times as well as to probe deep into a more holistic understanding of human consciousness. The novel does this by juxtaposing historical and experiential axes along which various orders of knowledge are reified, refuted, and reinstated through narratives of recognition and reconciliation.

The protagonist of *Saturday* is the neurosurgeon Henry Perowne – a man who repairs brains and is thus ceaselessly attached to the material world – an unreliable observer who believes 'that the supernatural was the recourse of an insufficient imagination, a dereliction of duty' (McEwan 2005, 67) and thus decries magic realism in literature as kitsch. Through the presentation of its neurosurgeon protagonist, McEwan's novel emerges as a covert critique of some versions of neo-Darwinism and neural determinism that suggest that 'we are born selfish' (Dawkins 1979, 3) and that the mind is 'packed with high-tech systems each contrived to overcome its own obstacles' (Pinker 1998, 4). Instead, what is offered in *Saturday* is an interface between phenomenology and neuroscience that articulates an ambivalence about the claims of scientific knowledge about the feeling self which is capable of curiosity, empathy, revision, and change. In essence, *Saturday* is about one day in the life of the neurosurgeon Henry Perowne, a socially successful middle-class white Londoner who loves his wife and has a talented blues musician as a son and a published poet as a daughter. The one day depicted in the novel happens to be the day of the London march against the 2003 Iraq War. Perowne wakes up and sees what he first thinks is a terrorist attack in the sky, is assured upon being informed later that it was a harmless aircraft accident, drives off to play a squash game with an American colleague, and has a car accident with a typical troublemaker named Baxter. Although he is certain he is not in the wrong about the accident, Perowne cannot convince Baxter and his mates and finds himself helplessly overpowered, with physical assault imminent. Perowne escapes the beating by using his medical knowledge, discerning and exposing Baxter's nervous condition (the incurable Huntington's disease) before his cronies, then flees the scene. He manages to keep his squash match appointment and wins the game with a combination of petulance and shameless cheating. He returns home to a happy gathering where his father-in-law Grammaticus and daughter Daisy are also present and subsequently finds his household invaded by Baxter, who seeks to avenge his humiliation earlier. Baxter has the whole of Perowne's family at knifepoint and commands Perowne's daughter Daisy to undress before noticing her book of poems titled *My Saucy Bark*. He then orders the naked Daisy to read from her book, and the latter, now revealed as pregnant, reads out Matthew Arnold's 'Dover Beach' to him.

Perowne then witnesses the power of affect as he sees Baxter moved by the beauty of the lyric, emotionally attaching himself to Arnold's lines about loss of faith and temporarily foregoing his initial intention of attacking Perowne's family. With his mood increasingly softening, Baxter 'changes his mind' temporarily, much to the consternation of his mate Nigel, who leaves the scene. Baxter appears to give in to Perowne's arguments for seeking medical treatment for his nervous condition but soon begins to get angry again. With his son Theo, Perowne swiftly captures the now outnumbered Baxter, rendering him unconscious in the process. He decides not to lodge a police complaint in order to give Baxter a second chance by performing surgery on him, moved by the latter's rich existential response to poetry and viewing it as his claim to life. The novel ends with the day coming to an end. Perowne returns from the operation theatre and begins to fall asleep, looking at his loving wife again and meditating on the mystery and majesty of the process through which the matter that makes the brain becomes emotions which in turn inform the feeling mind, one which extends to the uniquely changeable human self. He also realizes that the Western metropolis of London is not a grand biopolitical success or a biological masterpiece, as he had arrogantly imagined earlier, but a city of uncertainties and contingencies, like many other cities, waiting for its bombs.

Essentially a novel about changing human minds amid uncertain political climates, *Saturday* enacts an epistemic shift from rational scientific certainty to an affect-driven experiential frame grounded in the recognition of uncertainty and indeterminacy, where wonder at the magnificence of the human mind displaces empirical medical knowledge about the mappable functions of the neural brain. The narrative negotiates between different orders of signification – medical, social, and political – through the presentation of its protagonist's attempt to arrive at an epistemic recognition and reconciliation of various networks of knowledge. Such narrative negotiations offer a rich analysis of the sentient subject seeking to bridge scientific and philosophical modes of response and interpretation through an engagement with literature's affective abilities, corroborating David Lodge's view of the literary novel as 'man's most successful effort to describe the experience of individual human beings moving through space and time' (Lodge 2002, 10). With its complex narrative that is both unreliable and self-reflexive, *Saturday* enacts a 'postmodern work of realist fiction that, focalized through an intelligent though at times obtuse character, is concerned with depicting how an embodied, socially embedded, story-loving consciousness shapes everyday human acts of perception' (Thrailkill 2011, 176).

In examining how medical science can unlearn its privileged perspective and instead learn to look at liminality as the site where intentionality is informed by experiential feelings (Ratcliffe 2008, 30–31), *Saturday* investigates the interfaces between analytical and affective realms. More significantly, and at an intertextual level, such investigation locates McEwan in line with the tradition of Modernist writing he so conspicuously alludes to thematically as well as stylistically, in his role as 'the one contemporary literary writer who has most extensively and directly engaged with cognitive neuroscience [and] has also tended to perpetuate the myth of the Modernist "inward turn"' (Waugh 2011, 78). Perowne first appears in the novel assuming the neo-Darwinist position that is certain of its randomness principle and its irrefutable genetics of determinism based on cellular combination, one that leaves little room for legacy, existential agency, or change due to external intervention. His subsequent move – through empathy and affect – to an existential awareness of the unique ontology of the mind apropos of the mappable materiality of the brain, constitutes a combination of medical science and poetry with a backdrop of political changes. It is this uniqueness of multiple points of view, along with the affective epiphanic experience of the self-reflective mind, that emerges in McEwan's *Saturday* as subversive to the neural determinism and certainty of neuroscientific knowledge. In doing so, *Saturday* appears as a fictional narrative that eventually upholds affect's crucial role as a 'collective vehicle for self-reflection and as a shared source of cultural identity' (Donald 2006, 4–5).

The locations of affect and empathy in *Saturday* correspond closely to the works of cognitive psychologists who contend that 'affective feelings convey, in an embodied form, information about the interface between oneself and one's environment' (Gohm and Clore 2002, 91). Empathy emerges in the novel as a cognitive as well as a political condition, especially given its broader subtexts of political terrorism and war. McEwan himself places a high premium on empathy as a significant quality of humanity, one which he locates as a necessary casualty in the operative principle of terrorism. Referring to the 9/11 attackers, the author of *Saturday* had argued: 'Imagining what it is like to be someone other than yourself is at the core of our humanity. It is the essence of compassion, and it is the beginning of morality. The hijackers used fanatical certainty, misplaced religious faith and dehumanizing hatred to purge themselves of the human instinct for empathy. Among their crimes was a failure of the imagination' (McEwan 2001). McEwan's interpretation of empathy as an act of imagination whereby one perceives the pain in the other is substantially corroborated by current research in social neuroscience that how individuals perceive others in pain throws light on the neural mechanisms underlying empathy (Decety and Jackson 2006, 55).

Empathy in *Saturday* is not simply a literary motif or poetic trope but a cognitive response to the voice of the other that the sentient self can establish a dialogue with through the moving mind that exists as an epistemic excess to the materiality of the hardwired brain. Poetry in the novel thus emerges as a voice that speaks to the medically degenerate, as Baxter – the baddie from the street who happens to embody 'biological determinism in its purest form' (McEwan 2005, 93) – is moved by Daisy's reading of Matthew Arnold's 'Dover Beach', since it makes him think about where he grew up. The significance of the lyric as a construct that communicates the qualia of consciousness has been corroborated by neuroscientists and literary writers alike. The method of the lyric in constructing qualia has been classified as unique inasmuch as it uses 'language in such a way that the description of qualia does not seem partial, imprecise, and only comprehensible when put in the context of the poet's personal life' (Lodge 2002, 11–12). McEwan's novel about neurons and affect also underlines the affective abilities of literature and literary narratives to change feelings and minds. In their essay exploring the intersections of neurology and narratives, Kay Young and Jeffrey Salver propose that '[w]hen we choose to be in the company of narrative by reading a novel or seeing a film, the narrative sets itself off as narrative, not as part of our lives; we stand in relation to it as audience to its "performance" as an aesthetic work. However, the storytelling we experience as an event in life can lose its appearance as narrative by virtue of its integration in life' (Young and Salver 2001, 72). *Saturday* seems to break the borderlines between the affect inside the 'story' produced by the literary artefact and the reader's own empathetic understanding of the human selves within the fictional frame. Like Baxter's empathic engagement with the lyrical content of Arnold's 'Dover Beach' that arises out of the possibility of reunion, Perowne's daughter Daisy's emotional response to *Jane Eyre* earlier in McEwan's novel is premised on the affective experience induced by the literary work of art. The emotional response to art-affect appears as the ability through which empathy and agency emerge in ways which medical science cannot map. In positioning a neurosurgeon at the complex crossroads of agency and empathy, McEwan's novel enacts modern neuroscience's investigations into emotions and intentionality. The issue of agency in *Saturday* is in close yet complex correspondence with the structures of empathy in the novel, evinced spectacularly in the broader political scene by the massive public protests in London against the Iraq War and privately by Baxter's affective association with Matthew Arnold's nineteenth-century lyric of loss and love.

Therefore, when Baxter admits that he has *changed his mind*, the meaning is metaphorical as well as neurological, corroborating the close and complex correspondence between matter, metaphor, and memory in McEwan's novel. In responding to the art of poetry and in connecting to a nineteenth-century lyric about human emotions in times of cultural crises, the untutored Baxter shifts from a position of violence to one of empathetic association. In the process, he asserts his claim to life with the ability to enact what is defined by neuroscientists as the dual function of consciousness: the urge to address the concerns of the self and connect to other selves while improving the art of life (Damasio 2000, 5). It is this condition that the neurosurgeon Henry Perowne recognizes, despite his inability to comprehend the quality and depth of Baxter's emotional empathy with Arnold's poetry, and this constitutes the moment in McEwan's novel when phenomenal insight begins to mix with the medical gaze of neuroscience. Perowne comes to realize that some nineteenth-century poet 'touched off in Baxter a yearning he could barely begin to define. That hunger is his claim on life, on a mental existence, and because it won't last much longer, because the door of his consciousness is beginning to close, he shouldn't pursue his claim from a cell, waiting for the absurdity of his trial to begin' (McEwan 2005, 278–79). The role of the fictional narrative as inducing empathy in the human mind is the core issue in the narrative of cognition in *Saturday*, operating through dual cognitive frames: Baxter's phenomenological association with the emotional reverberation of Matthew Arnold's lyric, and Perowne's existential awareness of ambivalence that is born of his experience of witnessing Baxter's embodied dialogue with poetry. Just as Baxter's emotional engagement with the lyric reminds and reconnects him to his past, Perowne's recognition of Baxter's association provides him with a unique insight into the wonder of the human mind whose agency and intentionality cannot be explained by the neuroscience he knows and practises.

'Dover Beach' is more than a casually situated subtext in McEwan's *Saturday*, a novel which may be seen as a critique of neo-Darwinian notions of selection and agency in the twenty-first-century Western world. Arnold's nineteenth-century lyric of love and loss engages with the existential uncertainty of the human self experienced in the wake of the original Darwinian moment that corroded religious faith in the nineteenth century with the new discoveries in natural sciences. The final message of togetherness in love in 'Dover Beach' corresponded closely to the Arnoldian notion of culture as an '*internal* condition' that transcended the 'animality' of the human 'in the ever-increasing efficaciousness and in the general harmonious expansion of those gifts of thought and feeling which make the peculiar dignity, wealth and happiness of human nature' (Arnold [1869] 2006, 36). Such condition, based on the politics of communal and collective harmony, was ontologically undercut by the Darwinian notion of natural selection – by which 'the innumerable beings on the face of this earth are enabled to struggle with each other, and the best adapted to survive' (Darwin 2003, 10) – that left little room for free will and existential agency. In foregrounding a literary work as a producer of affect and empathy which moves the human subject away from violence, *Saturday* corroborates David Amigoni's argument that McEwan's works largely examine 'literature's role in generating and enhancing "civilization"' (Amigoni 2008, 151). The subtextual significance of Arnold's 'Dover Beach' in the broader political setting of *Saturday* is further compelling, as the Iraq War the novel is set right ahead of 'can be seen as the moment of truth when the "official" political distinctions are blurred' (Žižek 2004, 28) and ideological expectations are problematized. Thus, at a broader cognitive level, the narrative in *Saturday* evokes the classic Arnoldian image of ignorant armies clashing by night with its descriptions of the Taliban and Iraq crises where the angry youth of the Middle East 'are fighting over armies they will never see, about which they know almost nothing' (McEwan 2005, 190).

The epiphanic moment in *Saturday* occurs not in a dream or reverie but amid the medical materiality of the operating theatre where the brain and the mind meet as Perowne embarks on operating on the unconscious Baxter. The epiphany thus described is characterized by humility and constitutes an inward turn with Perowne's admission of the mystery of the mind:

> For all the recent advances, it's still not known how this well-protected one kilogram or so of cells actually encodes information, how it holds experiences, memories, dreams and intentions. He doesn't doubt that in years to come, the coding mechanism will be known, though it might not be in his lifetime. . . . But even when it has, the wonder will remain, that mere wet

stuff can make this bright inward cinema of thought, of sight and sound and touch bound into a vivid illusion of an instantaneous present, with a self, another brightly wrought illusion, hovering like a ghost at its centre. Could it ever be explained, how matter becomes conscious? (ibid., 254–55)

Perowne's epiphanic insight into the complexity of the human mind breaks away from his erstwhile rational biopolitical belief and anticipates the existential awareness of ambivalence with which *Saturday* ends. As the ghost in the machine, the human mind transcending the neural nets in the brain emerges as essentially unmappable by the medical gaze that Perowne initially embodied, enacted, and extended with markers of middle-class white privilege. The 'cinema of thought' spread and savoured by the self-reflective mind is situated at an epistemic excess in relation to the cellular reductionism of medical science. Moving away from the determinism of such a medical gaze, Perowne's phenomenal discovery of the complexity of consciousness and the philosophical enquiry about how matter becomes conscious connect to a sense of wonder about the mystery and majesty of the mind's unique agency. It is a mystery that he acknowledges will remain, despite the discoveries medical science may achieve in the future.

In his admission of wonder about the human mind as it is born out of the neural brain, Perowne, the professional reductionist, comes – unbeknownst to himself – to articulate how existential feeling of the highest order is an affective category of knowledge (Ratcliffe 2008, 56). The ambivalence that he experiences contributes to a deeper understanding of the human mind and an existential understanding of human self, agency, and intentionality in relation to intersubjective feelings. More significantly, Perowne's newfound knowledge of inwardness invests him with the insightful humility that the philosopher acquires through affective and embodied awareness (James 1979, 63). The acknowledgement of ambivalence informs Perowne's heightened recognition of the sentient self and its economy of empathy that had been brought to light before him by Baxter's connection with the lyric and his subsequent epiphany in the operation theatre. Perowne's existential insight into Baxter's brain thus seeks to look beyond matter in its philosophical questions about human life and consciousness. In the process he realizes that the transition from matter to meaning constitutes not just the mappable neural mechanism but the active agency of the feeling existential self that is unique in its self-reflexive location in broader narratives of shared language and culture. The inward cinema that brings meaning out of matter and consciousness out of a semi-solid mass is thus invested with a sentient quality that underpins its subjective situatedness and functional complexity. Such complexity, as Perowne comes to realize, transcends the empirical method of medical science and generates instead an ambivalence that is philosophical in its scope. *Saturday* thus emerges as a novel about ambivalence as an epistemic category, one that re-examines and revises the biopolitical complexities of its times.

As Perowne gazes into the gap between the mind and brain in the operation theatre, he inhabits the threshold moment where epistemic change occurs through a process of perception which blurs the borderlines between the inside and the outside. In trying to figure how the matter of Baxter's brain becomes conscious mind, Perowne in essence looks into his own. It is at this point that the novel brings together experientiality and existential agency in the same cognitive and epistemic plane. In the process, the other (as embodied by Baxter) is interiorized through an experience of empathetic understanding that breaks the barriers between the material and the phenomenal realms, between empirical and emotional states of being. The complexity of *Saturday* lies in its depiction of the manner in which such understanding extends into an unlearning of hegemonic biopolitical knowledge.

The smug satisfaction with which Perowne had woken up in the morning and seen the city as a biological masterpiece is now permanently unsettled, and Perowne's vision of the metropolis that is his home is significantly altered as 'London, his small part of it, lies wide open, impossible to defend, waiting for its bomb, like a hundred other cities' (McEwan 2005, 276). The metacognitive quality of human consciousness, like the self-reflexive quality of the literary narrative itself, is flagged up again as the thoughts of the sleepy Perowne are on sleep itself, which is cognized as 'a material thing, an ancient means of transport, a softly moving belt, conveying him into Sunday' (McEwan 2006, 279). Perowne's awareness of his existential change from the position of certainty to one of liminality – he 'feels skinny and frail in his dressing gown, facing the morning that's still dark, still part of yesterday' (McEwan 2005, 275) – is interestingly similar to Gabriel Conroy's realization of himself in James Joyce's 'The Dead' as 'a nervous well-meaning sentimentalist, orating to vulgarians and idealizing his own clownish lusts, the pitiable fellow he had caught a glimpse of in the mirror' (Joyce 2004, 229). It is perhaps a deliberately designed tribute to the one-day high-Modernist literary aesthetic that *Saturday*'s author draws heavily on, one which foregrounds the complex spatiotemporal markers of cognition and the moving mind.

Henry Perowne in *Saturday* may be viewed as the confused everyman in the post-9/11 neoliberal white Western world ceaselessly invaded by forms of fear manufactured, mediated, and disseminated by dominant structures of control. McEwan's novel may thus be read as a story of awakening which takes place at the level of medicine as well as philosophy, embodied by a neurosurgeon who is offered a glimpse into the mysterious underpinnings of the feeling and changing human mind in times of political indecision, violence, and unclear wars on terror. Ending with the admission of ambivalence and a phenomenal recognition of the feeling self, McEwan's unreliable neurosurgeon is eventually and existentially elevated with the knowledge of his liminality and lack.

Saturday ends with a literal stream of consciousness as Perowne savours the scent and the warmth of his sleeping wife, gets comfort from 'her beloved form, and draws closer to her' (McEwan 2005, 279) while slowly drifting into sleep. As the feeling subject dissolves away to sleep with a final affirmation of being alive to emotions, it also concedes the loss of another sentient day and the imminent move towards nothingness, thus furthering the entanglement of attainment and loss that McEwan's novel dramatizes. As *Saturday* ends with Perowne's consciousness, and as language melts into the purity of the senses, the narration accentuates an awakening of affect that corresponds to the agency of the feeling human self. The only certainty that Perowne appears to arrive at with his newly acquired knowledge of (medical and political) ambivalence is the affirmation of the *affective now*, the phenomenal moment that inhabits and informs the existential, feeling, and fluid self. Perowne's subjective awareness of his own existentiality as he drifts into sleep, corresponds to the neuroscientific notion of 'a mind with an autobiographical self capable of guiding reflective deliberation and gathering knowledge' (Damasio 2010, 307). In his movement from 'ignorance and innocence to knowingness and self' (Damasio 2000, 4), the neurosurgeon enacts the experience in feeling through which the self is embodied and extended not as 'a detached intellectual act but a way of cognitively *grappling* with the world' (Solomon 2004, 77). Emotions and agency emerge in *Saturday*, not merely as cognitive categories that cannot be mapped by the medical machines in Perowne's operation theatre but also as an evaluator of values through which human judgements are made through a process 'in which we acknowledge our neediness and incompleteness before those elements that we do not fully control' (Nussbaum 2004, 184). The narrative that informs Perowne's knowledge and subsequent articulation of ambivalence also voices the philosophical orientation of modern cognitive psychology. It is one that reinforces its claim to truth not by an additional baggage of medical data but by existentially inhabiting 'a sense of reality that is not accessible to the standpoint of empirical science' (Ratcliffe 2008, 241). Perowne's awareness of the arrival of ambivalence is medical as well as philosophical and corresponds closely to the issue of agency and its location in the contemporary political scene, where millions march in protest against a war which nevertheless happens, where ignorant armies clash against enemies they do not know, in fear of weapons which may or may not exist.

This reading of *Saturday* has attempted to examine the awakening of the self at a time of political and cognitive confusion as it changes from being a consumer to becoming an outsider to dominant notions of bioscientific certainty and neoliberal progress. By reading McEwan's fictional neuro-novel right after Fanon's critique of the biopolitics determining colonial violence and identity, this chapter has also attempted to show how learnt discursive knowledge is disrupted during moments of existential ambivalence that correspond to states of self-censorship and auto-critique (Žižek 2010, 401). Such moments reveal the constructed quality of hegemonic narratives, socially sanctioned emotional behaviour, and biopolitical identity, while leading the fluid feeling self to inhabit the schism between shared ideology and individual agency through an inward turn. This chapter attempted to study such an inward turn as represented in a complex literary narrative about changing existential and political identities in a cultural climate of confusing wars amid hegemonic Western notions of growth, health, happiness, and progress. In its reading of a complex work of fiction, the section has drawn on cognitive psychology and philosophy that examine the interface between neuroscience and affect, the mind and the brain. Such examinations of literary representations affirm that to be fully feeling and self-reflectively human is to be in doubt, uncertainty, ambivalence, and pain (Wittgenstein 1958, 200).

REFERENCES

Adler, Alfred. 1921. *The Neurotic Constitution*. Translated by Bernard Glueck. London: Kegan Paul.

Agamben, Giorgio. 1998. *Homo Sacer: Sovereign Power and Bare Life*. Translated by Daniel Heller-Roazen. Stanford, CA: Stanford University Press.

Amigoni, David. 2008. 'The Luxury of Storytelling: Science, Literature and Cultural Contest in Ian McEwan's Narrative Practice'. In *Literature and Science*, edited by Sharon Ruston, 151–68. Suffolk: Boydell & Brewer.

Arnold, Matthew. (1869) 2006. *Culture and Anarchy*. Oxford: Oxford Classics.

Bauman, Zygmunt. 2003. *Wasted Lives: Modernity and Its Outcasts*. Oxford: Polity.

Bhabha, Homi K. 1963. 'Foreword: Framing Fanon'. In *The Wretched of the Earth*, by Frantz Fanon, translated by Richard Philcox, vii–xii. New York: Grove.

———. 1986. 'Remembering Fanon'. In *Black Skin, White Masks*, by Frantz Fanon, i–xxii. London: Pluto Press.

———. 1994. *The Location of Culture*. London: Routledge.

Bradley, Arthur, and Andrew Tate. 2010. *The New Atheist Novel: Fiction, Philosophy and Polemic after 9/11*. London: Continuum.

Butler, Judith. 2004. 'Endangered/Endangering: Schematic Racism and White Paranoia'. *The Judith Butler Reader*, edited by Sara Salih and Judith Butler, 204–11. New York: Blackwell.

———. 2008. 'Violence, Nonviolence: Sartre on Fanon'. In *Race after Sartre*, edited by Jonathan Judaken, 211–32. Albany, NY: State University of New York Press.
Carothers, J. C. 1940. 'Some Speculations on Insanity in Africans in General'. *East African Medical Journal* 17:90–105.
———. 1947. 'A Study of Mental Derangement in Africans and an Attempt to Explain Its Peculiarities, More Especially in Relation to the African Attitude to Life'. *Journal of Mental Science* 93:548–97.
———. 1951. 'Frontal Lobe Function and the African'. *Journal of Mental Science* 97:12–48.
———. 1972. *The Mind of Man in Africa*. London: Tom Stacey.
Childs, Peter. 2006. *The Fiction of Ian McEwan*. Basingstoke: Palgrave Macmillan.
Clare, Stephanie. 2013. 'Geopower: The Politics of Life and Land in Frantz Fanon's Writing'. *Diacritics* 41(4): 60–80.
Damasio, Antonio. 2000. *The Feeling of What Happens: Body, Emotions and the Making of Consciousness*. London: Vintage.
———. 2010. *Self Comes to Mind: Constructing the Conscious Brain*. New York: Pantheon.
Darwin, Charles. (1859) 2003. *On the Origin of Species by Natural Means of Selection*. Peterborough: Broadview.
Dawkins, Richard. 1979. *The Selfish Gene*. New York: Oxford University Press.
———. 1982. *The Extended Phenotype: The Gene as a Unit of Selection*. Oxford: W. H. Freeman.
———. 2000. *The Blind Watchmaker*. London: Penguin.
Decety, Jean, and Philip L. Jackson. 2006. 'A Social-Neuroscience Perspective on Empathy'. *Current Directions in Psychological Science* 2:54–58.
Donald, Merlin. 2006. 'Art and Cognitive Evolution'. In *The Artful Mind: Cognitive Science and the Riddle of Human Creativity*, edited by Mark Turner, 3–20. Oxford: Oxford University Press.
Fanon, Frantz. 1967. *Towards the African Revolution: Political Essays* Translated by Haakon Chevalier. New York: Grove.
———. (1967) 2001. *The Wretched of the Earth*. Translated by Constance Farrington. London: Penguin.
———. 1980. 'Medicine and Colonialism'. In *A Dying Colonialism*, translated by Haakon Chevalier, 121–46. London: Writers and Reader.
———. 1986. *Black Skin, White Masks*. Translated by Charles Lam Markmann. London: Pluto Press.
———. 2000. 'The Fact of Blackness'. In *Theories of Race and Racism: A Reader*, edited by Les Back and John Solomos, 257–66. London: Routledge.
Foucault, Michel. 1972. *The Archaeology of Knowledge*. Translated by A. M. Sheridan. London: Tavistock.
———. 1980. *Power/Knowledge: Selected Interviews & Other Writings, 1972–1977*. Translated and edited by Colin Gordon. New York: Vintage.
———. 1990. *The Will to Knowledge*. Translated by Robert Hurley. London: Penguin.
———. 2003. *Society Must Be Defended: Lectures at the College De France, 1975–76*. New York: Picador.
———. 2009. *Security, Territory, Population: Lectures at the College de France, 1977–78*. Edited by Michael Senellart. Translated by Graham Burchell. Basingstoke: Palgrave Macmillan.

Frank, Arthur W. 1995. *The Wounded Storyteller: Body, Illness and Ethics*. Chicago: Chicago University Press.
Fuss, Diana. 1994. 'Interior Colonies: Frantz Fanon and the Politics of Identification'. *Diacritics* 24(2): 11–33.
Gohm, Carol L., and Gerald L. Clore. 2002. 'Affect as Information: An Individual-Differences Approach'. In *The Wisdom in Feeling: Psychological Processes in Emotional Intelligence*, edited by Lisa Feldman Barrett and Peter Salovey, 89–113. New York: Guilford.
Gordon, Lewis R. 1996. 'The Black and the Body Politic: Fanon's Existential Phenomenological Critique of Psychoanalysis'. In *Fanon: A Critical Reader*, edited by Lewis R. Gordon, T. Deean Sharpley-Whiting, and Renée T. White, 74–84. Oxford: Blackwell.
Gramsci, Antonio. 1985. *Selections from Cultural Writings*. Edited by David Forgas and Geoffrey Nowell-Smith. Translated by William Boelhower. Cambridge, MA: Harvard University Press.
Houen, Alex. 2010. 'Sacrificial Militancy and the Wars around Terror'. In *Terror and the Postcolonial*, edited by Elleke Boehmer and Stephen Morton, 113–40. Oxford: Blackwell.
James, William. 1979. *The Will to Believe and Other Essays in Popular Philosophy*. Cambridge, MA: Harvard University Press.
Joyce, James. (1914) 2004. *Dubliners*. New Delhi: Rupa.
Kaplan, E. Ann. 1999. 'Fanon, Trauma and Cinema'. In *Frantz Fanon: Critical Perspectives*, edited by Anthony C. Alessandrini, 130–51. London: Routledge.
Kennedy, Greg. 2007. *An Ontology of Trash: The Disposable and Its Problematic Nature*. Albany, NY: State University of New York Press.
Khanna, Ranjana. 2003. *Dark Continents: Psychoanalysis and Colonialism*. Durham, NC: Duke University Press.
Lemke, Thomas. 2011. *Bio-Politics: An Advanced Introduction*. Translated by Eric Frederick Trump. New York: New York University Press.
Lodge, David. 2002. *Consciousness and the Novel*. London: Secker & Warburg.
Mannoni, Octave. 1964. *Prospero and Caliban: The Psychology of Colonialism*. Translated by Pamela Powesland. New York: Praeger.
McCulloch, Jock. 1995. *Colonial Psychiatry and the African Mind*. New York: Cambridge University Press.
McEwan, Ian. 2001. 'Only Love and Then Oblivion. Love Was All They Had to Set against Their Murderers'. *The Guardian*, September 15, 2001. https://www.theguardian.com/world/2001/sep/15/september11.politicsphilosophyandsociety2.
———. 2005. *Saturday*. London: Jonathan Cape.
———. 2007. 'End of the World Blues'. In *The Portable Atheist: Essential Readings for the Non-Believer*, edited by Christopher Hitchens, 351–65. London: Da Capo.
Nethersole, Reingard. 2020. 'Shards of Hegel: Jean-Paul Sartre's and Homi K. Bhabha's Readings of the *Wretched of the Earth*'. In *Violence, Slavery, and Freedom between Hegel and Fanon*, edited by Ulrike Kistner and Philippe Van Haute, 117–40. Johannesberg: Wits University Press.
Nussbaum, Martha. 2004. 'Emotions as Judgements of Value and Importance'. In *Thinking about Feeling: Contemporary Philosophers on Emotions*, edited by Robert C. Solomon, 183–99. Oxford: Oxford University Press.

Parui, Avishek. 2018. '"Human Nature is Remorseless": Masculinity, Medical Science and Nervous Conditions in Virginia Woolf's Mrs Dalloway'. In *The Male Body in Medicine and Literature*, edited by Andrew Mangham and Daniel Lea, 120–36. Oxford: Liverpool University Press.
Pinker, Steven. 1998. *How the Mind Works*. London: Penguin.
Porot, Antoine, and C. Sutter. 1939. 'Le primitivisme des indigenes nord-sfricains: Ses incidences en pathologie mentale'. *Sud Medical et Chirurgica* 1:226–41.
Porot, Antoine, and Charles Bardenat. 1960. *Anormaux et malades mentaux devant la justice pénale*. Paris: Librairie Maloine.
Ratcliffe, Matthew. 2008. *Feelings of Being: Phenomenology, Psychiatry and the Sense of Reality*. Oxford: Oxford University Press.
Said, Edward W. 1989. 'Representing the Colonized: Anthropology's Interlocutors'. *Critical Inquiry* 15(2): 205–25.
Sartre, Jean Paul. (1967) 2001. Preface to Frantz Fanon's *The Wretched of the Earth*, translated by Constance Farrington. London: Penguin.
Siegel, Lee. 2005. 'The Imagination of Disaster'. *Nation*, March 24, 2005. https://www.thenation.com/article/archive/imagination-disaster.
Solomon, Robert C. 2004. 'Emotions, Thoughts, and Feelings: Emotions as Engagements with the World'. In *Thinking about Feeling: Contemporary Philosophers on Emotions*, edited by Robert C. Solomon, 76–90. Oxford: Oxford University Press.
Spivak, Gayatri Chakravorty. 1999. *A Critique of Postcolonial Reason: Towards a History of the Vanishing Present*. Cambridge, MA: Harvard University Press.
Thrailkill, Jane F. 2011. 'Ian McEwan's Neurological Novel'. *Poetics Today* 1:171–210.
Waugh, Patricia. 2011. 'Thinking in Literature: Modernism and Contemporary Neuroscience'. In *Legacies of Modernism: Historicizing Postwar and Contemporary Fiction*, edited by David James, 75–95. Cambridge: Cambridge University Press.
Wittgenstein, Ludwig. 1958. *Philosophical Investigations*. Oxford: Blackwell.
Young, Kay, and Jeffrey Salver. 2001. 'The Neurology of Narrative'. *SubStance* 30:72–84.
Žižek, Slavoj. 2004. *Iraq: The Borrowed Kettle*. London: Verso.
———. 2010. *Living in the End Times*. London: Verso.

Conclusion

This book began with a popular-culture reference to a recorded recitation by the tennis maestros Roger Federer and Raphael Nadal. It will start its conclusion with a reference to another speech act by the actor Tom Cruise. In the Seventy-Fourth Annual Academy Awards in 2002, taking place subsequent to the 9/11 attacks, the actor appeared as presenter of the Errol Morris montage of movie memories. Describing the 9/11 attacks as an event that 'changed us', Cruise mentioned a discussion with an actor-friend about the moral logic of celebrating cinema and its magic after such human horror and tragedy, before moving on to declare that such celebration of storytelling and magic in cinema was needed 'more than ever' in the wake of a colossal loss. As Cruise would go on to state in his brief but remarkably moving piece, in cinema 'a small scene, a gesture, even a glance between characters can cross lines, break through barriers, melt prejudice, just plain make us laugh' ('Tom Cruise's Post-9/11 Opening' 2008). The affective possibilities of the storytelling medium – operating as a celebration as well as subversion of culture as it is commonly consumed and shared – appear with heightened existential significance in the wake of a tragedy or crisis. The same could be said about literature and the act of storytelling, from Giovanni Boccaccio's *Decameron* where seven young women and three men escape from a plague-infested Florence and seek refuge in a deserted villa in Fiesole, filling in their crisis-ridden exiled space-time with the existential possibilities emerging out of performative fictional acts, to Salman Rushdie's *Haroun and the Sea of Stories* which situates the 'subversive function of magic and mimesis against a culture of coercion and political fascism that censors free speech and agency' (Parui 2017, 66). Fiction and the act of narration, this book has argued, are key categories which lend vital affective, experiential, and ideological investments in cultural materiality and identity, enacting what Martha Nussbaum defines as the 'third ability' of true citizenship along with negotiation with knowledge and logic, namely that of 'narrative imagination' which informs the 'ability to think what it must be like to be in the shoes of a person different from oneself' (Nussbaum 2010, 95–96).

The references to the Tom Cruise speech at the post-9/11 Oscars and to Boccaccio's *Decameron* are of course connected and deliberately situated. This book emerged from an ongoing pandemic which has defamiliarized and deterritorialized shared as well as private perception, knowledge, and experience of space, security, trust, and time. The COVID-19 crisis, a spectral as well as a fearfully real presence throughout the writing of this book, may in itself be considered an entanglement of dangerously mysterious and multidimensional matter, metaphor, and memory, emerging as an ironic and partial pointer to the subtitle of this book. This work has attempted to situate the literary medium as a creative and narrative form that offers a complex understanding of the contagious material and affective activity we call culture, its rituals of remembering and forgetting. The COVID-19 pandemic, with its suspension of shared space and time and its devastating effect on human life, has also forced an experience of exile on us all, the ones who have survived as yet but live with the knowledge that the deadly infection can happen any time, any place, from anybody we may or may not know, may or may not love, touch, or trust. This compares interestingly with Siegfried Kracauer's posthumously published book *History: The Last Things before the Last* (1969) where the historian emerges as a figure who is always in exile, a stranger (*Fremde*), one who inhabits and experiences *extra-territoriality* (Kracauer 1995, 83–84). For we too can perhaps only record and remember the *pandemic present* as *extra-territorial exiles* even as we witness its horror from its *infected space-time*. This liminal location between exile and witness, between extra-territoriality and lived reality, is the lens this book has attempted to take in espousing a philosophical framework that situated the narrative as a vital vector of culture and cultural activity.

As emergent as well as connective conditions, narrative and fiction have taken various forms in human evolution, from cave drawings to digital diagrams of events and experiences. The human brain, which can live, learn, and love on a mere twenty watts ('The Brain Works With 20 Watts' 2019) can embody, extend, and enact an experiential self through structures of storytelling that create, consolidate, and critique what constitutes culture, cultural activities, and identities. This book, which has drawn on memory studies, material engagement theory, and affect theory, among other frameworks, is an examination of the ontology of fiction and the storytelling mind that engages with the 'messy and ambiguous' quality of human reality (Bauman 1993, 32). The messiness and ambiguity – accentuated medically as well as culturally in the contemporary world today with the crisis of the COVID-19 pandemic – receive full and true human depictions in acts of fiction and narrativity which can open up 'the ontology of *givenness*, whereby the reified relationships between author and character, time and space, history and identity, substance and its absence, are debunked and deconstructed' (Parui 2018, 25). In its attempt to understand culture as a mutable material and affective process, this book has examined the realm of the literary as an entanglement of matter, metaphor, and memory, one which may function as a parable as well as a *parabole* in its negotiations with paradigms, indicating being 'beyond as well as alongside', whereby things and concepts may be calibrated by their controlled situationality as well as 'thrown more hazardously and dynamically together so that the paradeigmatic that emerges might open up the entire system' (Waugh 2021, 111). Fiction and narrativity, this book has attempted to argue, offer a *view of the beyond* as well as that of the *alongside* apropos of culture and cultural materiality, with a medium that can absorb as well as open, consolidate as well as critique, what we consume as meaningful materiality.

The COVID-19 crisis, out of which this book emerged, has brought about a cognitive remapping of reality as well as modes of remembering, as the 'matter produced and experienced during the current pandemic – including medical masks, sanitizers, vaccines, and essential and non-essential goods – generates special metaphoric and mnemonic associations in a defamiliarized cognitive frame' (Parui and Raj, forthcoming). As scientists continue to examine the nature of the virus that affects and infects us globally today and ironically connects us as one *precarious community*, a study of the narrative structures that may emerge out of this shared vulnerability is worth undertaking. Fritz Breithaupt's cognitive research on narrative and storytelling structures as forms of representations of the COVID-19 crisis offers such a study. The first narrative of the virus as a dent in normalcy, subsequently turning to normal life again, constitutes what Breithaupt calls the *narrative of assurance*. The narrative of *total control* and supreme surveillance as the only chance of survival forms the second category, one which is bleaker and more coercive in quality. The third narrative of *collective action* promotes sharing and co-creating and advocates a movement away from hoarding and selfishness towards collective action during the pandemic. The narrative of *depression* forms the fourth category where humans rely on virtual platforms to connect emotionally, where such machines of connectivity and interactivity also produce the painful awareness of actual disconnect and its resultant alienation. The fifth and final story structure classified by Breithaupt is one that foregrounds *failures of strong ego-driven leadership*, showcasing the collapse of megalomaniacal leaders and a move towards student-led global bodies that address causes such as the climate crisis (Breithaupt 2021).

The metaphoric and metonymic patterns emerging in Breithaupt's research on the narrative possibilities of COVID-19 highlight the range of associations the virus has assumed in contemporary cultural imaginary, from a shared sense of collective precarity to a revision and rejection of human hubris and totalitarian claims. The self-reflexivity in each of the narrative structures studied by Breithaupt foregrounds fiction's innate ability to transcend the materiality of its own medium and affectively represent the reality it critiques, enacting what Sara Ahmed argues may be described as a 'reach out of fiction, almost like a hand that comes up and comes out of the grave', marking a desire to establish 'connection to others' (Ahmed 2011, 249). The ability to imagine and animate lived experience and material reality offers fiction and narrative accounts a mode to remember events and experiences in ways which are creatively informative as well as emotionally evocative. Fiction's ability to *corporealize possibilities* through narratives makes it a unique medium to depict and deconstruct shared notions of space, time, security, and identity, especially at times of crisis that are collectively shared as well as privately suffered. The fluidity of the fictional frame 'lies in its liminality and its entanglement of materiality and metaphoricity, through which the remembered as well as the dismembered, the real and the spectral, can be stylized and stated' (Raj and Parui 2021, 346).

Drawing on the research possibilities in memory studies, Astrid Erll's examination of COVID-19 memories points to the necessity of imagination and representation in remembering a collective crisis, using the almost-forgotten Spanish flu as a case study. Highlighting how the earlier pandemic did not receive sufficient representations in literature to the extent of being metaphorized adequately in collective memory, Erll argues that as 'it was not a "pandemic imagined", it did not turn into a "pandemic remembered"' (Erll 2020, 865). The insufficient imagination and representation of the previous pandemic are also examined by the political scientist Bert Hoffmann who studies how the COVID-19 crisis, taking place a hundred years after the Spanish flu, 'forcefully reminds us that awareness of the ecological context in which we humans operate does not stop at resource extractivism and rain forest destruction, climate change and micro-plastics, but that it also encompasses our uneasy co-existence with nature's smallest beasts, the viruses, bacteria and germs that inhabit our world and our bodies' (Hoffman 2020, 209). Hoffman's study of collective co-existence situates mind, matter, and meaning as interchangeable categories in a planetary connectedness forcefully foregrounded by the prevailing pandemic, while also highlighting the ability to imagine it as an emergent as well as connective activity that can recreate and reanimate reality. This book, very much a product of the COVID-19 world of mysteriously multiplying matter, sudden deaths, and messy metaphors, situates storytelling and a study of narratives – both fictional and nonfictional – as a fundamental feature of the human self that is constituted by cultural matrices as well as being beyond the same. Culture *in* the literary is thus an embedded as well as an extended representational category, situated as well as proleptic, with an interplay of matter and metaphor that shapes modes of multidimensional memory, remembering what may or may not have happened while also anticipating what may or may not *take place*. This form of representation emerges with unique relevance and significance in the COVID-19 world today where human engagements are 'characterized by *incomplete intersubjectivity* and *interfacial interactivity* in a shared and contagious space-time' (Parui and Raj, forthcoming).

One of the finest literary responses to the culture of the COVID-19 crisis emerged from the 2020 science fiction symposium Thinking through the Pandemic. There, one primary argument underlined how the uniquely destructive nature of the COVID-19 fear rests less on 'the event of its emergence' and more on the 'totality of its effect on the imagination, one that rivalled the most ambitious tropes of sf and made apocalypse and dystopia the lexicon of scientists, policymakers, journalists, and storytellers alike' (Science Fiction Studies 2020, 323). The symposium also offered a list of words that have assumed new and more complex metaphoric meanings in the COVID-19 memory such as *contactless, essential goods, essential workers, virtual learning, social distancing*, and *economic impact payment* (ibid., 331–32). Due to its unique vocabulary, generating and investing new semantic and metaphoric entanglements out of old words, the language of the COVID-19 world is always already figurative and focalized, corresponding to defamiliarizing notions about corporeality, survival strategies, and sustenance, whereby the very ontology and experience of the social is defined and decreed by distance. This in turn connects to certain shared markers and metaphors of access, alienation, and absence. This book has also shown how the literary as a medium can enact and highlight fluidity as well as depth, interiority as well as interface, in its re-encoding of events and experiences. If fiction offers an amalgamation, as the cognitive theorist Lisa Zunshine argues, of points of view '*potentially available* to us but at a given moment *differing* from our own' (Zunshine 2004, 132), it creates focal points and perspectival positions through which commonly consumed cultural ideas and identities may be recognized and recalibrated through representations and proleptic projections. The literary, this book has attempted to argue, is a complexly coded form of representation, one which defamiliarizes, consolidates, and critiques the vectors and markers that constitute culture. Fiction and fictional representations offer an affective medium of imaginative intersubjectivity, empathy, and interactivity in figurative language that 'overcomes the challenges of cultural, national, and racial difference by offering opportunities for empathetic identification' (Keen 2007, 62).

In her essay on the ontological possibilities of the paradigm in *future theory*, Patricia Waugh studies how contemporary science is oriented towards the 'onto-epistemologies of the complex, the emergent and the artefactual' while humanities research is also advised to align and reorient itself 'towards the assemblage, the curated, the network, the open, unpredictable and the horizontal' (Waugh 2021, 109). While the celebration of surfaces, interfaces, and horizontal networks innovatively pervades humanities research today, there is an increasing need to reconnect to critique's conservative 'metaphors of depth' in order to avoid a view of 'creativity reduced to innovation and for-profit entrepreneurship, creative industries and performativity' (ibid., 109). The metaphors of depth offer a cognitive and existential dimension that shows minds processing matter and meanings with acts of anticipation and rituals of remembering. The double-helical temporal axes offered by fictional as well as nonfictional narratives – depicting episodic and embodied experiences and identities emerging out of memory and materiality – foreground lived reality as a form of representation as well as an anticipation. This book has attempted to engage with the possibilities produced by the literary and the narrative orders in describing, disrupting, and defamiliarizing the events, emotions, and experiences that create and constitute culture and cultural activities. If, following Slavoj Žižek, an event may be defined by *'the effect that seems to exceed its causes* – and the space of an event is that which opens up by the gap which separates an effect from its causes' (Žižek 2014, 3), the literary medium is perhaps best suited to capture such ontological gaps with its potential to be defamiliarizing, disruptive, and proleptic. The realm of the narrative – both fictional and experiential – contains the convergence of the retrospective, the immediate, and the anticipatory, remembering what happened while also shaping what might materialize and capturing the 'leap from the *not yet* to the *always already*' that defines contingency and ontological uncertainty (Žižek 2021, 213). In the process, the literary medium may remind us of what we forge to forget through our strategic structures of meaning and meaningful materiality, the fact that human and planetary life has emerged and continues to emerge from existential accidents, which are random, ontologically uncertain, and always already precarious and contingent. This precarity is spectacularly corroborated by the crisis of the COVID-19 pandemic that has brought about 'subject-object dis-orientations and defamiliarizations in space-time at ontological and experiential levels, which also affects the memory of events and experiences' (Parui and Raj, forthcoming). The function and reception of the literary, the complex form of representation that draws on matter, metaphor, and memory, are perhaps relevant, more than ever, in the culture of contingency we collectively inhabit and internalize today.

REFERENCES

'The Brain Works with 20 Watts. That Is Enough to Cover Our Entire Thinking Ability'. 2019. Munich RE, August 7. https://www.munichre.com/topics-online/en/digitalisation/interview-henning-beck.html.
'Tom Cruise's Post-9/11 Opening: 2002 Oscars'. 2008. YouTube video, 3:08, Oscars, February 20. https://www.youtube.com/watch?v=wb0KYB3Z8Ws.
Ahmed, Sara. 2011. 'Willful Parts: Problem Characters or the Problem of Character'. *New Literary History* 42(2): 231–53.
Bauman, Zygmunt. 1993. *Postmodern Ethics*. Oxford: Blackwell.
Breithaupt, Fritz. 2021. 'The Future Tells'. *Zeit Campus*. https://www.zeit.de/2020/18/corona-krise-studierende-professoren-narrative.
Erll, Astrid. 2020. 'Afterword: Memory Worlds in Times of Corona'. *Memory Studies* 13(5): 861–74.
Hoffman, Bert. 2020. 'Repressed Memory'. *European Review of Latin American and Caribbean Studies* 109:203–11. https://doi.org/10.32992/erlacs.10677.
Keen, Suzanne. 2007. *Empathy and the Novel*. Oxford: Oxford University Press.
Kracauer, Siegfried. 1995. *History: The Last Things before the Last*. Princeton, NJ: Markus Wiener.
Nussbaum, Martha C. 2010. *Not for Profit: Why Democracy Needs the Humanities*. Princeton, NJ: Princeton University Press.
Parui, Avishek. 2017. '"What's the Use of Stories That Aren't Even True?": Agency, Fabulation and the Epistemology of the Storytelling Self in Salman Rushdie's Haroun and the Sea of Stories'. *South Asian Review* 35(1): 55–73.
———. 2018. *Postmodern Literatures*. Hyderabad: Orient Blackswan.
Parui, Avishek, and Merin Simi Raj. Forthcoming. 'The COVID-19 Crisis Chronotope: The Pandemic as Matter, Metaphor, and Memory'. *Memory Studies*.
Raj, Merin Simi, and Avishek Parui. 2021. '"Not Knowing for How Much Longer": Requiem for the Living as an Act of Cultural Recovery of the Paranki Community in Kerala'. In *Anglo-Indian Identity: Past and Present, in India and the Diaspora*, edited by Robyn Andrews and Merin Simi Raj, 343–70. London: Palgrave Macmillan.
Science Fiction Studies. 2020. 'Thinking through the Pandemic: A Symposium'. *Science Fiction Studies* 47(3): 321–76.
Waugh, Patricia. 2021. 'Paradigm'. In *Future Theory: A Handbook to Critical Concepts*, edited by Patricia Waugh and Marc Botha, 93–114. London: Bloomsbury.
Žižek, Slavoj. 2014. *Event: Philosophy in Transit*. Harmondsworth: Penguin.

———. 2021. *Less than Nothing: Hegel and the Shadow of Dialectical Materialism*. London: Verso.

Zunshine, Lisa. 2004. 'Richardson's Clarissa and a Theory of Mind'. In *The Work of Fiction: Cognition, Culture, and Complexity*, edited by Alan Richardson and Ellen Spolsky, 127–46. Aldershot: Ashgate.

Index

aberrative space, 125
abject, 171, 192–93; abjection, 193; abjection of blackness, 193; image of the, 188; ontology of the, 181–82; production of the, 182
Academy Awards, 207
Adler, Alfred, 187
aesthetic narcissism, 164
affect theory, 7, 10, 173; affective apparatus, 184; affective insight through accident, 177–78; affective instrument, 42, 93, 160; affective now, the, 202; affective unlearning, 10, 178, 180 affect studies, 5, 34, 36
Agamben, Giorgio, 177–79
ageless artefact, 160
agency-less, 111, 125
agentic, 10, 93, 95, 116, 119, 132–33, 149, 156, 182; non-agentic, 184
Ahmed, Sara, 5, 210
AIDS, 165–66, 169–70
Alcoff, Linda Martin, 66
Algerian Muslim, 191
Algiers School of Psychiatry, 190
alienation, 12, 15, 17, 42, 50, 62, 67, 106, 110–12, 122, 125, 127, 165, 172, 210–11

Alldritt, Keith, 76,
Althusser, Louis, 7, 13–16, 29, 30–31
ambiguity, 14, 158, 165, 209
ambivalence as an epistemic category, 201
Ambrosini, Richard, 47, 57
Amigoni, David, 199
Amin, Shahid, 108; Chauri Chaura, 108
amnesia, 123, 131, 133, 137; amnesiac, 124
Amritsar, 120
Anderson, Benedict, 125
Anglo-American, 23
Anglo-French criticism, 17
Anglo-Indian, 70, 81, 87
ANT (Actor-Network Theory), 10, 151, 173
anti–Iraq War, 194
anti-Semitism, 77, 78
Appadurai, Arjun, 5, 147
apparition of the inapparent, 55
AR (augmented reality), 146, 154, 169
archive, 154
Arendt, Hannah, 113
Armstrong, Paul, 8
Armstrong, Tim, 167

Arnold, Matthew, 16, 143, 178, 193, 197–98; Arnoldian, 117, 99; *Culture and Anarchy*, 16–17, 19; 'Dover Beach', 178, 193, 195, 197, 199
artefact 13, 19, 24, 136, 150–52, 155, 160–64, 169, 171, 197; artefactual, 212; cultural, 13, 148; techno-artefact, 158–59
art form, 11, 143, 161, 168
Augé, Marc, 126; 'Oblivion', 126
Austen, Jane, 22, 31; *Pride and Prejudice*, 31
Austria-Hungarian Empire, 130
autonomy, 31; of affect, 153; relative, 7, 14

Baden-Powell, Robert, 2
Bakhtin, Mikhail, 23, 104
Banerjee, Maria Nemcova, 139
bare life, 179
baroque over-signification, 165
Barthes, Roland, 98–99, 136
Bartlett, Frederic, 94
Battle of Loos, 1
Baudelaire, 19
Baudrillard, Jean, 165, 171
Bauman, Zygmunt, 36, 177, 179
Beckett, Samuel, 15, 173–74; *Waiting for Godot*, 15
belatedness, 29
Belfast, 143
Belsey, Catherine, 6, 22, 31
Berlatsky, Eric, 135
Bertolazzi, Carlo, 14–15; *El Nost Milan*, 14–15
Bhabha, Homi, 9, 65, 68, 182, 192
Bhalla, Alok, 114
Bihar, 59, 76
biological self as technological experiment, 170
biological transcription, 185
biomedical, 10, 184, 189, 191; biomedicalization, 179
biopolitical, 59, 77, 177–80, 200–203
Birringer, Johannes, 173
blackness, 184, 191–93; ontology of, 180

blackwater fever, 75
Boccaccio, Giovanni, 207–8; *Decameron*, 207–8
body, mindless, 115; negotiable, 148
Boehmer, Elleke, 41, 43, 87
Boers (raid), 1; Jameson, Leander, 1
Bohemia, 130–31, 135; Communist, 135
Bombay, 110
Borges, Jorge Luis, 8
Bowker, Gordon, 61
Boy Scout, 2, 79
boys' magazines, 60
Bradbury, Peter, 116
Braidotti, Rosi, 152–53
brain, human, 97, 103, 148, 208; hardwired, 197; interpretative, 99; manipulatable, 148; neural, 196, 200; plastic, 148; situated, 102, 149
Brecht, Bertolt, 14–16
Breithaupt, Fritz, 209–10
Britain, 2, 69, 76, 78, 81
Broca, Paul, 157
Brooks, Cleanth, 143
Bruner, Jerome, 4, 11
Brussels, 48–49
Burma, 42, 59, 61, 62, 67, 70–71, 75–77, 80, 84, 87; British, 42; Lower, 62
burra memsahib, 86
Burroughs, Edgar Rice, 20; Tarzan, 20, 60
Butler, Judith, 5, 9, 36, 178, 184, 188, 193

Calvino, Italo, 95
camera, 158, 161, 168
capitalist, 14, 31, 59, 153, 165; high-capitalist, 158
carnivalesque, 123, 167
Carothers, John, 185–86, 190–91
Carroll, Joseph, 17
Cartesian, 147
cartography, 126; cartographic, 44, 107, 123, 124
Cassirer, Ernst, 96
cathodic ego, 164
censorship, 129, 131, 133, 135–36; self-censorship, 203

chronotope, 110; chronos and kairos, 99; chronotope-like quality, 123; complex, 129; crisis, 11
chunking, 96, 101, 108
cinema, 110, 167, 200, 207
city, 48, 119–20, 129–30, 167, 171; as a biological masterpiece, 201; fiction, 166; riot-torn, 117; textuality of the, 171; without memory, 130
Clare, Stephanie, 192
Clark, Andy, 6, 96, 148–50, 153
classic realism, 22
claustrophobia, 73, 182
Clifford, W. K., 156
Clinton, Alan, 154
clock time, 49, 99; and narrative time, 99
club, 66, 69; English, 68, 76; Englishman's, 72; European's, 84; imperial clubbability, 69
Cockney accent, 68–69
code field, 12
cognitive: absorption, 165; blankness, 121; deframing, 43; deterritorialization, 121; disruption, 146; dissonance, 50, 111, 124; economy, 160; flatness, 112, 127; instruments, 94; profiling, 167; reframing, 147; schema, 134
collective memory, 13, 36, 103, 106–7, 120, 133, 210; hegemonic, 128
colonial contact zone, 64, 67–71, 74–76, 78–80, 84, 86–87
colonial elsewhere, 43
colonial gaze, 10, 44, 48, 57, 59
comic, grotesquely, 123
Communist Party, 138; communism, 28; communist, 129–30, 135; in Czechoslovakia, 138
complementarity, 150
conceptual peg, 101
Congo, 42, 48–52
consciousness, the dual function of, 198
Conservative (party), 48
contagion, 5–7, 17, 165, 169, 172
contagious, 7, 93, 127; contagiousness of affect, 5; material and affective activity, 208; space-time, 211

continental philosophy, 30
contingency, 6, 45, 212–13
corporeality, 10, 77, 110, 115–16, 120, 122, 127, 144, 148, 153, 157, 159, 165–66, 174, 180, 184, 211; corporeal compression, 134; corporeal intervention, 161; corporeal schema, 184
corporealization of time, 123
corpse, recognition of a, 115
corpse-like, 121
counter-discourse, 188
counterpoint, 105
COVID-19, 11, 208–12
Cruise, Tom, 207–8
crystallize, 105
cyberspace, 152, 173
Czechoslovakia, 129, 131, 133, 136–38
Czech Reformation, 130

Damasio, Antonio, 102, 110–11
Daniel, Valentine, 115, 117
Dante, Alighieri, 19
Darwin, Charles, 17–18; Darwinian, 17; Darwinism, 17; neo-Darwinian, 199; neo-Darwinism, 194; neo-Darwinist, 178, 196; post-Darwinian, 23; social Darwinism, 61; social Darwinist, 46, 187
Das, Veena, 113
decadence, 20–21, 24, 61, 74–75, 110, 154, 163
decoding, 100; delayed, 33, 46–48, 50, 52–53, 57
defamiliarization, 32–33, 43, 48, 56, 145–46, 154
Defoe, Daniel, 43; *Robinson Crusoe*, 43
depragmatization, 105
Derrida, Jacques, 8, 15, 19, 25, 27–31, 36, 55; deconstruction, 9, 14–15, 19, 23, 25, 27–28, 30, 36, 51, 79, 82
Derridean, 14, 23, 25
determinism, 76, 77, 180; biological, 197; genetic, 80; neural, 194, 196; overdeterminism, 14, 16, 67
dialectical materialism, 34
dialectical treatment, 3

Diana, Princess, 167–68, 181
Dickens, Charles, 21
diegetic, 21
digital, 146, 154, 167–69, 172, 208; deathless, 167; post-digital, 170; self-fashioning, 168
discontinuity, 179
dislocation, 50, 56, 63, 70, 84, 106, 113, 153, 188, 190
distributive cognition, 150
Dollimore, Jonathan, 158
Donne, John, 169; 'The Flea', 169
double-helical, 212; narrative, 53
double inscription, 23, 68
Draaisma, Douwe, 101
drugs, 164, 166–67, 169–70, 172; addiction, 166

Eagleton, Terry, 19, 22–25, 31, 36
Eichenbaum, Howard, 95, 100
eighteenth century, 24
elasticity, 23; epistemic, 23; epistemological, 171
electrons and human minds, 97
Eliot, George, 22
Eliot, T. S., 13, 17–19, 22, 24–25, 36; *The Waste Land*, 20
Empire Annual for Boys, 83
emplotment, 102, 125, 138, 146, 149
Engels, Friedrich, 192
ennui, 155, 173
enunciative modality, 191
epidermalization, 181, 184, 188, 190; epidermal schema, 184
epiphany, 75, 177, 199–200
episodic memories, 47, 95
epistemic and ontological uncertainty, 178
Erll, Astrid, 8, 210
ethnography, 186
Eurasians, 76–78
extended cognitive process, 149

Fabrega, Horacio, 80
fabulation, 95, 99, 128, 133, 138, 185
fallacy, 25–26
Fashoda Incident, 48

Federer, Roger, 1, 207
feeling-less-ness, 171
feminine, 45, 80, 85; Left-feminist, 116
Ferrier, David, 157
fetish, 32, 156, 158, 160–62, 172; fetishization, 55, 135
fiction, medium of, 131–33, 137, 139
fictions about failures, 44
Fiesole, 207
fin de siècle, 10, 77, 154–64, 166, 172; cultural imaginary, 155; marketplace, 158
First World War, 1, 60–61
Florence, 207
fluidity, 45, 83, 97–98, 144, 152, 174, 210–11
focalization, 3, 43, 97, 106, 112
forgetting, president of, 133
forgetting, production of, 132, 136
forgetting, state-induced forms of, 134–35
formalist, 143; technological-formalist, 173
Forster, E. M., 67; *A Passage to India*, 67
Foucault, Michel, 9, 36, 41, 63, 145, 177, 185, 191–92; four types of technology, 146
Fowles, John, 32; *The French Lieutenant's Woman*, 32
Fremde, 208
French-Algerian, 180–81, 185, 191
Freud, Sigmund, 187; Freudian, 55
Fritsch, Gustav, 157
frontal lobe syndrome, African's, 190
frontal sluggishness, African's, 186
frozenness of the black body, 188
Fuss, Diana, 181

Gagnier, Regenia, 158
Gazzaniga, Michael, 98–99
Geertz, Clifford, 72–73
gender, 67; studies, 119
gendered vocabulary, 188
geopolitical, 18, 43, 48, 107, 127
German imperialism, 48
Goethe, Wolfgang von, 18
Gopal, Priyamvada, 116

Gottwald, Klement, 129, 135
Gramsci, Antonio, 12, 183
Gulag, 35
Gulf War, 165

half-breed, 77
Hardy, Thomas, 19, 143; 'Conversations of the Twain', 143
hauntology, 55; hauntological, 8, 58
Hayles, Katherine, 155
Hegel, 30–31; quasi-Hegelian, 17
Herman, David, 96, 101–2
heterotopia, 152; heterotopic, 173
highbrow culture, 82, 20
high-Modernist, 75, 86, 201
hippocampus, 95, 150
historicity, 184; historicize, 19, 188; historicizing, 193
Hitchcock, Alfred, 31
Hitchens, Christopher, 60–61
Hitzig, Eduard, 157
HIV, 165, 167–68
Hoffman, Bert, 210
Hogan, Patrick Colm, 103
Hollander, John, 144
hollow hedonism, 155
Hollywood, 20
Holmes, Sherlock, 60
Homo Sacer, 178–79
homosexuality, 159, 162, 164, 172
homosocial, 69, 72, 76, 87
Hübl, Milan, 135
hunting, 64, 66, 75, 80–81
Huntington's disease, 195
Husak, Gustav, 133, 135
Huxley, Aldous, 17–18
hybridity, 68, 76
hyper-: civil, 68; civility, 68; fictionalized, 137; heterosexual, 116; masculine, 115–19; masculinity, 120; mimetic, 168, 171; production, 21; sexuality, 191; simulated, 171–72; technological imaginary, 147
hyperreal, 172; hyperreality, 144, 165–67, 171
hypnosis, 160
hysteria, 51, 58, 70, 73, 82, 84–85, 187

identification, negative, 71
identity preservation, 132
imagination: anachronistic, 139; failure of the, 197
imperialism, as 'textual exercise', 41
inaccessible articulation, 55
India-Pakistan Partition, 10, 106, 110, 120; necropolis of, 118
infantocracy, 133
inferiority complex, 187
installation, 145, 147, 155, 164, 166, 170
interactivity, 6, 146–47, 149, 152–53, 155, 164, 209; interfacial, 211
intercorporeal, 109, 117, 149, 151; encounters, 115
intercorporeality, 153
interdisciplinary, 10–11, 93, 177
interpellation, 15–16, 29, 35–36, 43, 178
interrupted: cognition, 172; embodiment, 59, 109; identities, 44, 130; interpellation, 43; sentences, 181; storytelling, 53
interruption, 11, 15, 22, 44, 66, 110, 117, 120, 128, 132, 134, 147, 165
interstitial, 13, 55, 108, 113, 182; interstitiality, 153, 177
intersubjectivity, 6, 8, 35, 94, 144, 146–49, 153, 155, 211–12; incomplete, 211; intersubjective agency, 139
intertexts and interruptions, 165
intimacy through interactivity, 152
invalidated identities, 66
Iraq War, 194, 198–99
irresolution, 33–35
Iser, Wolfgang, 4, 9; fictionalizing acts, 9
iterability, 8, 29–30; reiterability, 31

Jackson, John Hughlings, 157
Jalal, Ayesha, 107, 109, 112
James, Henry, 22–23
James, Williams, 156; 'Are We Automata?', 156; 'On Some Omissions of Introspective Psychology', 156
Jameson, Frederick, 192
Jane Eyre, 198

Jayasena, Nalin, 82
jouissance, 33
Joyce, James, 22, 29, 201; 'The Dead', 201; *Ulysses*, 20, 22

Kafka, Franz, 33, 102–3, 129–30, 179; cognitive realism, 102; monsters and mutants, 179; statue, 129
Kafka, Hermann, 130
kalma-i-taassuf, 114
Kandel, Eric, 8, 97, 100
Kantian philosophy, 31
Kaplan, E. Ann, 188
Kennedy, Greg, 144, 177, 180
Kermode, Frank, 99–100, 105
Khanna, Ranjana, 189
Kiel Canal, 12
kinetic identities, 164
Kipling, Rudyard, 1–2, 16, 19, 29, 59; 'If', 1; Kiplingesque, 2, 67
kitsch, 194
Kittler, Frederick, 159
Kodak, 158. *See also* camera
Kolkata, 69
Kracauer, Siegfried, 208
Kroker, Arthur, 147
Kyauktada, 69, 76, 84–85, 87

Lacan, Jacques, 14, 30; Lacanian, 14, 30, 35, 165
Lahore, 111, 123–25, 127
Latour, Bruno, 151
Lawrence, D. H., 22
Leavis, F. R., 19–25, 36; *The Great Tradition*, 21–22; Leavisian, 22–23, 26
LeDoux, Joseph, 96, 100–102
Lehan, Richard, 171
Lenin, 25, 130; statues of, 25, 130
Levenson, Michael, 54,
Lévi-Strauss, Claude, 32
libidinal, 82, 118–19; intercorporeal space, 117
liminal, 138–39, 171, 178–79, 183, 208; liminality, 130, 177, 196, 201–2, 210; subliminal, 182
Linde, Charlotte, 8
liquid culture, 179; liquidation, 130, 135

literature, ontology, 145
litost, 137
Lodge, David, 45, 99, 196
Lombroso, Césare, 74, 162; criminology, 48, 51, 74, 77, 87; Lombrosian, 51, 191
London, 164–66, 194–95, 198, 201
Lotman, Yuri, 105–6
lowbrow, 20
Lukács, Georg, 35
Lyotard, Francois, 165

Macherey, Pierre, 25–26, 35
Mackenzie, John, 81
Maczynska, Magdalena, 166
Madagascar, 187
madness, 123, 185, 188, 50
magic realism, 194
Mallarmé, Stéphane, 158–59
Manichean allegory, 187
Mannoni, Octave, 186–87
Marghescou, Mircea, 11; regime of texts, 11
Massumi, Brian, 153
Marx, Karl, 14, 16, 21, 30, 62; Marxist, 13–14, 15, 24, 62
masculinity, 2, 54, 59, 79, 81–85, 87, 117, 154, 161; desirable, 2; imperial, 45, 79–81; melancholic, 42; military, 82; nervous, 53; normative, 79–81; plucky, 2; xenophobic, 83
material markers, 6–7, 9, 18, 36, 93–94, 111, 136, 158, 172
Mathari Mental Hospital, 185
matter-metaphor compound, 113
Maudsley Hospital, 186
McColloch, Jock, 186, 188, 191
McMullan, Anna, 173
media-induced conditions, 167
medico-anthropological, 185
medico-cultural, 87, 190
medium, the literary, 30, 145, 165, 173, 208, 212
melancholia, 46, 50, 51, 88, 190, 191; de-corporealized, 118; of forgetting, 130
Mellor, Philip, 116

memory: city without, 130; creative, 106; dialectic of, 105; fictions of, 105; forward, 100; informative, 105–6; markers, 128; memory of, 100; metonymic quality of, 135; multidimensional, 208, 211; multidirectional, 127; narrative, 61
memory-less-ness, 130
Menon, Jisha, 115
MET (material engagement theory), 5–7, 10, 34, 36, 146, 147–48, 151–52, 173, 208
metacognitive, 153, 169, 201; metacognition, 170
metafiction, 9, 170; metafictional, 136, 169–70, 172
metaphor, attrition of a, 101; dead, 101; good, 100; living, 100
metaphoric practice, 43–44
metaphors of depth, 212
Metaphysical Poets, 18; metaphysical, 162
metropolis, 49, 171–72, 201; European, 193
metropolitan literary culture, 43
middle class, 24, 194, 200
Middle East, 199
mimesis, 85, 131, 161, 172, 207
mimetic, 8, 57, 64, 84–85, 131, 164–65, 169, 172; pseudo-hysteric mimetic act, 85
mimic man, 84
mimicry, 64–65, 68, 158, 167, 182
mind, social, 104
misadventure fiction, 9, 16, 42, 59
mis-cognition, 56
mixed reality, 148
mnemonic, 95
modernity, 21, 23, 143, 179, 180
monstrosity, 34, 154, 158, 184
monument, 7, 95, 126–27, 129–30
Morris, Errol, 207
Motihari, 59, 76
Mountbatten, Lord, 107
Mughalpura, 120
mutability, 10, 83, 93, 124, 131, 136, 148, 156

Nadal, Rafael, 1–2, 207
narrative austerity, 112, 114, 127
narrative emergence, 24
narrativization, 103; narrativity, 8, 12, 98
nation-states, 107, 120, 123, 124–27
neoliberal, 193, 201, 203
nervous narration, 44, 48, 50, 58, 88
Neumann, Birgit, 105
neuromimetic performance, 64
neuro-novel, 10, 177–78, 180, 194, 203, 65
neuroscientific, 95, 194, 196, 202; gaze, 178
9/11, 10, 31, 207–8, 197
nineteenth century, 41
no-man's-land, 63, 123, 126
non-dialectical, 15
non-events, 15
nonhuman, 151
non-innocence, 19, 27
non-linear, 102–3
non-normative, 77
non-place, 126
non-synchronicity, 43
Nordau, Max, 162
North African syndrome, 182, 188–90, 192
nothingness, production of, 115
nuclear world, 166
Nussbaum, Martha, 71–72, 77, 83, 208

oblivion, 8, 94, 105–6, 126, 129
obscene, ontology of the, 171
Old Town Square (Prague), 135
ontological coalition, 7
ontological opacity, 15
orchestrated alterity, 187
Orientalist, 19, 187
otherness, 26, 51, 56, 68, 71, 74, 171, 178–80, 188; of the black subject, 184

Palmer, Alan, 104–5, 132
pandemic, 11, 208–12
paparazzi, 169
parabole, 209

parallax, 32–33
paranoia, 77, 194; paranoid, 178, 180–81, 194
pariah, 84
partial objects, 33–34
Pater, Walter, 23
perpetrator trauma, 116, 120
phantom limb, 55, 123–24
phenomenal self, 102; phenomenality, 154, 156
photography, 135–36; propaganda, 135
Pied Piper attribute, 51
Pied Piper signifier, 64
Pifer, Ellen, 128, 133
plasticity, 28–29 148, 150, 157, 170; of fiction, 144; metaplasticity, 148
point of view, 16, 19, 27–28, 32, 44–45, 51, 147
Polvinen, Merja, 103
popular-culture, 31, 167, 207
Porot, Antoine, 190–91
post-: communist era, 129; Darwinian, 23; digital, 170; human, 145, 152, 173; humanist, 151; industrial, 171; memorial agency, 127; memory, 107; 9/11, 194, 201, 208; 1960s Anglo-French criticism, 17; perception, 46; religious, 23; riot, 117; Second World War, 12; socialist Prague, 129; truth, 67
posthumous, 55; ignominy, 86; monument, 127; public identities, 115
postmodernist, 17, 29, 155, 169–70; centreless ontological quality of the postmodern, 171; postmodern historiographic metafiction, 9; postmodern sublime, 165
postmodern posthuman orders, 145
Prague, 129, 130, 135, 139; changing street names in, 130; Spring, 10
precarious community, 209
pre–Iraq War, 194
Propp, Vladimir, 94
prosthetic and plastic ontology of the body, 167
pseudo-hysteric, 85

pseudomelancholia, 182, 190–91
pseudo-neural, 150
pseudoscience, 77
psychiatry, 186, 190; African, 185; colonial, 188–89; ethnopsychiatry, 185–87, 191
psychoanalysis, 30–31, 189
psychology, 101, 156–57, 185, 194; cognitive, 202–3
psychosomatic, 187; pathology, 181
public school, 59–60, 83; Edwardian, 60; St. Cyprian's, 61
pukka sahib, 62, 64, 67, 70, 73, 75, 78–79

quantum self, 97
quasi-cannibalistic, 158, 163; consumerist culture, 167
quotidian, 192

reanimate, 211
race studies, 5, 10
racial: degeneration, 76; hybridity, 76; identity, 177; miscegenation, 78; politics, 177; reification, 59, 192; supremacy, 79
racialization of medicine, 185, 191–92
racialized: discourses, 10, 186–87; panic, 78; pseudoscience, 77; psychiatry, 190; space, 87
racially reified: gaze, 10, 188; identity, 182; setting, 184; space, 88; subject, 181
racism, dynamic, 185
Raid, Jameson, 48
Raj (the British), 61, 63
Ramachandran, V. S., 104, 148
re-becoming, 100
recalibrate, 144
recognizability, 180
reification, 4, 27, 41–42, 55, 59, 62, 67, 79, 156, 186, 188–89, 192; strategic, 138
reified: identity, 182; imperial space, 75; product, 62
relative ontology, 6–7
remembering: and forgetting, 4–5, 7–9, 93–95, 98, 101, 105, 109, 124, 127,

129, 132, 135, 138, 208; the precarity of, 139
remembering and un-remembering: structures and silences of, 130
remembrance, 88, 100, 104, 109, 129, 131, 134–35, 138
reshuffling, 151
re-simulation, 103–4
Ricoeur, Paul, 3, 8–9, 100–102
Robbins, Kevin, 173
roman à clef, 169–71
Rothberg, Michael, 127
Rushdie, Salman, 207; *Haroun and the Sea of Stories*, 207
Ruskin, John, 23
Ryan, Judith, 157

Said, Edward, 2, 36, 42, 47, 53, 74, 187, 193
Salisbury, Lord, 48
Salver, Jeffrey, 197
Sartre, Jean-Paul, 183, 186, 192
Saussurean, 16
Schachter, Daniel, 99–100
schema, 94; cognitive, 134, 148, 173; corporeal, 184; epidermal, 184
Schilling, Chris, 116
Second World War, 12; post–Second World War, 12, 17
semiotic, 4, 12, 16, 20, 105–6, 147, 151; instability, 171; slipperiness, 171
semi-solid, 200
sexuality, 116, 118, 167; deviant, 159; hedonistic, 165; performative, 156
Shakespeare, 19, 24; Shakespearean, 187
shaming, 70, 72, 88
shell-shocked, 189
shrinking, 133; and blurring, 134
sign production, 34
simulacra, 164, 166, 168
simulation, shallow, 154, 164
Sinha, Mrinalini, 69
situational meaning, 97
slowness, 130, 135; as a strategy of remembrance, 135
social distancing, 211

socialist, 35, 61
software, primal, 145
Solzhenitsyn, Alexander, 35; *One Day in the Life of Ivan Denisovich*, 35
space-time, 33, 110, 125, 127, 207–8, 213; contagious, 211
Spanish flu, 210
spatiotemporal, 33, 97, 110, 127, 131, 134, 137, 168, 201; alienation, 125
spectral, 8, 53, 55, 108, 111, 117, 119, 122, 127, 163, 208, 210; techno-spectral, 159
spectrality, 8, 54, 107, 109, 111, 115–17, 120, 124, 128, 130, 159, 161–62, 166, 174; recognition of, 115
Spivak, Gayatri Chakravarti, 190; epistemic violence, 11, 124, 135, 188, 190, 192
split-brain patients, 98
staggered storytelling, 48, 50, 59
state apparatus, 14, 125; ideological, 15; repressive, 14
Stile, Ann, 157
Stoker, Bram, 150, 155, 162
subject, the situated, 147
subjectivity, 6–7, 57, 94, 97, 136, 148, 151, 153–54, 160, 174; fractal, 147; nomadic, 152
subjectivity-effect, 14
sub-Saharan, 191
subtextual, 199
Sullivan, Shannon, 79
supermarket, 151
surveillance, 68, 209, 130, 133
Sutton, John, 150
symbolic investments, 42
synaptic plasticity, 96, 148
synthetic, 153, 158, 159, 160, 161, 162, 163

Taliban, 199
techno-: artefact, 158; corporeal interface, 159–60; culture, 152; cultural, 156; economic, 147; spectral, 159
technological violence, 155
technologies, self-enhancing, 145

technologized self, 147
technology, transformative, 160–61
television, 10, 155, 164, 166–68; televised, 164, 167–68, 171
Terdiman, Richard, 7
territorialization, 46, 48, 56, 108, 134, 155; deterritorialization, 31, 43, 112–13, 116, 121; extra-territoriality, 208
textuality of memory, 134, 136
thingness of things, 149
thing theory, 5, 27
Thomas, Alfred, 129
Thurschwell, Pamela, 155, 159–60
Titanic, 143
Todorov, Tzvetan, 192
Tolstoy, Leo, 25
Tom & Jerry cartoons, 34
toxic bodies and designer aesthetics, 147
Transvaal, 1, 48
trash, 144, 177, 180
Trilling, Lionel, 23
Troscianko, Emily, 102–3
truth, 33–34, 47, 49, 63, 72–73, 182, 185, 199, 202; narrative, 99; official, 137; post-truth, 67; scientific, 17
twentieth century, 20–21, 23, 60–61, 74, 81, 83, 86, 156, 161, 172, 185, 189
twilight territory, 127
typewriter, 159

un-becoming, 100
Unheimlich, 55
unnarrated, 109
unprocessed, 109, 128
Upanishads, 18
urban, 155, 166–67, 171–72, 191; masculine identities, 164

vampiric terror and xenophobic panic, 162
vanishing subject, the, 157
Vedas, 18
Verne, Jules, 25

video, 1; installation, 164; portrait, 167
violent otherness, 180
virtuality, 10, 165, 173
virtual object, animated, 164
virtual reality, 160, 171, 173
virtual synesthetic perspectives, 153
voyeurism as visual mode, 158, 164, 168

Warhol, Andy, 164
waste, 5, 10, 42, 144, 162–63, 177, 179–80
wasted identity, ontology of, 177
Watt, Ian, 47
Watts, C. T., 51
Waugh, Patricia, 53, 212
Wells, H. G., 47
Wertsch, James V., 95
Western Europe, 41, 157
white supremacy, 42, 64
WHO (World Health Organization), 185
wideware, 149
Wilde, Constance, 158
Williams, Raymond, 12–13, 23, 71
Wimbledon, 1
Woolf, Virginia, 47, 87; *Mrs. Dalloway*, 87
Wordsworth, 18;
Wordsworthian, 20–21

X-rays, 161
xenophobia, 19, 60, 155
xenophobic, 77; imperialist, 68; masculinity, 83; panic, 162

Yebra, Jose M., 164–65, 171
Young, Kay, 197

zeitgeist, 18
Žižek, Slavoj, 14, 30–35, 63, 212
Zohar, Danah, 97–98
Zunshine, Lisa, 211

www.ingramcontent.com/pod-product-compliance
Lightning Source LLC
Chambersburg PA
CBHW031549300426
44111CB00006BA/238